Praise for *Mooncakes and Milk Bread*

"Kristina's book is a trip down memory lane, an evocative look at the foods that made me happy as a child and that are laced with nostalgia for me as an adult. Every page of *Mooncakes and Milk Bread* is a treat, with beloved cakes and not-too-sweet favorites that felt unattainable to create myself at home, until now. Kristina's stories about growing up in her family's Chinese restaurant and greeting her 'aunties and uncles' at dim sum are full of heart and soul, providing a window into a vibrant part of American culture that has brought joy to so many. And *joy* is a good word to sum up Kristina's book. It is more than a Chinese baking book—it is a triumphant celebration of how food brings people from different generations and cultures together. I've never been so excited to bake and steam!"

—HETTY MCKINNON, FOOD WRITER, AUTHOR OF FOUR BESTSELLING COOKBOOKS
INCLUDING *TO ASIA, WITH LOVE*, AND EDITOR OF *PEDDLER JOURNAL*

"This book brought tears to my eyes. Some of my tastiest childhood memories were at Chinese bakeries, and these photos, stories, and recipes have both transported me back in time and provided fresh inspiration to re-create these memories at home. I am truly in awe of Kristina's ability to evoke nostalgia while also infusing new life into this genre of food that hasn't, until now, gotten the attention it deserves. *Mooncakes and Milk Bread* is a stunning, thorough, delicious, and important piece of work."

—MOLLY YEH, COOKBOOK AUTHOR AND FOOD NETWORK HOST

"Kristina Cho's book is a long overdue collection of the artistry and sweet and savory flavors of Chinese baking. I can't think of another book that made me want to make every single thing!

Delving into the history of Chinese bakeries, visits to and recipes from popular traditional Chinese bakeries, including her grandfather's own almond cookie recipe, Kristina makes everything accessible—no easy feat for pastries that always leave me in awe, wondering, *How do they make that?!* This book is an absolute treasure."

—LIZ PRUEITT, FOUNDER, TARTINE

"*Mooncakes and Milk Bread* serves as a love letter to the Chinese bakeries of our childhoods but also as a guide for a new generation of fans, who can now bake their own pineapple buns (always with a slice of cold butter), the most perfect Chinese sponge cake, and everything else on the bakery rack—all from the comfort of their own homes."

—BIN CHEN AND ANDREW CHAU, COFOUNDERS OF BOBA GUYS AND AUTHORS OF *THE BOBA BOOK*

"You can almost smell the magical aroma of freshly baked buns and steamed dumplings through the pages as you thumb through *Mooncakes and Milk Bread*. Kristina takes readers on a journey from Hong Kong to Cleveland to San Francisco and beyond, guiding us through the many typologies of Chinese American bakeries, like grab-and-go and takeaway. This book is filled with a beautiful blend of traditional recipes and new takes and twists on nostalgic classics. Ready your heart and belly for what's sure to be an instant favorite."

—ALANA KYSAR, AUTHOR OF *ALOHA KITCHEN*

Mooncakes & Milk Bread

Sweet & Savory Recipes
Inspired by Chinese Bakeries

Kristina Cho

HARPER HORIZON

Published by Harper Horizon, an imprint of HarperCollins Focus LLC.

Any internet addresses, phone numbers, or company or product information printed in this book are offered as a resource and are not intended in any way to be or to imply an endorsement by Harper Horizon, nor does Harper Horizon vouch for the existence, content, or services of these sites, phone numbers, companies, or products beyond the life of this book.

Photography by Kristina Cho
Illustrations by Minnie Phan

Unless otherwise noted, profiles in this book were taken from personal interviews in 2020.

ISBN 978-0-7852-3900-0 (eBook)
ISBN 978-0-7852-3899-7 (HC)

Library of Congress Control Number: 2021930696

Printed in South Korea
21 22 23 24 25 SAM 10 9 8 7 6 5 4 3 2 1

*To Goong Goong and Pau Pau,
my selfless grandparents,
who sacrificed so much
to make this dream a reality.*

Contents

introduction

From Hong Kong to Cleveland

Nestled along Payne Avenue, between the East 20th and East 40th Street blocks of downtown, is Cleveland's Chinatown. Compared with the densely packed streets and alleys of New York City's and San Francisco's Chinatowns, the Cleveland Chinatown feels teeny-tiny, but for my family, it was home. Our family lived right in the very heart of it for fifty years. When I was growing up, though I wasn't raised in Chinatown, I spent almost every weekend there visiting my grandparents. It was the home of our go-to dim sum spot, where my family gathered around large, round tables full of steamers every Sunday, and frequented the few Asian grocery stores, to pick up vegetables and ingredients we couldn't find at the local Giant Eagle.

My grandparents first moved to Cleveland from Hong Kong in the late 1960s. A lot has changed since then. Cleveland's little Chinatown transitioned from few Asian-owned businesses to an ever-growing number of Chinese restaurants and grocery stores. But what we lacked for many years was a stand-alone bakery. All we had was a bakery case the size of a small closet, in one of the local Asian markets. It was enough for us—most of the time. Each year we'd pack up the minivan for our annual road trip to Chicago. The Chinatown there was more robust, and its bakeries indulged our cravings for baked buns and rolled cakes.

Trips to the local bakery case and vacation visits to Chinatown bakeries in other cities are some of my favorite childhood memories. It was exhilarating, getting the chance to pick out a new, shiny baked good or crisp cookie, each bite connecting me a little more to my family's culture. Sipping on tea and pulling apart our haul of treats bit by bit, my parents and grandparents would regale us with their own memories of living in Hong Kong or even older stories of my grandparents in Taishan, China.

Maybe that's why Hong Kong has always felt like a second home to me. Both my parents are originally from Hong Kong and grew up in the same apartment complex. The food I ate while growing up is firmly rooted in Cantonese flavors and techniques, and the unique Western influences found only in Hong Kong.

My maternal grandfather, Goong Goong, was a schoolteacher and calligrapher, but when he decided to move his entire family, including his mother, wife, and five young children, to the United States, he knew he needed another plan, so he learned to cook. He learned to do more than just cook, though. When he arrived in the States and started working in kitchens, his first job was baking endless trays of almond cookies. He had an incredible work ethic (having seven mouths to feed will do that to you) and worked his way up in restaurant kitchens until he had saved up enough money to open his own restaurant. One restaurant turned into several more. Working in the restaurant became the family business. My maternal grandmother, Pau Pau, washed dishes and helped cook, and my mom and her siblings were the waiters, carry-out runners, prep cooks, and bartenders, when they weren't studying, at college, or working another full-time job in a completely different field.

We were, and still are, a Chinese American restaurant family blessed with masterful cooks. I grew up watching my goong goong roast huge slabs of pork and wield a giant, fiery wok. I spent hours making dumplings with my pau pau and studying the way she formed her *joong*—a sticky rice tamale wrapped in bamboo leaves—to

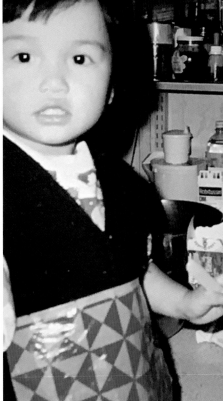

celebrate the Dragon Boat Festival. Evenings at the restaurant meant huge staff dinners in the kitchen. During holidays, I was inspired by my mom's ability to single-handedly whip up a feast featuring more than a dozen dishes for the entire family. I may have missed making traditional all-American memories—baking homemade brownies with my grandma, say, or baking a pumpkin pie to celebrate Thanksgiving. Nonetheless, my Chinese American upbringing in the Midwest was filled with an abundance of incredible food made with care and lovingly tied to tradition.

For a long time I wanted to be a chef just like my goong goong, but when it came to choosing a college major, architecture felt like the right path for me. I have always loved art and creating beautiful things with my hands. While I was in architecture school, food and cooking for others still took up every spare moment I had. Between all-nighters building models in the studio and struggling through structures homework, I fed my friends at weekly dinner parties with minimal ingredients, baked midnight blueberry muffins to de-stress, started an embarrassingly hipster supper club in my professor's artist studio, and attempted to skew every architecture assignment into a project that involved making, growing, or dispensing food. You could say I was *mildly* obsessed with food.

After college, I moved to foggy San Francisco to become a "real" architect. I met my partner, Reuben (also an architect), soon after I arrived, on a rainy morning over dim sum (naturally). For a few years, I worked as a designer at a couple of firms in the Bay Area. I tried to give architecture my all, but spending my days tweaking construction drawings and coordinating with engineers didn't satisfy me creatively. I was still cooking and baking regularly. I was the girl who brought in baked goods for my coworkers on a weekly basis or volunteered to make waffles for the whole office on Bike to Work Day.

At the peak of my creative frustration, I started a food blog to document my ongoing kitchen adventures (and prove to my mom that I was able to properly cook for myself). *Eat Cho Food* started off mainly as a way to channel all the creative energy, which wasn't being utilized at work, into noodles, dumplings, and baked goods. At the same time, Reuben and I moved to the Inner Richmond neighborhood, one block north of Clement Street. Inner Richmond is San Francisco's unofficial second Chinatown, and Clement Street, the main drag, is packed with restaurants, bars, markets, and bakeries. It was the first time I'd ever lived anywhere most of the people walking up and down the street looked like me! I heard Cantonese more frequently than English, and all my favorite Asian foods and ingredients were minutes from our door. Years later, I'd realize what a profound effect this environment had on me and my cooking.

I found so much joy exploring the aisles of the local Asian markets and figuring innovative ways to use the ingredients in my recipes. A lot of these recipes were inspired by my family's classic Cantonese cooking, while others are completely unique twists on my favorite foods. When I'm cooking, I'm often inspired by what's in season, memorable meals from my travels, and memories of growing up in the Midwest. On my blog, I shared recipes and snippets of our life each week, even if the only people reading it were my mom and Reuben's mom. I transferred my design approach from architecture to photography, food styling, and dumpling pleats. What was most helpful in the transition from architecture to food was the unrelenting process of iteration and development. Architecture gave me the discipline to continually test and create recipes that are efficient, thoughtful, flavorful, and workable. It also taught me to balance artistry with precision when explaining techniques, presenting dishes, and writing recipes.

I was amazed when more and more people started visiting EatChoFood.com and following me on social media. What started off as a hobby soon became my full-time dream job. I discovered that the recipes that resonated most with my readers were the ones that connected them to a flavor from their childhood. This became super clear when I shared a recipe for Chinese Bakery-Style Hot Dog Flower Buns (page 94). Hot dog flower buns were one of my favorite Chinese bakery treats growing up—the flower shape alone evokes pure childhood nostalgia—so I made them on a whim. Apparently, a lot of other people love them too, as I was inundated with requests for more Chinese bakery bun recipes. That's when the wheels started turning on this cookbook.

Cookbook sections in bookstores are packed with dessert books, like cookie tomes with recipes for short-bread and the absolute best chocolate chip cookies. But you likely won't find a recipe for Chocolate-Hazelnut Macau-Style Cookies (page 212), tender, beautifully pressed cookies that melt in your mouth, in any American cookbook. I spent years searching for recipes for the perfect Chinese Sponge Cake (page 138), for Shao Bing (page 30)—a small bread encrusted with sesame seeds and filled with either sweet or savory options—and for crispy yet fluffy Sheng Jian Bao, pan-fried steamed buns filled with juicy pork. These recipes are hard to come by, and if anything exists, it's via a few untrustworthy web links. I wanted to change that and share a collection of thoughtful, well-tested recipes dedicated to my beloved Chinese bakeries and cafes.

Between recipes for the more iconic mooncakes and milk bread loaves, you'll find specialties of my pau pau that are near and dear to my heart: playful dumplings, clever ways to fold and twist buns, new ingredients to stock your pantry, and stories from growing up in my family's kitchen. I'm grateful for the opportunity to share these recipes, flavors, and stories. Whether Chinese baking is new or familiar to you, you'll find plenty of recipes that feel nostalgic, comforting, adventurous, and even whimsical. Maybe you'll find the inspiration to bake egg tarts with your own grandparents (and finally get them to turn on their oven) or introduce the gloriousness of pork floss to your family. I hope some of the recipes find a tender spot in your heart and even become baking traditions for years to come. I treat these recipes with endless respect toward my heritage but also apply my own perspective, as a first-generation Chinese American from the Midwest who now lives in California. So you know it's going to get interesting.

Cafe Culture

If you walk through the main drag of any Chinatown in the United States, you'll see bright-colored awnings and neon signs with the word **BAKERY** in large, bold lettering. Instead of buttery croissants, baguettes, and cupcakes, you'll find buns filled with taro, coconut, and red bean paste. The air is thick with the aroma of strongly brewed tea. Crisp cookies are chock full of seeds and nuts, and cakes are slathered with light-as-air whipped cream and glossy fruit that looks so perfect you might think it's fake. Most Chinese bakeries offer savory foods along with sweet treats. Some shops sell dim sum favorites like *siu mai* (page 223), *har gow* (page 219), and *lo bak gao* (page 240). Bakeries might also serve classic Chinese breakfast staples like *jook* (page 230), a creamy, slow-cooked rice porridge made by stirring rice in chicken or pork stock for hours. It's typically served with fried dough called *youtiao* (page 27)—think of it as a savory Chinese doughnut to dip in your jook.

Not all the food offered at bakeries is even baked at all. The art of baking and using ovens is only a recent cooking method in Chinese culture; most households were without ovens for the longest time. This is because in Hong Kong, where apartments are compact, large appliances like ovens are typically omitted from the floorplan. It's a running joke in my family that Pau Pau's oven is just an elaborate storage cabinet (I don't think she's ever turned the thing on). Steaming, frying, and boiling are more widely used cooking methods. This might explain why Chinese bakeries became so popular in Hong Kong, and ultimately that popularity traveled over to the States. Since families lacked ovens to make baked goods, going to the bakery became a special treat, offering indulgences they couldn't make at home.

Chinese bakeries first gained popularity in Hong Kong, which absorbed a hefty dose of Western culture during 150 years of British rule. Chinese bakers adapted recipes brought over from European bakers for brioche, custard pies, biscuits, and cakes, using the ingredients they had access to and incorporated flavors and ingredients more aligned with the Asian palate. Sugar levels were reduced, cakes became lighter, and ingredients like black sesame seeds and mango worked their way into everything. Thus, the classic Chinese bakery style is a quirky melding of Western and Eastern cultures. It's interesting that my dad and other Hong Kongers still refer to Chinese bakeries as "Western bakeries."

Aside from copious amounts of food, you'll also find community in a Chinese bakery. Asian Americans and immigrants flock to bakeries for treats that taste like home and invoke nostalgia. In the early hours of the day, groups of uncles and aunties sit gossiping. A lot of times you'll hear the happy chatter in a bakery or cafe before you see it. Mornings are when Chinese bakeries really buzz with energy, but they're also a perfect stop for an afternoon treat or a great place to pick up dessert for later.

Sharing Chinese American Stories through a Chinese American Lens

It wouldn't be right to introduce the magical world of Chinese bakeries without also highlighting the stories of the bakers, owners, and families that bring these bakeries to life. The spotlight and culinary accolades have primarily been focused on European and traditional American bakeries, but the professionals in Chinese bakeries deserve a round of applause for perfecting the softest buns, twisting dough into the most ingenious shapes, decorating the most whimsical cakes, and brewing the best cup of milk tea.

There are dozens of Chinatowns across the United States. Some, like San Francisco's, stretch on for blocks and blocks and make you feel as though you've been transported to another country. Other, smaller Chinatowns, like the one in Cleveland where my family lived, may have only a handful of restaurants and groceries. But even small towns have become part of the Chinese diaspora, where a lone grocery might include a bakery counter tucked into the corner. What all these Chinatowns and communities provide is a sense of familiarity for those far from home—and a connection with kindred spirits.

I've had the honor of speaking with bakery professionals from across the country, in San Francisco, Los Angeles, New York City, Philadelphia, and my hometown of Cleveland. They were all vastly different: Different origins. Different career paths. Different business styles. What connected them was a true passion for feeding people exceptional food and a dedication to wholesome ingredients and the virtues of making dishes from scratch and skipping shortcuts. In return, each has built a loyal customer base spanning generations.

Even though my family never owned a bakery, I felt a kinship with those who did. We're all part of an enormous *restaurant family club*. The fervor and joy these bakers expressed for their businesses reminded me of my goong goong's love for his restaurants and his journey from immigrant to business owner. When I spoke with the bakers' children, who are now adults helping run the family business, I could relate to their afternoons and weekends spent at the bakery—it was their form of daycare. And like the recipes in this book, their approach to products and recipe development deftly balances Western and Eastern influences.

It was important for me that their stories be shared through a lens similar to their own. Chinese bakeries are not something to be "discovered." They are not something new and trendy, but a beautiful facet of Chinese American life. Chinese bakeries have been around for a long time and deserve time in the spotlight.

Typologies

The term "Chinese bakery" can be very specific, but it's also broad in the sense that a number of different establishments provide bakery fare. Of course, some bakeries and cafes fall somewhere between these types, because just like buns, each one is unique.

Grab and go

This is the most common style of Chinese bakery. Rows of acrylic display cases are filled with every bun and pastry you can imagine. The first thing you do is grab a cafeteria tray and a pair of tongs and start browsing the cases. As you make your way past each one, you slowly fill up your tray, until you're ready to check out or you can't carry any more—whichever comes first.

Specialty shops

Instead of a one-stop-shop model, some bakeries specialize in only one item or a handful of items. A specialty bakeshop could be dedicated to elaborately decorated fruit and cream cakes, say, or offer the best cocktail bun in the city, or simply open for a few months out of the year, perhaps making mooncakes for Mid-Autumn Festival.

Takeaway

Takeaway restaurants are hybrids of bakeries and dim sum parlors. My favorites in San Francisco are Good Luck Dim Sum and Xiao Long Bao, both on Clement Street. In the mornings, it's worth waiting in the long lines for your pick of steamed buns, flaky egg tarts, juicy soup dumplings, and noodles, all sold in a tight space.

Sit-down cafes

Taking inspiration from *cha chaan tengs*, or Hong Kong–style diners, in these often bustling cafes you can sit down and enjoy a warm pastry and a spot of tea. Menus are generally more robust than what you find at traditional bakeries or takeaway restaurants.

Ingredients for a Better Bake

Coming from a background in architecture, I like to geek out and learn how each component of a recipe works together. Understanding why and how ingredients react to others helps me figure out how to make the best bread, cookie, and cake. Here, I've broken down the standard ingredients I use in my recipes, including why, how, and when to use them. Note that most of the recipes in this book feature everyday ingredients that most home cooks and bakers already have in the kitchen or can find in the neighborhood grocery store.

Flour

Flour is the building block of many recipes in this book. Each flour variety contributes inherent properties that allow you to create a successful baked good. The type of flour specified in each recipe is intentional and cannot be swapped out for another without some compromise in the results.

Bread flour is a wheat-based flour with a high protein content (11 to 14 percent). Higher protein content produces more gluten, which in turn gives bread chewiness and a strong structure. It has a higher absorption rate, which makes it ideal for breads that need a lot of milk, butter, and eggs.

All-purpose flour is another wheat-based flour with a slightly lower protein content (9 to 10 percent) than bread flour. It's wonderful for dumpling dough, green onion pancakes, puff pastry, steamed buns, and cookies. As the name implies, it works in almost any recipe.

Cake flour is on the lower end of the protein content spectrum (7 to 8 percent), which makes it ideal for airy sponge cakes and soufflés. I also prefer to use cake flour in my waffles and crepes because the batter hydrates much better and yields a more delicate texture.

Rice flour is made from finely milling grains of rice. It lends crispy and chewy textural notes, depending on how you cook it. Rice flour is often used for making bouncy rice noodles and as a breading for crispy fried tofu. When combined with water, it creates a batter for White Sugar Cake (page 132) and for suspending savory bits of Chinese sausage and green onions in a Turnip Cake (page 240). When buying rice flour, I recommend sticking with brands found in Asian markets; these tend to be ground to a finer, almost powdery consistency that works better in the recipes in this book than rice flours that are sold in American supermarket sections of "alt ingredients."

Glutinous rice flour is made from milling short-grain sticky rice. It behaves much differently than regular rice flour and is sometimes labeled as "mochiko" or "sweet rice flour." Glutinous rice flour is the base for Japanese mochi and other chewy treats. Koda Farms is my favorite brand because it delivers the best and most consistent results.

Sugar

Granulated sugar is white cane sugar with a neutral sweetness. It obviously sweetens recipes, but it also helps cookies spread in the oven, incorporates air into butter and egg whites, and caramelizes into beautiful shades of amber. As with every other ingredient in this book, the amount of sugar specified is intentional, so resist the urge to reduce the amount of sugar because you think it might be a little too sweet—trust me, it's not.

Brown sugar is cane sugar that has been combined with molasses. I typically use dark brown sugar for its deeper color and stronger flavor, but light brown sugar works fine as a substitute. When measuring brown sugar, you want to make sure to firmly pack it into the measuring cup.

Dairy and Eggs

Whole milk is what I typically use when a recipe calls for milk. However, 2% usually works as a substitute. Avoid skim or 1% milk in recipes because the fat content is too low. The higher fat content is necessary for the recipe's success.

Heavy cream is essential for whipped creams and is also my preferred liquid for egg washes—the fat from the heavy cream caramelizes into a beautiful dark-brown color in the oven.

Evaporated milk has about 60 percent of the water removed. It is sold in cans, and though it may feel like a slightly antiquated baking ingredient, it still gets heavy use in Chinese bakeries and cafes. It has an inherent caramelized flavor and extra-silky texture from the evaporation process, which makes it essential for Hong Kong Milk Tea (page 255) and to enhance the caramel flavors in Malay Cake (page 128).

Sweetened condensed milk is often confused with evaporated milk. It also has about 60 percent of its water content removed, but it has added sugar. The result is a rich, super creamy, and very sweet mixture. I look for any and every opportunity to drizzle it onto something.

Coconut milk is made from the pulp of mature coconuts. It is rich and creamy, with a strong coconut flavor. Full-fat coconut milk is the only coconut milk you should ever buy; avoid those marked "lite" or "reduced fat" or any that contain additives (the only ingredients on the label should be coconut and water). My favorite brands, Aroy-D and Chaokoh, are typically found in Asian grocery stores.

Butter for baking should be unsalted. I use salted butter when I'm sandwiching a patty inside a warm pineapple bun (page 45) or spreading it over a piece of bread, but not for baking. Unsalted butter in a recipe allows you to control exactly how much salt goes into it. Temperature is also incredibly important to a recipe's success—some call for chilled, softened, or melted butter. Be sure to allow your butter to soften at room temperature in advance (an hour or so in a warm spot is a good general rule), rather than trying to soften it in the microwave at the last minute. Once butter has melted, it doesn't quite behave the same way again, even if you let it firm back up.

Eggs should always be large and fresh. These recipes are designed with large eggs in mind. Save the beautiful heirloom eggs for brunch.

Oil

Canola oil is what I reach for again and again in the kitchen. It is often used to create crispier and more supple bread, brushed onto cutting boards and in between layers of dough for thin and flaky pancakes, and added to cakes for moisture. In most baking scenarios, stick with canola oil or another neutral-flavored oil, like vegetable or grapeseed, so it doesn't interfere with the flavors of your bake. Reserve more robust olive oil for savory cooking or dipping crusty bread in.

Sesame oil is nutty and aromatic. It's one of my favorite ingredients to incorporate into marinades, sauces, dressings, and dumpling fillings. A little sesame oil goes a long way in flavoring your food.

Other

Yeast is a nonchemical leavening agent (unlike baking soda or baking powder) that helps breads rise. Active dry yeast and instant yeast are the most commonly available types. Active dry yeast needs to be activated in warm water or liquid before it's combined with other ingredients, while instant yeast can be added directly to dry ingredients without any initial activation. In most cases, the types of yeast can be substituted without any problems. I typically use active dry yeast because when added to water and sugar (known as "proofing" the yeast), you can see bubbles popping up, indicating that it's alive and well. But every so often a recipe (like the steamed bun dough on page 17) calls for instant yeast because it works better for that specific method and recipe.

I prefer to buy jars of yeast (both active dry and instant) instead of individual packets and refrigerate them for freshness. I've been burned numerous times when packets of yeast have gone bad well before their expiration date. You can end up wasting an entire batch of bread if your yeast isn't doing its job.

Salt comes in many shapes and sizes. I exclusively use coarse salt for cooking, specifically Diamond Crystal kosher salt. The large, coarse grains dissolve quickly. Table salt is finer in texture, so if that's all

you have, use a little less than the recipe calls for, to avoid the risk of oversalting (more grains of table salt can fit into a measuring spoon than the coarser kosher salt grains). Save flaky sea salt for finishing touches, like sprinkling over a batch of salty-sweet cookies or topping buttery buns.

White pepper is more prevalent in my cooking than black pepper—purely based, I believe, on watching my mom cook with it my entire life. White pepper is more common than black pepper in Chinese cooking. It's a little spicier, and it's also ground into a fine powder, which makes it ultra-airborne when you sprinkle it. (I always sneeze when I cook with white pepper.)

Cornstarch is ubiquitous in Cantonese cooking. It's often used as a sauce thickener for glossy stir-fries, in marinades to help tenderize tough cuts of meat, and in batters for fried foods to produce extra-crunchy coatings. In baking, cornstarch acts as a stabilizer and thickener. It gives cakes an extra-tender crumb and custards their thick and creamy consistencies.

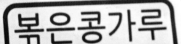
볶은콩가루

Roasted Soy Bean Powder

Distributed by

C.H. TRADING CO.
San Mateo, CA 94402

3 576500 812827

Nutrition Facts
Serv. Size 3 Tbsp (28g)
Servings about 20
Calories 160
Fat Cal. 0

Amount/Servings	%DV*	Amount/Servings	%DV*
Total Fat 17g	26%	Total Carb. 39g	13%
Sat Fat 2g	10%	Fiber 4g	16%
Cholesterol 0g	0%	Sugars 5g	
Sodium 0mg	0%	Protein 20g	
Vitamin A 0% • Vitamin C 0% • Calcium 15% • Iron 20%

*Percent Daily Values (DV)
are based on a 2,000
calorie diet.

NET WT. 8 oz (227 g)
PRODUCT OF USA

海苔の香
NORI KOMI FURIKAKE
ふりかけ

RICE SEASONING

Serving Suggestion

NET WT. 1.7oz (50g)

RICE FLOUR
แป้งข้าวเจ้าชนิดดีพิเศษ
水磨白粘米送粉
FARINE DE R
BỘT TẺ TI

AROY
COCONUT
NƯỚC CÔ

KIMBO 金寶肉酥
KIMBO BRAND PORK SUNG
COOKED SHREDDED DRIED PORK PRODUCT

INGREDIENTS: PORK, SUGAR, SOY FLOUR,
SOY SAUCE (WATER, SOYBEANS, WHEAT,
SALT (SODIUM BENZOATE LESS THAN 1/10
OF 1% AS A FOOD PRESERVATIVE)), LARD,
SALT, MONOSODIUM GLUTAMATE.

Manufactured for / Distributed by
WALONG MARKETING, INC.
BUENA PARK, CA 90621

16 OZ.
16 ออนซ์
16 安士
16 OZ.

NET WT. 4 OZ.

NET CONTENTS 14

BLACK & WHITE
Friesian Cow

SWEETENED CONDENSED FILLED MILK
LECHE CONDENSADA AZUCARADA LLENADA
NET WT / PESO NETO 14 OZ (396g)

· the cooking milk ·
Nestlé
Carnation

Evaporated Milk
淡奶

Vitamin D
Added
維他命D加
No rBST*

KSA
Gluten-Free

KODA ✿ FARMS®

A Family Legacy in California Farming Since 1918

MOCHIKO
Sweet Rice Flour
BLUE STAR® BRAND

もちこ

CALIFORNIA
Grown
& Milled

farine de riz doux
Net Wt 16 oz (1Lb) 454 g

Product
of USA

How to Shop at an Asian Grocery Store

On occasion, a recipe will call for some ingredient that can only be found at an Asian grocery store, but that's part of the fun in learning about Chinese baking. As a kid, I was obsessed with going to the Chinese grocery store near my grandparents' house because it was where all my favorite snacks and candies lived.

I realize that not every town has an Asian grocery store. Not to mention that "Asian grocery store" is a broad term; you might find a Korean, Japanese, or Cambodian grocery closer to you than a Chinese one. You'll be able to find many of the same ingredients you need across all the store varieties, plus everyday groceries. These stores usually carry all the essentials, like eggs, butter, milk, and regular flour.

I frequent Asian grocery stores and love to explore new ones when I travel. Once you arrive, give yourself some time to get the lay of the land, especially if this is your first time shopping there. Remember: this is still a grocery store, although the products and labels may look different to you. If you can't find something, ask an employee for help or show them a photo of the product you're looking for.

Some Asian grocery stores are huge and vast, while others are small and compact. Just remember to take your time and enjoy the opportunity to explore—meandering around the store has its own pleasures. Keep an open mind and try to shake any preconceived notions of what defines "weird" or "exotic" (my least favorite word) flavors and foods. They might be new to you but considered a kitchen staple for many other home cooks and are absolutely deserving of space in your kitchen.

Produce

Let's start with my favorite area (sorry, instant ramen aisle—I still love you!), the produce section. I love the vast variety of fruits and vegetables sold in Chinese groceries. You'll likely find all the conventional varieties of broccoli and oranges, but in the bin right next to sweet potatoes will be lotus root and taro. The leafy green section holds rows and rows of bok choy, yu choy, gai lan (Chinese broccoli), cabbages, amaranth, pea shoots, and mustard greens. In the fruit area, the most delicious mangos, crisp and juicy Asian pears, spiky rambutan, and neat bundles of lychee are yours for the choosing. Take your time scanning the bins, grab bundles that look fresh and crisp, and pick up a few new-to-you fruits and vegetables to experiment with.

Also, for the record, green onions and scallions are the same thing. I grew up calling them green onions and will continue to do so throughout the book!

Tea

Making and enjoying tea is a beloved practice in Asian cultures, and the tea section has options for every occasion. You'll need Ceylon tea to make a strong cup of Hong Kong Milk Tea (page 255). Jasmine and hojicha are beautiful blends for steeping in heavy cream to whip for desserts. Matcha is one of my favorites—for an occasional matcha latte, naturally, but also for adding to dough or batter to make bright emerald-hued buns and sponge-cake layers. With the exception of matcha (which is stone ground), I prefer to buy loose-leaf teas, which let me scoop up as much as I need and not have to deal with individual bags. If you can only find varieties in individual tea bags, that's fine—snip the tea bags and measure out as much tea as you need for your recipe.

Sauces

I like to take my time exploring the sauce aisle. The savory, salty, funky, sweet, and sour notes of sauces instantly elevate your cooking. I always keep light and dark soy sauce, oyster sauce, sriracha, fish sauce, hoisin sauce, chili crisp, and spicy bean paste (*doubanjiang*) in my fridge. With those staple sauces, I feel like I can cook anything. I also like to pick up the occasional shrimp paste or a jar of something I haven't tried before. I'm a big fan of Lee Kum Kee and Koon Chun for sauces and pastes, and Lo Gan Ma for chili crisp.

Starches

Starches play an important role in Chinese cooking and baking. They're used to make noodles, dumpling wrappers, and shiny sauces. They bind fillings together and lend a chewy texture to cookies and breads. Cornstarch is easily found in most grocery stores, but it's not the only starch in town. Wheat starch, tapioca starch, and sweet potato starch are always in my pantry. You will find all three in the same section, most likely adjacent to wheat-based flours.

Dried Foods

The practice of preserving and drying food has been a part of Chinese culture for centuries, so it's no surprise that the aisle of dried beans, seeds, nuts, vegetables, and medicinal herbs is expansive. If you can preserve or dry it, you'll most likely find it here, in a vacuum-sealed bag. I use dried red or aduki beans, black and white sesame seeds, and white lotus seeds to make all the sweet pastes for buns and mooncakes. Look for dried mushrooms close to the medicinal herbs section. Expect to see lots of varieties, from wood ear and white fungus to the more commonly used dried shiitake.

Cured and Salted Meats

Along the same line as dried foods, Asian grocery stores offer plenty of cured and salted meats. Pork floss is one of my absolute favorite toppings for jook, salads, and buns. Think of it as fluffy dried pork that is salty and a little sweet. It's much like crumbled bacon bits, offering a salty bite but with a softer, more airy texture. Pork floss is normally stored in a plastic tub, probably sold closer to the dried foods. (I like to keep a tub in the pantry for sneaky snack breaks.) Also in the cold cases are more substantial salted meats like dried shrimp and Chinese sausage (*lap cheong*). Add either to soups, rice dishes, and stir-fries for a kick of savory, salty flavor. Kam Yen Jan is my preferred brand for Chinese sausage. Both dried shrimp and Chinese sausage keep well in the refrigerator.

Oh! Don't forget to check out the instant ramen aisle to stock your pantry with quick meals and the snack aisle to load up for the drive home!

Essential Equipment

Aside from standard mixing bowls, a whisk, and measuring cups, I keep a collection of tools I consider essential for a well-equipped baker. Some are tools all bakers have on hand, and others are more specific for the Chinese bakery–inspired recipes in this book. I try to run a lean kitchen, without extraneous tools taking up space in my limited drawers and cabinets. Each of the tools listed here is well used and beloved.

Digital scale

This is the tool I use most in my kitchen. I wasn't always a devoted digital scale user. Before I got seriously into baking, I was a proud cook-by-feel type. I still very much am, *except* when it comes to baking, and *especially* when it comes to making pastry. I toggle between cooking by feel and with precision, depending on what I'm making. If a recipe provides weighted measurements, you'll get the most accurate and consistent results if you bake by weight. That mainly comes down to how people measure their ingredients like flour, of which any variance will start to change the consistency of the end result. One baker's cup of all-purpose flour might weigh 125g, while another cup might weigh 150g, if it wasn't aerated and spooned into the measuring cup (see below). That 25g variance will make a difference and also adds up if a recipe calls for more than 1 cup of flour. Once you start baking by weight, it's hard to go back. You're rewarded with dependable results, and cleanup is so much quicker without using all the extra measuring cups and spoons.

Measure your flour correctly: If you don't have a digital scale, the best practice for measuring flour is to aerate the flour with a fork or a whisk, spoon the flour into the measuring cup, and then level the flour with a straightedge (like a metal spatula or back edge of a butter knife). Scooping flour directly into the cup measure will pack in too much. And be sure to measure using a set of graduated measuring cups designed specifically for this purpose; never use a liquid measuring cup for dry ingredients.

Ruler

I still have my metal ruler from architecture school. It lives right above my spice rack, and I use it all the time to check for dough thickness and to guide straight, even cuts when working with pastry. I find straight lines, right angles, and consistently sized multiples incredibly satisfying.

Dowel rolling pin

I frequently use my dowel rolling pin for dumpling wrappers, but it comes in handy for many other kitchen tasks. This small rolling pin is the same thickness from end to end (not tapered) and measures about 12 inches long and about 1 inch in diameter. It's the perfect size for most of my kitchen projects, fitting my hand comfortably when rolling out dough for buns, mochi, cookies, and green onion pancakes. If you only have a larger rolling pin (designed for pastry and pie dough, primarily), you can certainly use it, but I highly recommend adding a dowel rolling pin to your kitchen arsenal.

Bench scraper

A bench scraper will become your best friend in the kitchen, helping you transfer chopped vegetables into a fry pan, divide dough into equal portions, lift pastry dough from your work surface, and clean up the floury mess left at the end of a big baking project.

Cookie scoop/dishers

I constantly use my 1-tablespoon and 1 1/2-tablespoon cookie scoops for effortlessly portioning the filling for buns and dumplings and, of course, for scooping cookie dough. It's not a completely necessary tool to have when you have regular old spoons at your disposal, but I appreciate how much cleaner and more efficient the process is when I use my cookie scoops.

Offset spatulas

My mini offset spatula is perfect for helping to release cakes from pans and spreading red bean paste onto dough. Its big brother, the full-size offset spatula, is excellent for smoothing out whipped cream for cakes and spreading cake batter into a level surface for Swiss rolls.

Bamboo steamer

A sturdy steamer is vital for making traditional Chinese steamed buns and cakes. Although I prefer to use bamboo steamers over metal steamers (the bamboo steamer doesn't condensate on the interior like metal steamers), either will work. When steaming food, you want to make sure there's some sort of nonstick barrier between the surface of the steamer and the food—cabbage leaves, small squares of parchment paper, reusable silicone steamer sheets, or a light spritz of nonstick spray. Otherwise, your buns or dumplings will securely stick to the steamer, and that's no fun.

When setting up a bamboo steamer, there's always the question of how far away the water should be from the steamer. The answer is: it doesn't matter, as long as the bottom of the steamer has enough water that it will boil continuously for as long you need to steam your food, whether that's 5 minutes or 45 minutes. The amount of water is more dependent on the type and size of the vessel.

My typical steamer setup: I set bamboo steamers over a heavy-bottomed pot that's the same diameter as the steamer (about 10 inches for both, in my case). It's simple and straightforward, and it prevents the bamboo steamer from burning or catching on fire. A tight seal between the steamer and the pot traps the steam, to cook the food inside. I normally fill the pot with 3 to 4 inches of water, which should allow for continuous steaming for 10 to 30 minutes. You can always refill the water between batches, if needed.

If you don't have this exact setup, don't worry. Some pots come with a metal steamer insert, and those work perfectly fine. If you have large pots and a steamer, but they aren't the same diameter, that's okay too. Some home cooks use woks, which are tapered with a wider mouth and narrower base, to boil water (although that will remove the seasoning on a steel wok) and snuggly place the steamer inside the mouth of the wok. You can create this same setup even if you don't have a wok. Find a pot that's slightly bigger than your steamer, and it should work in much the same way.

Pineapple cake molds

These molds aren't quite as multipurpose as mooncake molds. They're specifically used for making Taiwanese Pineapple Cakes (page 199), to help them hold their signature rectangular shape. A mold set will come with ten or so metal frames and a press. You place the cookie inside the frame and use the handled press to apply pressure to fill the mold with the dough.

Pineapple cake molds are sold at Asian houseware stores and definitely online.

Mooncake molds

Classic mooncake molds are beautiful and intricately carved out of wood. Mooncake masters have perfected the art of carefully pressing the mooncake dough into the mold and then smacking it with just enough force to release the mooncake in one piece. These days, commonly available plunger-style plastic mooncake molds are much easier to use. If you have an heirloom mooncake mold, by all means use it, but I highly recommend the plastic molds for overall ease and flexibility. Mooncake molds are obviously used for mooncakes, but you can also use their patterns as gorgeous cookie presses.

Molds typically come in 50g and 100g sizes. I consider 50g molds small mooncakes and 100g molds large mooncakes. Molds are round or square, but you can also find more unique shapes like wedges, flowers, fish, hearts, and leaves.

Mooncake molds are sold in Asian houseware stores, occasionally in grocery stores, and all over the internet.

Individual cupcake and tart molds

Loose individual cupcake and tart molds are crucial for making steamed cupcakes, because you can't fit a muffin tin inside a steamer. Back in the day, before the internet made every kitchen tool available with a simple click, my pau pau took it upon herself to cut individual molds out of a muffin tin with a pair of metal cutters. She still uses them today. Thankfully, you don't need to do that! The individual molds are also perfect for making cute little egg and coconut tarts.

I use two kinds of individual molds. My small fluted molds made from aluminum or carbon steel (about 2 ½ inches in diameter) give tart crusts a decorative texture. I also have slightly larger smooth-edged cupcake tins, about 3 inches in diameter and a little deeper than the fluted molds. These make slightly larger tarts than the fluted molds.

Parchment paper and silicone baking mat

For most baked goods you're on constant defense, trying to prevent buns, cookies, and cakes from sticking to the surface of pans. Occasionally, you *want* things to stick, like the side of sponge cake or soufflé cheesecake, which rely on the batter to grip onto the walls of the cake pan, so they bake nice and tall. For everything else, parchment paper should be all you need for a clean release. I almost always line baking sheets and cake pans with parchment paper. Squares of parchment paper act as a barrier between buns and steamer baskets, to prevent sticking. When I note that you should use a silicone baking mat instead, it's either because the recipe you're making is very sticky or the heat distribution provided by a silicone mat is essential for the recipe.

bread, bing, bao

Chapter 1

In Chinese, "bread" translates phonetically to *mianbao*, literally "packages" (*bao*) of "flour" (*mian*). That's an apt description of bread, if you ask me. Bread is treated differently across China. Some breads aren't even baked at all. Until recently, home kitchens in Hong Kong and other parts of Asia lacked conventional ovens. Because of this, steamed, deep-fried, and skillet-seared breads are common. In parts of northern and central China, varieties of *bing*, or crackery flatbreads, are baked in tandoor-like ovens and are popular street foods. The fried dough known as *youtiao* is a breakfast staple in any home—and well worth the effort of heating up a big vat of frying oil. Thankfully, most Chinese kitchens are now equipped with a stovetop *and* oven, so the challenges of making your own fresh bread, bing, or bao are a thing of the past—and baking a classic milk bread is that much easier.

Mother of All Milk Bread

It's fitting that the first recipe in this book is for milk bread. In the world of pillow-soft white enriched breads such as challah, brioche, and even Wonder Bread, I consider milk bread the reigning queen. It is an enriched bread, meaning that it has a higher fat content from the addition of eggs, butter, and milk. When done right, it has a lovely, sweet flavor and almost cotton-candy texture. It's the mother bread for practically all Chinese baked buns, whether stuffed and pinched into perfectly round and perky buns, or twisted into shapes and designs coyly hinting at the filling inside. Its versatility goes way beyond buns. Use the dough as the base for cinnamon rolls or bake a tall loaf for a week of turkey sandwiches and the best-ever grilled cheeses.

Milk bread is similar to Hokkaido milk bread or shokupan, which was popularized by Japanese bakeries. Different names, slightly varied recipes, but it's essentially the same bread. What sets these Asian enriched breads apart from other enriched breads is the use of *tangzhong*, a roux made of milk and flour. Tangzhong makes a huge difference in the quality of the bread. Think of it as a concentration of moisture. When you add tangzhong to the dough, the dough is able to retain a higher moisture content, and the result is a fluffy bread with a delicate crumb and ethereal softness that lasts for days—if it lasts that long at all.

The Foundations of Milk Bread

The concept of baking bread from scratch seems to intimidate some people. In the beginning of your bread-making journey, it's more about the technical process than feel. You may have to bust out a digital scale and learn how to tell if your yeast is properly activated by looking for tiny bubbles on the surface. I cook by instinct, but I love the methodical process of making bread. Once you have a solid recipe that you know and trust (I've got you covered there) and get into the practice of making bread, any trepidation should start to melt away, like butter on freshly toasted milk bread. Eventually, you'll rely on those kitchen instincts again and be able to simply feel when the dough is just right.

I approach many of my baking projects the same way I approached my past work in architecture: going through many iterations, eliminating extraneous components for the sake of efficiency, and studying how every small part reacts with the next. When I dove into the world of milk bread, everything started to click once I understood how each of the individual components worked together. So let's break it down:

Milk

You can't make milk bread without milk! Milk gives the bread richness, a soft crust, and a delicate, creamy flavor.

Do you need to scald the milk? You should. Milk contains whey protein, which prevents gluten from developing properly when you leave your dough to proof. Scalding the milk will deactivate or kill the whey protein in the milk. Better gluten formation results in a springier and softer bread texture. Once you scald the milk, let it cool until it's warm to the touch (or about 110°F, if you want to be precise), to activate the yeast. Milk that is too hot can kill the yeast.

Eggs and Butter

Like milk, eggs and butter enrich the dough. Both provide moisture to help you knead a supple and workable dough, while also providing fat and flavor.

Sugar

As previously mentioned, yeast feeds off sugar. So the presence of sugar in the dough will feed the yeast and produce carbon dioxide to make the dough rise. Slightly sweet milk bread is delicious on its own, but it also complements barbecue roast pork and makes a mighty melty grilled cheese. So resist the urge to reduce or even omit the sugar in the recipe if you plan to stuff it with your own savory filling creation. You will want the sweetness for balanced flavor and a proper rise.

Bread Flour

The high-protein content of bread flour makes it the best choice for milk bread. The higher protein levels in this heavily enriched dough provide the structure needed to support the fat from the milk, butter, and eggs. Bread flour contains between 11 and 14 percent protein, so it will produce more gluten, developing a sturdy, elastic dough that rises properly and produces a soft and chewy crumb. Note that you *could* swap out bread flour for an all-purpose flour in the milk bread recipe, but the results won't be the same. The bread will still be tasty, but it will also be more dense. For best results, stick with bread flour.

Yeast

Yeast is what makes bread rise. Don't let the thought of dealing with yeast intimidate you. Yes, it can make or break your bread, but remember that *you're* in charge here.

First, check the date on the jar or packet of yeast and make sure it's fresh. Most of the recipes in this book call for active dry yeast. This type of yeast requires that you "bloom" it in warm water or warm milk, with a pinch of sugar, before you mix it with flour. The yeast feeds off the sugar and produces carbon dioxide, resulting in lots of tiny bubbles on the surface of the liquid. If you see tiny bubbles, your yeast is alive and well! If you don't, throw out the yeast mixture and try again. Better to repeat blooming the yeast than to ruin an entire batch of bread.

If all you have is instant yeast, that's fine to use too. Instant yeast doesn't require blooming. Instead, you add instant yeast to the dry ingredients and continue with the recipe as instructed. I prefer using active dry yeast because I like to visually ensure the yeast is alive and doing its job.

Tangzhong

Tangzhong is a type of roux, made with a 1:5 ratio of flour to milk. The mixture is stirred together and cooked over low heat until it reaches the texture of creamy mashed potatoes. Cooking the milk and flour together gelatinizes the starches in the flour and traps in all that moisture, which will in turn give your bread a beautiful, soft texture.

Mother of All Milk Bread

MAKES 1 LOAF OR 12 BUNS

For the Tangzhong

100g (¼ cup plus 3 tablespoons) milk

20g (2 tablespoons) bread flour

For the Milk Bread

125g (½ cup plus 1 tablespoon) warm (110°F) milk

1 teaspoon active dry yeast

50g (¼ cup) granulated sugar, plus a pinch

335g (2 ⅔ cups) bread flour, plus more for work surface

½ teaspoon coarse salt

1 large egg

55g (4 tablespoons) unsalted butter, cut into pieces and softened

1 teaspoon canola or other neutral-flavored oil, for bowl

For the Egg Wash

1 large egg

1 tablespoon heavy cream

Make the tangzhong: In a small saucepan over low heat, combine the flour and milk and cook, whisking constantly, until thickened to a paste, 2 to 3 minutes. Immediately transfer the paste into a small bowl, scraping the sides of the saucepan with a flexible spatula; let cool until warm, 5 to 10 minutes. Texture should resemble mashed potatoes.

Make the milk bread: In a clean or new small sauce pan, scald the milk over medium heat, bringing the milk to a gentle simmer (watch carefully as milk tends to boil over). Pour milk into a small bowl and cool until warm to the touch (about 110°F). Stir in yeast and a pinch of sugar, and set aside until the surface of the mixture is foamy, 5 to 10 minutes.

In the bowl of an electric mixer fitted with a dough hook, combine the sugar, flour, salt, and egg. Add the tangzhong and milk and mix on low until shaggy. Add the softened butter one piece at a time, mixing until fully incorporated before adding the next. Increase the speed to medium-high and continue to knead the dough until it is tacky and slightly sticky, 8 to 9 minutes. Transfer the dough to a lightly floured work surface. Wet your hands to prevent the dough from sticking, pinch and pull the ends of the dough to form a smooth ball.

Coat a large mixing bowl with the 1 teaspoon of oil. Add the dough to the bowl, gently turning it to cover with oil. Cover the bowl with plastic wrap and set in a warm spot to proof until doubled in size, about 2 hours (or place in the refrigerator to proof for at least 8 hours or overnight).

Transfer the proofed dough onto a lightly floured work surface. Punch down the dough to deflate it. Pinch and pull the ends of the dough to form a smooth ball (see photos).

Variations

Whole-Wheat Milk Bread:
Reduce bread flour to 250g (2 cups) and add 85g (⅔ cup) whole-wheat flour.

Chocolate Milk Bread:
Add 16g (3 tablespoons) cocoa powder to the dry ingredients.

Kneading by hand: A heavily enriched dough, like this one, will naturally be on the stickier side. Using an electric stand mixer for kneading will be a lot easier, but it is not impossible to knead this dough by hand. All you need is an extra ¼ cup of bread flour on standby.

In a large mixing bowl, whisk to combine the flour, sugar, and salt. Add the tangzhong, milk/yeast mixture, egg, and softened butter. Using a flexible spatula, mix everything together to form a shaggy dough. Start kneading with your hands until you have a smooth dough ball, 13 to 15 minutes. Have an extra ¼ cup of bread flour off on the side to lightly dust the dough and the work surface whenever you find the dough too sticky to work with. Try not to use more than a ¼ cup of extra flour, though, to prevent the bread from being too dry.

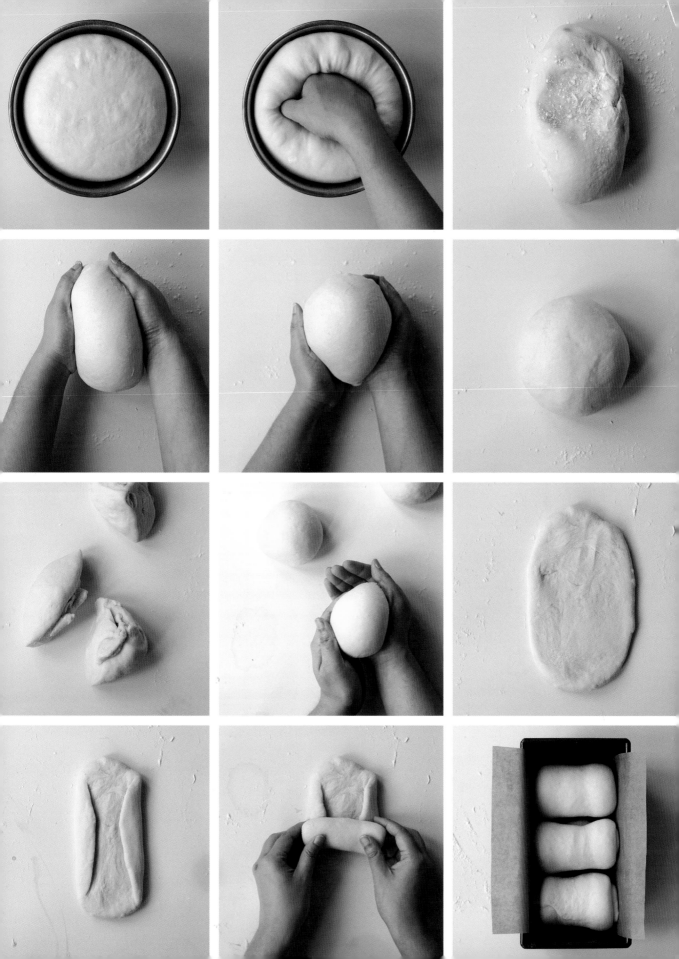

There's More than One Way to Form a Loaf

To Make a Classic Three-Segment Loaf

Line the bottom and long sides of a 9 x 5-inch loaf pan with parchment paper. (If baking in a pullman pan there's no need to line with parchment paper.) Divide the dough into three equal pieces. Form each piece into a smooth ball. Roll out a piece of dough into a 5 x 8-inch oval. Fold the long edges of the dough over by 1/2 inch and then roll into a 4-inch log, starting at one of the short ends. Place the dough seam-side down, in the loaf pan. Repeat with the remaining two pieces of dough, placing them side by side in the pan. Cover the pan loosely with a damp, clean kitchen towel or plastic wrap and allow the dough to proof in a warm spot until it reaches just above the rim of the pan (or just below the rim for a pullman pan), 60 to 90 minutes. Preheat the oven to 350°F. To make the egg wash, whisk together the egg and heavy cream in a small bowl. Brush the top of the dough with egg wash. (Omit the egg wash if using a pullman pan.) Bake on the center rack of the oven until the top is golden brown, 30 to 33 minutes. Transfer the pan to a wire rack and allow the bread to cool in the pan for 10 minutes. Use the edges of the parchment paper to help lift the bread from the pan, then transfer to the rack to cool completely.

To Make a Split-Top Loaf

Line the bottom and long sides of a 9 x 5-inch loaf pan with parchment paper. Divide the dough into eight equal portions with a bench scraper (for accuracy, weigh with a digital scale if you have one). Form each piece into a smooth ball. Place the dough balls in the pan, in two rows of four. Cover the pan loosely with a damp, clean kitchen towel or plastic wrap and allow the dough to proof in a warm spot until it reaches just above the rim of the loaf pan, 60 to 90 minutes. Preheat the oven to 350°F. To make the egg wash, whisk together the egg and heavy cream in a small bowl. Brush the top of the dough with egg wash. Bake until the top is golden brown, 30 to 33 minutes. Transfer the pan to a wire rack and allow the bread to cool in the pan for 10 minutes, then transfer the bread to the rack to cool completely.

To Make Pull-Apart Milk Bread Buns

Line the bottom and sides of a 9 x 9-inch baking pan with parchment paper. Divide the dough into 9 equal portions with a bench scraper (for accuracy, weigh with a digital scale if you have one). Form each piece into a smooth ball. Arrange the dough balls in the pan and cover loosely with a damp, clean kitchen towel or plastic wrap. Allow the buns to proof until doubled in size, 45 minutes to 1 hour. Preheat the oven to 350°F. To make the egg wash, whisk together the egg and heavy cream in a small bowl. Brush the tops of the buns with egg wash and sprinkle with flaky sea salt, or other toppings (see below) if you wish. Bake until the tops are lightly golden brown, 22 to 25 minutes. Remove the pan from the oven and allow the buns to cool completely on a wire rack.

To Make Milk Bread Buns (great for cheeseburgers and sandwiches)

Line two large rimmed baking sheets with parchment paper. Divide the dough into 12 equal portions with a bench scraper (for accuracy, weigh with a digital scale if you have one). Form each piece into a smooth ball. Place the dough balls on the baking sheets, spacing at least 3 inches apart, and cover loosely with a damp, clean kitchen towel or plastic wrap. Allow the dough to proof in a warm spot until doubled in size, 45 minutes to 1 hour. Preheat the oven to 350°F. To make the egg wash, whisk together the egg and heavy cream in a small bowl. Brush the tops of the buns with egg wash and bake until the tops are golden brown, 18 to 20 minutes. Transfer the buns to a wire rack to cool completely.

Topping Options: furikake, everything bagel seasoning, black pepper, sesame seeds, shredded cheese, Parmesan cheese

Matcha and Black Sesame Marbled Milk Bread

MAKES 1 LOAF

Matcha and black sesame make a flavor power couple, like chocolate and vanilla. You'll find the emerald and gray duo in soft serve ice cream cones and swirled into cheesecakes. Matcha, a stone-ground green tea powder, has a distinctive earthiness that accentuates the nutty and slightly bitter black sesame paste. The combination is also delicious—and strikingly colorful—in bread form. Half of the dough for this loaf incorporates matcha powder and the other half black sesame paste. The two doughs are layered together for a marbled effect, making each slice one of a kind.

This bread isn't necessarily sweet. It is, however, amazing with butter and salt, a smear of cream cheese, or a big swoop of peanut butter and drizzle of honey.

For the Tangzhong

100g (¼ cup plus 3 tablespoons) milk

20g (2 tablespoons) bread flour

For the Milk Bread Dough

125g (½ cup plus 1 tablespoon) warm (110°F) milk

1 teaspoon active dry yeast

50g (¼ cup) granulated sugar, plus a pinch

335g (2 ⅔ cups) bread flour, plus more for work surface

½ teaspoon coarse salt

1 large egg

55g (¼ cup) unsalted butter, cut into pieces and softened

3g (2 teaspoons) food-grade matcha powder

1 teaspoon canola or other neutral-flavored oil, for bowl

18g (1 tablespoon) Black Sesame Paste (page 14)

For the Egg Wash

1 large egg

1 tablespoon heavy cream

Make the tangzhong: In a small saucepan over low heat, combine the milk and flour and cook, whisking constantly, until thickened to a paste, 2 to 3 minutes. (The texture should resemble smooth mashed potatoes.) Immediately transfer the paste to a small bowl, scraping the sides of the saucepan with a flexible spatula; let cool until warm, 5 to 10 minutes.

Make the dough: In a small saucepan, scald the milk over medium heat, bringing it to a gentle simmer, about 1 minute (Watch carefully, as milk tends to boil over). Pour the milk into a small bowl and cool until warm to the touch (about 110°F). Stir in the yeast and a pinch of sugar, and set aside until the surface of the mixture is foamy, 5 to 10 minutes.

In the bowl of an electric mixer fitted with a dough hook, combine the sugar, flour, salt, and egg. Add the tangzhong and milk/yeast mixture and mix on low until shaggy. Add the softened butter, one piece at a time, mixing until fully incorporated before adding the next. Remove half of the dough (about 355g if using a digital scale) and transfer to a medium mixing bowl.

Add the matcha powder to the bowl of the electric mixer and continue to knead on medium-high speed until the dough is tacky and slightly sticky, 7 to 8 minutes. Transfer the dough to a lightly floured work surface. Wet your hands to prevent the dough from sticking, and pinch and pull the ends of the dough to form a smooth ball. Coat a medium mixing bowl with ½ teaspoon oil. Add the dough to the bowl, gently turning it to cover with oil. Cover the bowl with plastic wrap and set in a warm spot to proof until doubled in size, about 2 hours (or place in the refrigerator to proof for at least 8 hours or overnight).

In the bowl of the electric mixer (no need to clean), add the remaining dough and the black sesame paste. Repeat step 4 for the black sesame dough.

Once both the matcha and black sesame doughs have proofed, punch them down to deflate them, then transfer them to a lightly floured work surface. Pinch and pull the ends of the two doughs to form two smooth balls.

Line the bottom and long sides of a 9 x 5-inch loaf pan with parchment paper. (If baking in a pullman pan, no need to line with parchment paper.) Divide each dough into three equal pieces. Form each piece into a smooth ball. Roll out a piece of matcha dough into a 5 x 8-inch oval. Top with black sesame dough and roll it out into a 5 x 8-inch rectangle. Fold the long edges of the dough over by 1/2 inch and then roll into a 4-inch log, starting at one of the short ends. Place the dough, seam-side down, in the loaf pan. Repeat with the remaining pieces of dough (alternating the matcha and black sesame dough in one segment, for contrast), placing them side by side in the pan. Cover the pan loosely with a damp, clean kitchen towel or plastic wrap and allow the dough to proof in a warm spot until it reaches just above the rim of the pan (just below the rim for a pullman pan), 60 to 90 minutes.

Preheat the oven to 350°F.

To make the egg wash, whisk together the egg and heavy cream in a small bowl. (Omit the egg wash if using a pullman pan.)

Brush the top of the dough with egg wash. Bake on the center rack of the oven until the top is golden brown, 30 to 33 minutes. Transfer the pan to a wire rack and allow the bread to cool in the pan for 10 minutes, then transfer the bread to the rack to cool completely. Store in an airtight container (a resealable bag works great) for up to 4 days.

Black Sesame Paste

MAKES ABOUT 1 CUP

120g (1 cup) roasted black sesame seeds

20g (2 tablespoons) sugar

45g (¼ cup) canola or other neutral-flavored oil

In the bowl of a food processor, pulse the sesame seeds and sugar until the mixture is coarse and sandy. While the food processor is still running, add the oil and blend until smooth, 1 to 2 minutes. Store in an airtight container and refrigerate for up to 1 month.

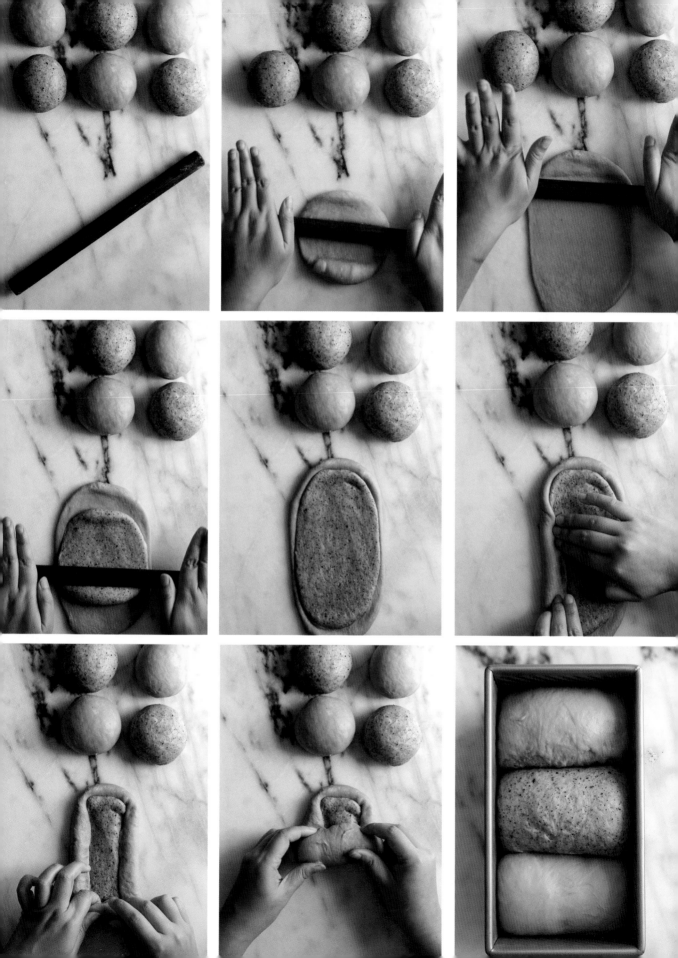

Fluffy Steamed Bun Dough

MAKES 12

Another cornerstone of Chinese bakeries are steamed buns. They are the paler, softer, and squishier sibling to baked milk bread buns. Were you one of those kids who preferred their peanut butter and jelly sandwich with the crusts trimmed off? Maybe the crusts had a little too much "texture" for your six-year-old palate. If you were that kid (I sure was), then steamed buns are definitely for you. Even if you weren't that kid, you'll still love these squishiest of squishy buns. Because they are cooked with steam, the exterior of the dough doesn't form a crust—the entire bun stays soft throughout.

Unstuffed buns are called mantou and are served at breakfast to dip into condensed milk, soup, soy milk, and jook. It's easy to pop in half a dozen mantou without thinking about it because it feels like eating little clouds. Stuffed steamed buns are called baozi and the stuffing options are virtually endless. Stuffing the buns with a simple red bean paste (page 53) or black sesame paste (page 14) is delicious, but so is a more laborious char siu bao filling (page 86). It's easy to stock up on frozen buns from any Asian market, but the texture just doesn't compare to that of fresh, homemade buns. Like Milk Bread, this steamed bun dough is versatile and can be formed into all kinds of imaginative shapes.

300g (2 1/2 cups) all-purpose flour

50g (1/4 cup) sugar

1 teaspoon instant yeast

1/2 teaspoon baking powder

1/4 teaspoon coarse salt

160g (scant 3/4 cup) warm water (about 110°F)

1 teaspoon canola or other neutral-flavored oil, for bowl

In the bowl of an electric mixer fitted with a dough hook, whisk to combine the flour, sugar, instant yeast, baking powder, and salt. With the mixer on low, pour in the warm water and mix to form a shaggy dough. Increase the speed to medium-high and knead until the dough is tacky and very smooth, 8 to 9 minutes. (Alternatively, you can knead this dough by hand until smooth, 10 to 12 minutes.) Transfer the dough to a lightly floured work surface. Pinch and pull the ends of the dough into a smooth ball.

Brush a large bowl with the oil and add the dough to the bowl. Gently turn the dough in the oil to coat, then cover the bowl with plastic wrap. Allow the dough to proof in a warm spot until doubled in size, 1 to 1 1/2 hours, or in the refrigerator for at least 6 hours or up to overnight.

Once the dough has proofed, punch down to deflate the dough and transfer it to a lightly floured surface. Pinch and pull the ends of the dough into a smooth ball.

To Make Unstuffed Steamed Buns (Mantou)

Cut twelve 4-inch squares of parchment paper.

Divide the dough into 12 equal portions with a bench scraper (for accuracy, weigh with a digital scale if you have one). Working with one piece at a time, pinch and pull the ends of the dough under to form a smooth ball. Place on a 4-inch square of parchment paper.

Cover the buns with a damp, clean kitchen towel and allow them to proof until they are 1 ½ times larger, 30 to 45 minutes.

Set up your steamer (page xxviii) and bring water to a boil. Arrange the buns in the bamboo steamer baskets, spacing 2 inches apart. If you can't fit them all, work in batches and keep remaining buns in the fridge to prevent overproofing. Steam buns over boiling water for 10 minutes. Turn off the heat and leave the buns in the covered steamer for 5 more minutes to prevent collapsing. Remove the buns from the steamer and let cool slightly before serving.

To Make Stuffed Buns

Cut twelve 4-inch squares of parchment paper.

Divide the dough into 12 equal portions with a bench scraper (for accuracy, weigh with a digital scale if you have one). Working with one piece at a time, pinch and pull the ends of the dough under to form a smooth ball. Using a dowel rolling pin, roll the dough into a 4-inch round, making sure the edges are thinner than the middle. Fill the dough with the desired filling (see chapters 2 and 3) and pleat the edges closed. Place on a 4-inch square of parchment paper (either pleat side up or pleat side down).

Place formed buns on a large rimmed baking sheet or cutting board. Cover the buns with a damp, clean kitchen towel and allow them to proof in a warm spot until they are 1 ½ times larger, 30 to 45 minutes.

Set up your steamer (page xxviii) and bring water to a boil. Arrange the buns in the bamboo steamer baskets, spacing 2 inches apart. If you can't fit them all, work in batches and keep the remaining buns in the fridge to prevent overproofing. Steam the buns over boiling water for 10 minutes. Turn off the heat and leave the buns in the covered steamer for 5 more minutes to prevent collapsing. Remove the buns from the steamer and let cool slightly before serving.

To Make Gua Bao (Steamed Slider Buns)

Cut twelve 4-inch squares of parchment paper.

Divide the dough into 12 equal portions with a bench scraper (for accuracy, weigh with a digital scale if you have one). Working with one piece at a time, pinch and pull the ends of the dough under to form a smooth ball. Roll out the dough into a 3 x 6-inch oval. Brush the surface of the dough with canola oil and gently fold the dough in half. Place on a 4-inch square of parchment paper.

Cover the buns with a damp, clean kitchen towel and allow them to proof until they are 1 ½ times larger, 30 to 45 minutes.

Set up your steamer (page xxviii) and bring water to a boil. Arrange buns in the bamboo steamer baskets, spacing 2 inches apart. If you can't fit them all, work in batches and keep the remaining buns in the fridge to prevent overproofing. Steam buns over boiling water for 10 minutes. Turn off the heat and leave the buns in the covered steamer for 5 more minutes to prevent collapsing. Remove the buns from the steamer and let cool slightly before serving.

Flavor Variations

Matcha Dough: Add 1 tablespoon (7g) food-grade matcha powder to the dry ingredients.

Spinach Dough: In a blender or food processor, puree 3 cups packed fresh spinach with $^3/_4$ cup warm water. Strain the puree through a fine mesh sieve set over a bowl until you have 160g (a scant $^3/_4$ cup) of spinach water. Discard the pulp. Use the warm spinach water in place of regular warm water in the recipe.

Sweet Potato Dough: Reduce warm water to 113g ($^1/_2$ cup) and add 120g ($^1/_2$ cup) sweet potato puree along with the dry ingredients.

Whole-Wheat Dough: Reduce all-purpose flour to 225g (1 $^3/_4$ cups) and add 75g ($^2/_3$ cup) whole-wheat flour.

How to Avoid Collapsed Dough

Turning off the heat and allowing the steamed buns to sit covered in the steamer for 5 additional minutes will help the buns maintain a smooth surface. If you lift the lid too soon, the sudden change in temperature will probably cause your buns to collapse and wrinkle.

If your buns turn out wrinkly on the surface, even if you let them sit in the steamer with the heat turned off, this may be because you either didn't knead the dough enough or the dough overproofed. Too many air bubbles in the dough will weaken its structure and cause wrinkles, which is why the initial proof is only 1 to 1 ½ hours, and the second proof is only 30 to 45 minutes. Make sure your dough is well kneaded and smooth, to remove any air bubbles. You also should aim to roll out each dough round so it's thicker in the middle and thinner at the edges before you form the buns; if it's too thin in the middle, the bun is more likely to collapse after steaming.

Crispy Chinese Sausage and Cilantro Pancakes

MAKES 6

These Chinese sausage and cilantro pancakes are a deviation from the beloved classic green onion pancake. I would take a plateful of crispy green onion pancakes topped with a big spoonful of chili oil over a stack of buttermilk pancakes any day. They should be salty, crispy, and a little greasy (in a good way). Some people like them thin and crunchy, bordering on cracker territory, while others prefer them thick and doughy. In my world, the perfect pancake is light and flaky on the outer rings and progressively doughier and chewier toward the center. That chewy center nugget of dough is *the best* piece to dunk into a generous amount of chili oil.

Thin layers of unleavened dough are rolled up with sesame oil and chopped fillings to create a quick lamination of sorts to create all those layers. The Chinese sausage renders into crunchy bits of sweet and salty pork, and the cilantro brings a welcome freshness. The combination is so delicious, complex, and textually more exciting than the classic green onion pancake.

Don't stop at Chinese sausage and cilantro though—consider filling your pancakes with other tender herbs such as basil, dill, and tarragon, and maybe swap out the Chinese sausage for crisp bacon or crunchy fried garlic.

300g (2 1/2 cups) all-purpose flour

1/2 teaspoon coarse salt

170g (3/4 cup) warm water

1/4 cup canola or other neutral-flavored oil, plus extra for brushing

3 Chinese sausages, finely chopped

2 tablespoons toasted sesame oil

1 cup fresh cilantro leaves and tender stems, finely chopped

Classic Green Onion Pancake Variation

Replace the Chinese sausage and cilantro with 4 green onions, trimmed and finely chopped.

In a medium bowl, combine the flour, salt, and warm water. Mix with a pair of chopsticks or flexible spatula until a shaggy dough forms. Knead with your hands until you form a smooth ball, 6 to 8 minutes. Lightly brush a medium bowl with canola oil. Transfer the dough to the bowl, turn to coat, and cover with plastic wrap. Rest at room temperature for at least 30 minutes, or up to 8 hours. (The longer the dough rests at room temperature, the flakier the pancakes will be.)

In a medium skillet over medium-high heat, cook the sausage, stirring occasionally, until the fat renders and sausage is crispy, 3 to 4 minutes. Transfer the sausage to a bowl to cool completely.

On a lightly floured surface, divide the dough into six equal pieces, preferably with a digital scale. Lightly brush a wooden cutting board with canola oil. Roll one piece of dough into a roughly 6 x 10-inch rectangle. Brush the dough with some sesame oil and sprinkle some sausage and cilantro evenly over the surface. Starting at a long edge, tightly roll up the dough into a 10-inch-long rope, pressing out trapped air. Starting at one end, form the rope into a coil shape, tucking the opposite end underneath at the end. Set aside and repeat with remaining dough, sesame oil, sausage, and cilantro to form six pancakes. (Brush the cutting board with more canola oil as needed.) When you've formed the last pancake, cover the coils with a kitchen towel and allow them to rest for

15 minutes. (Don't be tempted to skip this step, as the pancakes will not roll out as easily without a proper rest.)

Working with one piece at a time, gently flatten each coil with the palm of your hand, then roll into a 6-inch round. Place on a parchment paper–lined baking sheet. If the pancake bursts in some places, don't panic! That's natural! It will still cook just fine. In a heavy-bottomed skillet, heat the ¼ cup canola oil over medium-high until shimmering. Cook one pancake in the oil until the underside is golden brown, 1 to 2 minutes, then flip and cook the other side until golden brown, 1 to 2 minutes more. Place the pancake on a baking sheet fitted with a wire rack. Repeat with the remaining pancakes and serve. (The pancakes are best eaten soon after frying.)

Uncooked pancakes can be stored in the freezer for up to 3 months. Sandwich the pancakes between 7-inch squares of parchment paper, then place the stack in a resealable plastic bag and freeze. Do not thaw the pancakes before cooking and frying as you would fresh pancakes.

Cooked pancakes can be refrigerated in an airtight container for up to 3 days. Reheat the pancakes on a baking sheet in a 400-degree oven until hot, 8 to 10 minutes.

Why Use a Wooden Cutting Board?

This pancake dough rolls out best (read: thinnest) on a wooden cutting board brushed with canola oil. The dough is able to grab onto the texture of the wood, allowing it to stretch out easier. It doesn't roll out as easily on a solid surface countertop because there's nothing to grip onto.

Youtiao (Chinese Doughnut)

MAKES 6

What is it about fried dough that makes it so alluring for breakfast? Like their sweet glazed American cousins, Chinese savory fried doughnuts are a breakfast staple. *Youtiao* are airy sticks of fried dough that are often served alongside a breakfast porridge called jook (page 230), wrapped in sticky rice in Fan Tuan (page 234), or eaten plain with a glass of soy milk to wash them down. Whenever my mom made a giant pot of creamy jook in the morning, she'd ask us if we wanted a fried ghost on the side. Hearing this made us chuckle—youtiao sounds like "fried ghost" in Chinese. The answer was always yes!

Our family would order youtiao from our local dim sum parlor or stockpile them in the freezer after an epic bakery run to Chicago. These days, I've found that making youtiao from scratch is quite easy. It just requires a bit of patience. The dough needs ample time to rest and relax, so it has the flexibility to stretch into the fried ghosts we know and love. To split up the work, make the dough the night before (the longer the dough rests, the better) and then fry them in the morning for the best breakfast treat.

300g (2 1/2 cups) bread flour, plus more for dusting

1 tablespoon baking powder

1/2 teaspoon baking soda

1/2 teaspoon coarse salt

1 large egg

150g (2/3 cup) milk

20g (2 tablespoons) canola oil, plus extra for frying

In the bowl of an electric mixer fitted with a dough hook, combine the flour, baking powder, baking soda, salt, egg, milk, and oil. Mix on low speed to form a shaggy dough, then increase to medium speed and continue mixing until the dough is tacky and pulling away from the sides of the bowl, 8 to 9 minutes.

Transfer the dough to a lightly floured surface and form into a smooth ball. Cover with a clean kitchen towel and allow the dough to rest for 20 minutes.

Roll out the dough into a roughly 6 x 12-inch rectangle. Place a large piece of plastic wrap on your work surface. Transfer the dough onto the plastic wrap and wrap tightly in plastic. Set the dough on a plate or small baking sheet and allow the dough to rest overnight in the fridge (at least 8 hours or up to 24 hours).

The next day, let it come to room temperature on the counter, at least 1 hour. (The dough will be very soft.)

In a large heavy-bottomed pot, heat 3 inches of canola oil over medium-high heat until a deep-fry thermometer registers 370°F.

While the oil heats up, uncover the dough. Use the plastic wrap to help flip the dough onto a lightly floured surface. Cut the dough in half, into two 6 x 6-inch pieces. Then cut each half into six 1 x 6-inch strips. Stack two strips on top of each other and gently press a chopstick down the center of the dough, making sure not to fully cut through it. Pinch either end of the dough (so

the pieces don't separate in the oil) and gently stretch it until it is about 8 inches long. Place the stretched dough on a lightly floured surface and repeat with the remaining strips of dough.

Working in batches of one or two, fry the strips in the hot oil (adjust the heat in order to maintain 370°F). Once they float to the top (after about 5 seconds) turn them continuously with chopsticks or kitchen tongs until golden brown, 60 to 90 seconds. With tongs, transfer the doughnuts to a wire rack set in a large rimmed baking sheet. Continue to fry the remaining strips of dough, allowing time between each batch for the oil temperature to return to 370°F. Serve the youtiao warm.

Youtiao is best served fresh but freezes well. Place cooked youtiao in a resealable bag and freeze for up to 3 months. Reheat youtiao on a large rimmed baking sheet in a 400°F oven for 10 minutes.

Brown Sugar Shao Bing

MAKES 10

Shao bing is a popular street snack and breakfast item in northern China. The sesame seed–crusted breads are made from laminated dough stuffed with a variety of sweet and savory fillings. The style of shao bing depends on the city. Sometimes the dough is leavened, sometimes it's thin and cracker-adjacent, and sometimes it's filled with pork instead of sugar. What's consistent is that street vendors make them fresh every morning in makeshift tandoor-like ovens. Shao bing are baked on the walls of the barrel-shaped ovens and then peeled off when perfectly crisp. For those of us without tandoor ovens, a regular oven and baking sheets work fine. I'm a fan of the addition of nutty whole-wheat flour to the dough and simple brown sugar and butter filling, which tastes a little luxurious, like a cinnamon roll.

For the Dough

275g (1 ¼ cups) warm water (about 110°F)

1 teaspoon active dry yeast

Pinch of granulated sugar

300g (2 ½ cups) all-purpose flour

125g (1 cup) whole-wheat flour

½ teaspoon coarse salt

30g (3 tablespoons) canola oil, plus more for the bowl and board

For the Brown Sugar Filling

113g (½ cup; 1 stick) unsalted butter, softened

90g (½ cup) firmly packed brown sugar (light or dark)

For the Topping

20g (1 tablespoon) honey

20g (2 tablespoons) canola or other neutral-flavored oil

¼ cup toasted white sesame seeds

Make the dough: Place the warm water in a small mixing bowl. Stir in the yeast and pinch of granulated sugar, and set aside until the surface of the mixture is foamy, 5 to 10 minutes.

In the bowl of an electric mixer fitted with a dough hook, combine the all-purpose flour, whole-wheat flour, and salt. Pour the yeast mixture into the bowl and mix on low for 1 to 2 minutes. Add the oil, increase the speed to medium, and knead until the dough is smooth and tacky, 8 to 9 minutes. Transfer the dough to a lightly floured work surface. Pinch and pull the ends of the dough into a smooth ball.

Lightly coat a large bowl with 1 teaspoon oil. Transfer the dough to the bowl, turning to coat. Cover the bowl with plastic wrap. Allow the dough to proof in a warm spot until doubled in size, 1 ½ to 2 hours, or overnight in the refrigerator.

Make the brown sugar filling: While the dough rests, combine the softened butter and brown sugar in a medium bowl. Mix with a flexible spatula until well blended. Set aside at room temperature until ready to fill the bread.

Once the dough has proofed, punch down to deflate it and transfer it to a lightly floured work surface. Pinch and pull the ends of the dough into a smooth ball. Divide the dough into ten equal portions with a bench scraper (for accuracy, weigh with a digital scale if you have one). Form each portion of dough into a smooth ball.

Working on a wooden cutting board lightly brushed with oil, roll out one portion of dough into a 3 x 10-inch oval. Spread 1 tablespoon of the filling on the dough, leaving at least a ½-inch border around the edges. Fold the dough in half lengthwise. Gently pat down the dough to remove any air bubbles. Starting along a short end, roll the dough into a tight coil, tuck the end of the coil underneath, and set aside on the counter. Repeat with remaining portions of dough and filling to form ten shao bing. Cover the dough coils and allow them to rest for 15 minutes. (Don't be tempted to skip this step because the dough will not roll out as easily without a proper rest.)

Line two large rimmed baking sheets with parchment paper.

Firmly flatten one coil with the palm of your hand. Roll out the coil into a 5-inch round. The dough might fight back a little, but be patient or let the dough rest for a few more minutes. Place the formed shao bing on the prepared baking sheet. Repeat with the remaining portions of dough. Cover the sheets with damp, clean kitchen towels and allow the dough to briefly proof in a warm place, 25 to 30 minutes.

Make the topping: Mix the honey and oil together in a small bowl. With a pastry brush, top the shao bing with the honey mixture. Sprinkle the tops with the sesame seeds.

Preheat the oven to 400°F. Bake the shao bing until golden brown, 17 to 19 minutes. Transfer the sheet to a wire rack and let the shao bing cool on the sheet for 5 minutes before transferring to the wire rack to continue cooling. Serve warm or at room temperature.

Shao bing are best enjoyed fresh from the oven but can be stored in an airtight container (a resealable bag works great) for up to 3 days, or in the freezer for up to 3 months. Reheat on a baking sheet in a 350°F oven for 5 to 10 minutes, until crisp and warmed through.

Moo Shu Wrappers

MAKES 16

Growing up, moo shu pork was a favorite item on the menu at my family's restaurant. However, I was particularly fond of eating the moo shu wrappers simply with a light brush of hoisin, a fresh cucumber spear, and thinly sliced green onions. The wrappers are super thin and delicate, almost akin to flour tortillas. Making your own wrappers takes little effort, and straight from the pan, they taste so much better and have a delightful chewy texture.

You make the dough by kneading together flour, water, and oil. After a brief rest to allow the gluten to relax, you portion the dough into 16 pieces, then stack two pieces of dough with a layer of oil in between, and roll them out super thin. I prefer to roll out the wrappers while simultaneously cooking them, but if time management and multi-tasking is an issue, you can stack the wrappers in between sheets of parchment paper until you're ready to cook them (just don't let them sit too long because the wrappers will start to stick to the parchment paper). The wrappers are quickly cooked in a skillet until slightly blistered on both sides. The dough might puff up into a balloon when cooking because hot air causes the two layers to separate. When all the wrappers have finished cooking, peel the two layers apart and get stuffing! You could take my favorite route of hoisin, cucumbers, and green onions, or stuff with roast duck, pork belly, or your favorite veggie stir-fry.

300g (2 ½ cups) all-purpose flour, plus more for dusting

170g (3/4 cup) warm water

20g (2 tablespoons) canola oil, plus more for brushing

Place the flour in a large mixing bowl and make a well in the center. Pour the warm water and oil into the well and stir the flour into the water with a pair of chopsticks or flexible spatula, working from the outside in. Mix until the water has been absorbed and the dough is shaggy. Knead the dough with your hands for 5 minutes, until you have a smooth ball.

Lightly brush a medium bowl with oil. Transfer the dough to the bowl, toss to coat, and cover the bowl with plastic wrap. Rest at room temperature for at least 30 minutes, or up to 2 hours.

Cut eight 9-inch squares of parchment paper.

On a lightly floured surface, unwrap the dough and divide it into 16 equal portions with a bench scraper (for accuracy, weigh with a digital scale if you have one). Form each piece into a smooth ball. Dust the dough with more flour to prevent sticking. Flatten two pieces of dough with the palm of your hand into 3-inch rounds. Brush the surface of one dough round with oil, up to the edges. Stack the other dough round on top and gently press down to flatten the dough. Roll out the two dough layers into an 8-inch round. Place on a sheet of parchment paper. Repeat with remaining dough to form eight stacked rounds.

Heat a large skillet over medium-low heat. When the skillet is warm, flip one dough round into the skillet and peel away the parchment paper. Cook until the underside is blistered, with golden brown spots, 1 to 2 minutes. Flip and cook until the underside is blistered golden brown spots, 1 minute. (The dough may puff up and then deflate.) Stack the cooked moo shu wrappers on a plate and continue to cook the remaining dough rounds.

Peel apart each set of wrappers and serve them warm with your choice of filling.

Place cooked wrappers in a resealable bag and keep in the refrigerator for up to 5 days. Reheat in the microwave until warmed through, 30 to 45 seconds.

Mo

MAKES 12

I was first introduced to *mo* during the summer I spent as an intern in Beijing. I spent 25 percent of my time modeling futuristic buildings on the computer, 25 percent of the time attempting (and failing) to learn Mandarin, and 50 percent of the time eating absolutely everything. The food in northern China was vastly different from the Cantonese food I grew up eating. It was spicy, herbaceous, and lacking in . . . rice.

I had recently graduated from architecture school and felt like my knowledge of food was advanced for a twenty-one-year-old from Ohio. I was so naive. The flavors, smells, textures, and sensations (*Wait, why is this sauce making my mouth numb?*) were so exciting I couldn't help but spend every extra dollar I had on food.

Rou jia mo was one of my go-to meals in Beijing because it was cheap, portable, and meaty. In the crudest way, expats called rou jia mo "Chinese hamburgers." The *mo* is the bun. It sort of looks like an English muffin and cooks like an English muffin, but it isn't an English muffin. The bun's flavor is neutral, but the bread is perfect for sopping up all the sauce and juicy fat from the filling. The most traditional filling is braised pork belly with warm spices and cilantro, but I love the Xi'an-style filling of braised lamb with cumin and Sichuan peppercorns. My recipe (below) is pure heaven. If you find juicy lamb fat running down your arms while you're eating these, you'll know you made them right!

227g (1 cup) warm water (about 110°F)

1 teaspoon active dry yeast

Pinch of sugar

450g (3 2/3 cups) bread flour

1/2 teaspoon coarse salt

30g (3 tablespoons) canola oil, plus more for the bowl and rolling

Place the warm water in a small mixing bowl. Stir in the yeast and pinch of sugar and set aside until the surface of the mixture is foamy, 5 to 10 minutes.

In the bowl of an electric mixer fitted with a dough hook, combine the flour and salt. Add the yeast mixture and mix on low to form a shaggy dough. Add the oil and increase the speed to medium. Continue to mix until the dough is smooth, firm, and tacky, 8 to 9 minutes more.

Coat a large bowl with 1 teaspoon oil. Transfer the dough to the bowl, turning to coat it with oil, and cover the bowl with plastic wrap. Set aside to proof in a warm spot until the dough is doubled in size, 1 1/2 to 2 hours (or in the refrigerator overnight).

Punch down to deflate the dough and transfer to a lightly floured surface. Pinch and pull the ends of the dough into a smooth ball.

To form the buns, divide the dough into 12 equal portions with a bench scraper (for accuracy, weigh with a digital scale if you have one). Form each portion of dough into a smooth ball. On a wooden cutting board lightly brushed with canola oil, roll out one portion of dough into a 3 x 10-inch oval. Fold the oval in half lengthwise, then roll it into a coil, tuck the end of the coil underneath, and set aside on the counter. Repeat with remaining portions of dough. Cover the coils and allow them to rest for 15 minutes. (Don't be tempted to skip this step, as the dough will not roll out as easily without a proper rest.)

Gently flatten one coil with the palm of your hand, and then roll it into a 4-inch round. Place the round on a baking sheet lined with parchment paper and repeat with the remaining dough to form 12 buns. Cover the buns with a damp, clean kitchen towel and allow the dough to proof in a warm spot until doubled in size, 30 to 45 minutes.

Heat a cast-iron or heavy-bottomed skillet with a tight-fitting lid over medium-low heat. Working in batches of three or four, cook the buns until lightly toasted on one side, about 5 minutes. Flip, cover the pan, and cook until the buns are lightly toasted on the other sides, 5 minutes more. Transfer the toasted buns to a wire rack to cool while you cook the remaining buns.

Buns can be stored in an airtight container (a resealable bag works great) at room temperature for up to 5 days, or in the freezer for up to 3 months. Reheat the frozen buns on a baking sheet in a 400°F oven for 10 minutes.

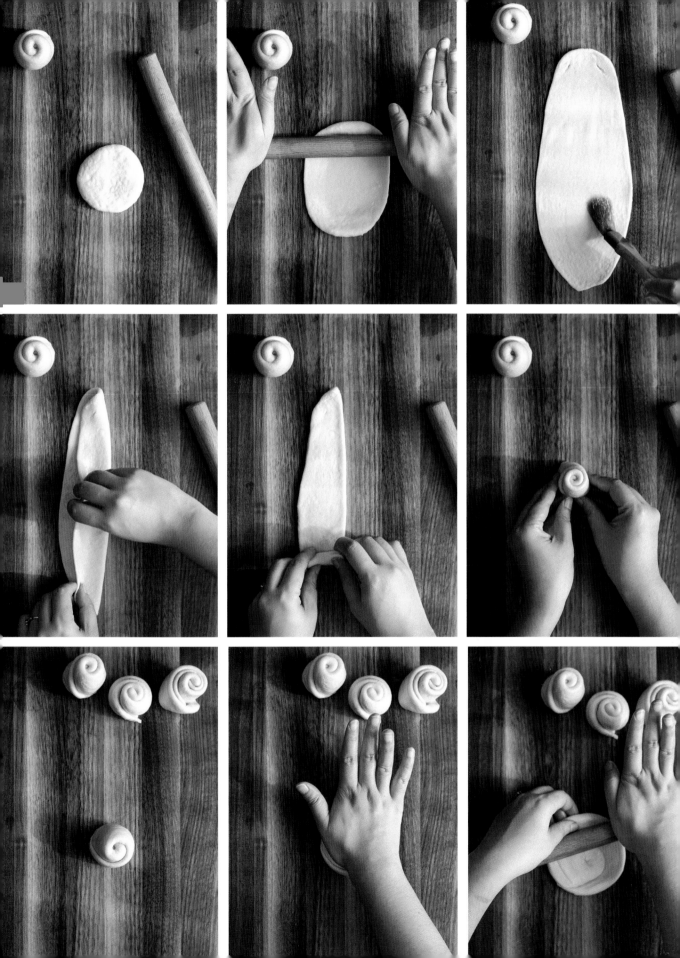

Xi'an-Style Braised Lamb Ro Jia Mao

MAKES 12

2 pounds boneless lamb shoulder, cut into 2-inch pieces

1 $1/2$ teaspoons salt

$1/4$ cup olive oil

1 tablespoon brown sugar

2-inch piece fresh ginger, peeled and sliced thin

$1/2$ teaspoon cumin seeds

$1/2$ teaspoon Sichuan peppercorns

4 cups water

$1/4$ cup Shaoxing cooking wine

$1/4$ cup soy sauce

1 bay leaf

2 serrano peppers, minced and stems removed

$1/2$ cup coarsely chopped fresh cilantro

Mo (above), for serving

In a large bowl, toss the lamb with the salt. In a large heavy-bottomed pot, heat the oil over medium-high heat. Add the lamb and sear until browned on all sides, about 5 minutes. Stir in the brown sugar, ginger, cumin seeds, and peppercorns and cook until fragrant, about 5 minutes.

Add the water, wine, soy sauce, and bay leaf and bring to a boil. Reduce the heat to low, cover, and simmer until the lamb is fall-apart tender, 50 minutes to 1 hour.

With a slotted spoon, remove the lamb from the braising liquid and transfer to a cutting board. Chop into $1/2$-inch pieces. In a medium mixing bowl, toss the chopped lamb with the serrano peppers, cilantro, and 3/4 cup of the braising liquid to combine.

To serve, split each bun in half almost all the way through, leaving one side connected. Fill the bread with the braised lamb and serve immediately.

Place lamb in an airtight container and keep in the fridge for up to 3 days. Reheat in the microwave until warmed through, 2 to 3 minutes, or sauté in a pan over medium heat.

Fay Da Bakery

A trip to New York City isn't complete without a stop at a Fay Da before heading to the airport. I'll pick up a barbeque pork bun (which I consume within a block of walking out the door) and a few other buns to keep me company on the flight home. Fay Da is a New York Chinatown institution, with thirteen locations in Manhattan Chinatown, Brooklyn, Flushing, and Connecticut. Despite the large-scale production and multiple locations, the bakeries are still family operated. Chi Chou (the founder's daughter) and her family oversee the production and logistics of their bakery network, to ensure fluffy, beautiful buns and expertly decorated cakes at every location.

Her father, Han Chou, opened the first location in 1991 and still plays a vital role in Fay Da's maintenance and expansion. Han is a lifelong baker. He started working in bakeries at the age of twelve, first out of necessity to help provide for his family. Necessity then grew to a deep love for the culinary arts. He learned most of his bakery skills from his *sifu*, or master, in Taiwan and later connected with him again after immigrating to the United States in 1983. He worked in other bakeries for a few years, even moving to Virginia to work with his *sifu*. After a few years of getting his bearings in the States, he opened his own bakery in Manhattan Chinatown. Fay Da's popularity quickly grew, and a second location was opened.

Fay Da's loyal community has helped the business reach icon status in the city. The buns are always made fresh, and the energy in every location just feels right. It feels like home, if you grew up going to Chinese bakeries. Locals spend their morning chatting with neighbors over tea and pastries, and families stop by to pick up birthday cakes. For a Chinese bakery newbie, it feels like a candy store, with varieties of classic and whimsical buns filling every acrylic case.

Eagle-eye attention to quality control and focus on wholesome ingredients are top priorities for Han. All the dough and fillings are made at a central production kitchen and then distributed to the various locations. It's an impressive infrastructure, with machinery and conveyor belts creating perfectly perky buns in a matter of seconds. Ingredients are simple and straightforward: fresh butter, milk, eggs, and sugar. Han is passionate about avoiding artificial dough stabilizers—he believes they leave a funny aftertaste. Even without dough stabilizers, Fay Da's buns stay soft and fluffy for a few days (even though most buns don't last more than a few minutes). When developing new products, Han always tests to see how they taste two to three days after being prepared.

The offerings at Fay Da truly embody the spirit of Chinese bakeries. They sell classics like pineapple buns and egg tarts, but the Fay Da test kitchen works on creative seasonal buns year after year. Han is in charge of the traditional treats, but his children, who grew up in the States, integrate the flavors they've learned to love over the years. The baked goods are a balance of Western and Eastern flavor influences. So you might find a cheesy ham and jalapeño bun next to a tried-and-true classic like a barbeque pork bun.

With each bite, you can tell how much care Han puts into his bakeries. Two of his three children work with him in the family business, but he considers the bakery his first child. Han believes the key to Fay Da's growth is that "you have to really love what you're doing," and you have to feel the passion to continue pushing forward. Han doesn't open new locations lightly. Every detail needs to feel right, because each bakery is a representation of him. For Han, being a baker is so much more than a job.

not-too-sweet buns

Chapter 2

It's a big misconception that the Chinese palate favors savory over sweet. Many Cantonese dishes walk a fine line between sweet and savory. A scoop of brown sugar is used in marinades for *char siu* (barbecued pork) for example, to produce a caramelized and shiny exterior while also mellowing out the saltiness in the marinade. When it comes to actual sweets and desserts, we just don't enjoy our sweets *too* sweet. It's all about balance (with a thoughtful pinch of salt here and there) and relying on the inherent sweetness from fruit instead of pure sugary sweetness. My family avoided desserts like American-style cakes covered in buttercream and milkshakes studded with brownie bites. For years, the highest compliment I'd hear from my family when I shared a baking experiment was, "Mmmm, it's not too sweet!"

Still, as an Asian-American child growing up in the Midwest, I desperately wanted the chocolatiest, fudgiest, and most frosting-heavy birthday cake in the Greater Cleveland area. Now I shudder at the very thought. These days, I prefer something far less cavity-inducing. I appreciate the natural sweetness and nuttiness of red bean paste, how delicate and rich fresh tea-infused whipped cream can be, and that salted egg yolks absolutely belong in pastry cream.

In this chapter of not-too-sweet buns, you'll find classic Chinese bakery stars, like the Almighty Pineapple Bun and Cocktail Buns. I took a few liberties and channeled the creativity and whimsy I see in many bakeries into a few unique creations of my own. A sweet bun can be paired with almost every occasion. If you're in the mood for a baking project with multiple components, the Milk Bread Doughnuts with Salted Egg Yolk Cream might be more your speed. Or if you're feeling like a literal loaf and want a direct route to fluffy, sweet buns while staying in your PJs all day, turn to the Very Chill Jam Buns. Each bun in this chapter and the savory bun chapter following will teach you a new technique and flavor pairing, to help expand your bun horizons. Bun's the limit!

The Almighty Pineapple Bun (Bo Lo Bao)

MAKES 12

Every Chinese bakery must have a pineapple bun in their case. Despite the name, the bun has no pineapple—it's a soft milk-bread bun with a sweet, buttery, crackly cookie-like top that, after it's baked, resembles pineapple skin. The simple, iconic treat has a loyal following, even beyond Asian cultures: everyone loves a good pineapple bun. When I was younger, I'd slyly pick off the cookie topping and leave the plain bun behind for my brother. (When you're the older sister, you can get away with things like that.)

Few things transcend enjoying a fresh pineapple bun still warm from the oven. You can eat it plain, or if you want to be like a true Hong Konger, slice the bun in half and stick a thick slice of cold butter inside. And for a true delicacy, use the buns as the base for Crispy Panko Pork Chop Sandwiches (page 105).

For the Buns

Mother of All Milk Bread Dough (page 6), made through step 4

All-purpose flour, for dusting the work surface

For the Topping

250g (2 cups) all-purpose flour

1/4 teaspoon baking soda

1/4 teaspoon coarse salt

113g (1/2 cup; 1 stick) unsalted butter, softened

100 g (1/2 cup) sugar

1 large egg

1/2 teaspoon pure vanilla extract

2 drops yellow food coloring

For the Egg Wash

1 large egg, white and yolk separated into two small bowls

While the dough is proofing, line two large rimmed baking sheets with parchment paper.

Make the buns: After the first proof, punch down to deflate the dough and transfer it to a lightly floured surface. Pinch and pull the ends of the dough to form a smooth ball. Divide the dough into 12 equal portions with a bench scraper (for accuracy, weigh with a digital scale if you have one). Form each portion of dough into a smooth ball by pulling the ends of the dough underneath and then rolling between the palms of your hand, and arrange on the prepared sheets, spacing at least 3 inches apart. Cover with a damp, clean kitchen towel and set aside in a warm spot until the buns are doubled in size, 45 minutes to 1 hour.

Meanwhile, make the topping: In a small bowl, whisk together flour, baking powder, and salt. In a medium bowl, combine the softened butter and sugar with a flexible spatula until smooth. Add the egg, vanilla, and food coloring, mixing until smooth. Fold the flour mixture into the butter mixture to form a sandy dough, then knead by hand until smooth. Pat into a disc and divide the dough into 12 equal portions with a bench scraper (for accuracy, weigh with a digital scale if you have one). Roll one piece into a smooth ball, then flatten into a 4-inch round with a dowel rolling pin. Score a crosshatch pattern into the dough with the edge of a bench scraper or knife, being careful not to cut all the way through. Use the edge of the bench scraper to lift the topping off the work surface. Repeat with remaining topping dough, setting each round aside until ready to top the buns. (Alternatively, you can skip making the crosshatch pattern. The topping will still crack beautifully as it bakes, just not as neatly.)

Preheat the oven to 350°F. Brush the tops of the buns lightly with the egg white to help the topping adhere. Place one topping dough round on each bun, gently pressing to cover the entire outer edge (you want the dough to fully encase the top of the bun, if possible). Whisk the egg yolk in a small bowl and lightly brush over the topping of each bun.

Bake the buns until golden brown, 18 to 20 minutes. Transfer the sheets to a wire rack. Let the buns cool for 5 minutes on sheets, then transfer to the rack to cool. Serve warm or at room temperature.

Buns can be kept in an airtight container (a resealable bag works great) at room temperature for up to 4 days, or in the freezer for up to 3 months. Reheat room temperature buns in the microwave for 15 to 20 seconds or on a baking sheet in a 300°F oven for about 5 minutes, until soft and warmed through. Reheat frozen buns on a baking sheet in a 350°F oven for 10 to 15 minutes.

"Pinching and Pulling" the Dough

Throughout these recipes, you'll read the instruction to "pinch and pull the ends of the dough into a smooth ball." But what does that mean, and does it really make a difference? The answer is yes, if you want smooth and perky buns.

Proper handling is important when forming and proofing buns. When working with dough, it's essential to create tension at the surface, which allows the dough to proof more evenly and develop the proper gluten structure. It will also result in a smoother surface (and thus, prettier buns) once baked. If you haphazardly form loose and bumpy balls of dough, you run the risk of slightly deflated and dense buns.

So when a recipe instructs you to "pinch and pull the ends of the dough into a smooth ball," you'll want to pull the edges of each portion of dough toward the center, rotating as you go, and then tuck them underneath. The tucking process creates that all-important tension and smooth surface. It will take some practice, but eventually you'll get the hang of forming the smoothest, perkiest buns!

Score and Twist

Each bun recipe in this chapter and the following chapter is intended to highlight a different style of forming buns and treating the ingredients. Some methods are as simple as spreading store-bought ingredients like peanut butter and jelly inside a portion of dough and calling it a day. Other recipes will encourage you to bring out a ruler and flex your origami skills. Many of the recipes and dough treatment associated with it are flexible and could be interchanged with another style. So just because the Red Bean Swirl Buns are shown in swirls, it doesn't mean you can't form them like the striped Sambal and Parmesan Buns. I highly encourage you to play around with all the design options!

Swirl Buns

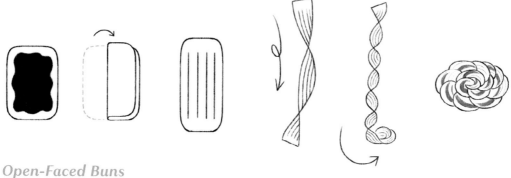

Open-Faced Buns

Sliced Rolls

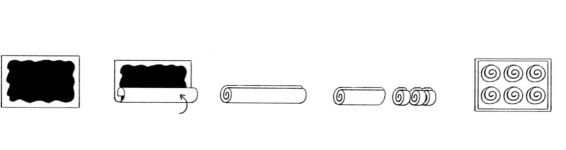

Leaf Buns

Score and Roll

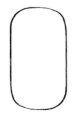   

Braided Loaf

Simply Stuffed Buns

Cocktail Buns (Gai Mei Bao)

MAKES 12

For the Buns

Mother of All Milk Bread Dough (page 6), made through step 4

All-purpose flour, for dusting the work surface

For the Coconut Filling

40g (²/3 cup) unsweetened shredded coconut

85g (6 tablespoons) unsalted butter, melted, plus more if needed

30g (¹/4 cup) dry milk powder

50g (¹/4 cup) granulated sugar

20g (2 tablespoons) all-purpose flour

¹/4 teaspoon coarse salt

For the Egg Wash

1 large egg

1 tablespoon heavy cream or milk

For the Topping

21g (1 ¹/2 tablespoons) unsalted butter, melted

18g (2 tablespoons) all-purpose flour

10g (1 tablespoon) confectioners' sugar

Gai mei bao is my favorite baked bun. There, I said it. I love a good pineapple bun as much as the next person, but I'm in the minority that enjoys a buttery, coconut-heavy cocktail bun a little more. Cocktail buns originally were created as a way for bakers to salvage day-old buns. The stale buns were ground into crumbs, then mixed with sugar and shredded coconut as a filling for fresh dough (like a "cocktail" of bakery leftovers). Nowadays, bakers make the filling fresh.

Cocktail buns are traditionally formed into long buns that resemble chicken tails, which might also be how they got their name. You could bake these as individual buns (spaced apart), but these are baked together in a deep baking dish for a pull-apart approach, with a bonus of less pressure to perfectly form each bun. They also stay incredibly soft when cozied up and baked together. My issue with a lot of cocktail buns is that there is never enough filling (the best part, in my opinion). You won't have that issue with this recipe. Every bite possesses plenty of butter, sugar, and shredded coconut.

Make the buns: While the dough is proofing, line a deep baking dish with parchment paper.

After the first proof, punch down to deflate the dough and transfer it to a lightly floured surface. Pinch and pull the ends of the dough to form a smooth ball. Divide the dough into 12 equal portions with a bench scraper (for accuracy, weigh with a digital scale if you have one). Form each portion of dough into a smooth ball by pulling the ends of the dough underneath and then rolling between the palms of your hand.

Make the filling: In a medium bowl, mix all the filling ingredients together with a flexible spatula until crumbly. (The filling may look a little dry, but if you scoop a tablespoon of filling and press it, it should stick together. If not, add another tablespoon of melted butter.) Set the filling aside at room temperature until you're ready to fill the buns.

Roll out one ball of dough into a roughly 3 x 5-inch oval. Scoop a heaping tablespoon of the filling and press it in the palm of your hand to form a small log. Center the log lengthwise on the dough. Bring up the edges of the dough and pinch together to seal around the filling, forming an oval log shape. Repeat with remaining dough and filling. Place the buns in the baking dish, creating two rows of six buns. Cover with a damp, clean kitchen towel and set aside in a warm spot until the buns are doubled in size, 60 to 90 minutes.

Preheat the oven to 350°F.

Just before baking, make the egg wash: In a small bowl, whisk together egg and cream. Brush the egg wash over tops of buns.

Make the topping: In a small bowl, combine the melted butter, flour, and confectioners' sugar with a flexible spatula until smooth. Place the topping in a small resealable bag, pressing toward one corner. Snip the tip off the corner of the bag and pipe a line along the short ends of each bun.

Bake the buns until golden brown, 28 to 30 minutes. Transfer the dish to a wire rack to cool. The buns can remain in the dish as they continue to cool. Serve warm or at room temperature.

Buns can be kept in an airtight container (a resealable bag works great) at room temperature for up to 4 days, or in the freezer for up to 3 months. Room temperature buns can be reheated in the microwave for 15 to 20 seconds or on a baking sheet in a 300°F oven for about 5 minutes, until soft and warmed through. Reheat frozen buns on a baking sheet in a 350°F oven until soft and warmed through, 10 to 15 minutes.

Red Bean Swirl Buns

MAKES 12

It might surprise you to see beans as an ingredient in something sweet, but I promise you it works. Red beans, or adzuki beans, is a common ingredient in many Chinese and Japanese desserts. You can find them in bubble tea, frozen ice pops, and all sorts of pastries. My mom makes a lovely, sweet dessert soup with red beans and tapioca pearls. You can purchase red bean paste at an Asian market or online, or make your own (page 53). Homemade red bean paste is simple to make and has a deeply roasted, almost nutty flavor that's not sugary sweet. The thick, creamy paste is perfect for swirling into milk bread dough. Or, instead of red bean paste, try filling the spiral buns with the same amount of Taro Paste (page 77), Nutella, peanut butter, or jam. The process of scoring and twisting the dough into hypnotizing spirals is an easy and creative way to form buns. Through the scores, you also catch a glimpse of the sweet filling.

Mother of All Milk Bread Dough (page 6), prepared through step 4

All-purpose flour, for dusting work surface

1 cup Red Bean Paste (page 53)

1 large egg

1 tablespoon heavy cream

1/4 cup water

1/4 cup sugar

While the dough is proofing, line two large rimmed baking sheets with parchment paper.

After the first proof, punch down the dough to deflate it and transfer it to a lightly floured surface. Pinch and pull the ends of the dough into a smooth ball. Divide the dough into 12 equal portions with a bench scraper (for accuracy, weigh with a digital scale if you have one). Form each portion of dough into a smooth ball by pulling the ends of the dough underneath and then rolling between the palms of your hand.

On a lightly floured surface, roll out one ball into a roughly 5 x 7-inch rectangle. With an offset spatula, spread a heaping tablespoon of red bean paste over the dough into a thin layer, leaving a 1/2-inch border all around. Fold the dough in half lengthwise, then gently pat to remove air bubbles and tightly pinch the edges to seal. With a sharp knife or pastry wheel, cut four or five slits, spaced 1/2 inch apart, along the length of the dough. Holding the two short ends of dough in either hand, twist to form a spiral rope and then roll the rope into a coil, tucking the end underneath. (See the swirl buns diagram on page 48.) Repeat with remaining dough and red bean paste to form 12 buns. Arrange the buns on the prepared sheets, spacing at least 3 inches apart. Cover with a damp, clean kitchen towel and set aside in a warm spot until doubled in size, 45 minutes to 1 hour.

Preheat the oven to 350°F. Just before baking, make the egg wash by whisking together the egg and cream in a small bowl. Brush the egg wash over the buns.

Bake the buns until golden brown, 18 to 20 minutes.

Meanwhile, make the glaze by combining the water and sugar in a small saucepan over medium heat. Bring to a simmer and cook until the sugar is dissolved and mixture has thickened, 1 to 2 minutes.

Transfer the baking sheets to a wire rack. Immediately brush the hot buns with glaze to cover completely. Let the buns cool on the sheets for 5 minutes, then transfer to the wire rack to cool. Serve warm or at room temperature.

Buns can be kept in an airtight container (a resealable bag works great) at room temperature for up to 4 days, or in the freezer for up to 3 months. Room temperature buns can be reheated in the microwave for 15 to 20 seconds or on a baking sheet in a 300°F oven for about 5 minutes, until soft and warmed through. Reheat frozen buns on a baking sheet in a 350°F oven until soft and warmed through, 10 to 15 minutes.

Red Bean Paste

MAKES ABOUT 3 CUPS

200g (1 cup) dried red beans, rinsed and picked over

100g (1/2 cup) sugar

90g (1/2 cup) canola oil

In a large bowl, cover the beans with 4 inches of water and let soak at least 8 hours or overnight. Drain and rinse the beans.

In a medium saucepan, combine the beans and enough water to cover by 2 inches. Bring the water to a simmer and continue to cook until the beans are tender, 40 to 50 minutes. Drain the beans and rinse under cold water.

Transfer the beans to the bowl of a food processor and add the sugar. Puree until smooth.

Transfer the paste to a medium nonstick skillet. Add 1/4 cup of the oil and cook over medium-low heat, stirring with a flexible spatula until blended and smooth. Add the remaining 1/4 cup oil and cook, stirring, until the paste is darker in color and the oil is completely blended in, 8 to 10 minutes. Transfer paste to a heat-proof container and set aside to cool completely. Refrigerate until ready to use. Paste can be refrigerated in an airtight container for up to 2 weeks or frozen for up to 3 months.

Coconut Jasmine Cream Buns

MAKES 12

I have a tendency to infuse tea into any recipe I can. I grew up sipping aromatic chrysanthemum tea (page 252) at dim sum and have a strong affinity toward matcha and hojicha. I start most mornings with a warm mug of jasmine tea, a gentle tea that immediately makes me think of springtime and walking through our old neighborhood of Inner Richmond, while our neighbors' jasmine vines were starting to blossom. I can't get enough of its subtly sweet and strong floral flavor.

Infusing tea into baked goods is simple. One option is to add the dried tea leaves to whatever dough you're working with, preferably something enriched or with a high percentage of butter or another fat, so the tea flavor can soak in. Or you can steep the tea in warm milk, cream, or melted butter—as you would in hot water—to extract all those flavors from the leaves. This latter method is wonderful for flavoring whipped creams, custards, and buttercreams.

For this recipe, you steep tea leaves in heavy cream. Once the cream is fragrant, all you have to do is chill it, then whip it up as you would regular whipped cream. I add a bit of confectioners' sugar to sweeten things up, and a pinch of salt for balance. You don't want to add much else, to allow the tea flavor to shine. The jasmine whipped cream is a lovely way to elevate the classic coconut cream bun.

Mother of All Milk Bread Dough (page 6), made through step 4

All-purpose flour, for dusting work surface

1 large egg

1 tablespoon heavy cream or milk

1/4 cup water

1/4 cup sugar

1/2 cup finely shredded unsweetened coconut

Jasmine Whipped Cream (page 57)

Line two large rimmed baking sheets with parchment paper.

After the first proof, punch down to deflate the dough and transfer it to a lightly floured surface. Pinch and pull the ends of the dough into a smooth ball. Divide the dough into 12 equal portions with a bench scraper (for accuracy, weigh with a digital scale if you have one). Form each portion of dough into a smooth ball by pulling the ends of the dough underneath and then rolling between the palms of your hand, then roll the dough between your hands to form a small, football-shaped bun. Arrange the buns on the prepared baking sheets, spacing at least 3 inches apart. Cover with a damp, clean kitchen towel and set aside until doubled in size, 45 minutes to 1 hour.

Preheat the oven to 350°F. Right before baking, make the egg wash by whisking together the egg and cream in a small bowl. Brush the egg wash over the buns.

Bake the buns until golden brown, 18 to 20 minutes.

Meanwhile, make the glaze by combining the water and sugar in a small saucepan over medium heat. Bring to a simmer and cook until the sugar is dissolved and glaze has thickened, 1 to 2 minutes. Remove from the heat.

Transfer the baking sheets to a wire rack. Immediately brush the hot buns with the glaze to cover completely, then sprinkle with the coconut. Let the buns cool on the sheets for 5 minutes, then transfer to the rack to cool completely.

Split the buns in half down the middle, like a hot dog bun, leaving the bottom intact. Place the whipped cream in a pastry bag or a heavy-duty resealable bag, pressing toward one corner. Snip the tip off the corner of the bag and fill each bun with cream, piping side to side to form a squiggly line.

Store the buns and whipped cream separately and assemble them just before serving. Buns can be kept in an airtight container (a resealable bag works great) at room temperature for up to 4 days or in the freezer for up to 3 months. Store the whipped cream in an airtight container in the refrigerator for up to 3 days or in the freezer for 3 months.

Room temperature buns can be reheated in the microwave for 15 to 20 seconds or on a baking sheet in a 300°F oven for about 5 minutes, until soft and warmed through. Reheat frozen buns on a baking sheet in a 350°F oven until soft and warmed through, 10 to 15 minutes. Allow to cool again before filling with whipped cream.

Jasmine Whipped Cream

MAKES 2 1/2 CUPS

1 1/4 cups heavy cream

2 tablespoons jasmine tea leaves

2 tablespoons confectioners' sugar

1/4 teaspoon coarse salt

In a small saucepan, combine the cream and tea leaves. Bring to a simmer over low heat and simmer for 5 minutes. Turn off the heat, cover with a lid, and allow the tea to steep for 15 minutes.

Strain the cream into a bowl and discard the tea leaves. Cover the cream and refrigerate until chilled, at least 2 hours or up to 3 days.

In the bowl of an electric mixer fitted with the whisk attachment, beat the chilled cream, sugar, and salt on medium speed to form medium-stiff peaks, 3 to 4 minutes.

Egg Custard Buns (Nai Wong Bao)

MAKES 12

2 large eggs

65g (⅓ cup) sugar

20g (2 tablespoons) cornstarch

150g (⅔ cup) heavy cream

1 teaspoon pure vanilla extract

Pinch of salt

Fluffy Steamed Bun Dough (page 17), matcha variation, made through step 2

Buns can be kept in an airtight container (a resealable bag works great) in the refrigerator for up to 4 days, or the freezer for up to 3 months. Refrigerated buns can be reheated in the microwave for 30 seconds or steamed for about 2 minutes, until soft and warmed through. Reheat frozen buns by steaming until soft and warmed through, 10 to 12 minutes.

I love to end a morning dim sum feast with at least a few orders of egg custard buns. It's incredibly easy to eat half a dozen without even thinking about it because the buns are so light and pleasantly sweet. The custard tucked inside is unlike custard you would serve in a pie or doughnut—it's on the firmer side, which makes forming the buns easier. Once steamed, the custard will soften slightly and create a heavenly combination with the matcha steamed bun dough.

Make the filling: In a small bowl, whisk together the eggs, sugar, and cornstarch until smooth. In a small saucepan, whisk together the cream, vanilla, and salt. Bring to a gentle simmer over medium heat. Remove from the heat and slowly pour the warm cream mixture into the egg mixture, whisking constantly. Pour the mixture back into the saucepan and cook over medium-low heat, whisking constantly, until just starting to thicken, 3 to 4 minutes. Turn off the heat and continue to whisk until the whisk leaves a trail in the custard, about 1 minute. Transfer the custard to a small bowl and cover the surface with plastic wrap (to prevent a skin from forming). Refrigerate for at least 2 hours or up to overnight (it should be solid enough to scoop).

Cut twelve 4-inch squares of parchment paper.

Make the buns: After the first proof, punch down to deflate the dough and transfer it to a lightly floured surface. Pinch and pull the ends of the dough into a smooth ball. Divide the dough into 12 equal portions with a bench scraper (for accuracy, weigh with a digital scale if you have one). Form each portion of dough into a smooth ball by pulling the ends of the dough underneath and then rolling between the palms of your hand.

Roll out one ball of dough into a 4-inch round with a dowel rolling pin, thinner on the outside edge and thicker in the middle. Place a heaping tablespoon of the chilled custard into the center, pull up the edges, and pleat closed. Place the bun, pleat side down, on a parchment paper square. Repeat with remaining dough and filling. If it's taking you a long time to form the buns, cover the formed buns with a kitchen towel and place in the fridge to prevent overproofing. Otherwise, cover the buns with a damp, clean kitchen towel and let them rest in a warm spot until they are 1½ times larger, 30 to 45 minutes.

Prepare your steamer setup (page xxviii) and bring water to a boil. Place buns in the bamboo steamer baskets, spacing at least 2 inches apart. Cover and steam buns over boiling water for 10 minutes. Turn off the heat and leave buns in the covered steamer for 5 minutes longer to prevent collapsing. Remove the buns from the steamer and allow to cool for 5 minutes before serving.

After-School PB&J Buns

MAKES 12

If you grew up as a child of immigrants, you may have an uncomfortable school lunch story, as I do. While everyone else was eating peanut butter and jelly sandwiches, I usually had steamed buns or a small container of leftover fried rice. I was sometimes met with judgy, eight-year-old faces that made me feel a little embarrassed and confused as to why my lunches looked different from everyone else's. I now appreciate the food my mom packed for me, but at the time my desire to fit in was stronger than my taste buds.

I like to think my PB&J buns are a way of preventing those types of awkward moments for my future kids. It's the perfect weekend baking project and will leave you with self-contained PB&J "sandwiches" to keep you or your kids going all week! Enjoy at least one bun warm right from the oven, with a glass of cold milk—it's mind-blowing!

This simple bun doesn't require any special shaping or twisting. It's a humble bun. However, it still needs to be handled with care and attention. I prefer to use a creamy, unsweetened peanut butter, because I personally love smooth peanut butter and the savory richness heightens the tart and sweet flavor of a good-quality fruit jam. Also, for crunch, don't skip the salted peanut topping, a small detail that adds nice texture and provides a clue to the filling.

Mother of All Milk Bread Dough (page 6), made through step 4

All-purpose flour, for dusting the work surface

1/2 cup smooth peanut butter

1/4 cup fruit jam or preserves (your favorite flavor!)

1 large egg

1 tablespoon heavy cream or milk

3 tablespoons roasted unsalted peanuts, chopped

1 tablespoon flaky salt

Buns can be kept in an airtight container (a resealable bag works great) at room temperature for up to 4 days or in the freezer for up to 3 months. Room temperature buns can be reheated in the microwave for 15 to 20 seconds or on a baking sheet in a 300°F oven for about 5 minutes, until soft and warmed through. Reheat frozen buns on a baking sheet in a 350°F oven until soft and warmed through, 10 to 12 minutes.

Line two large rimmed baking sheets with parchment paper.

After the first proof, punch down to deflate the dough and transfer it to a lightly floured surface. Pinch and pull the ends of the dough to form a smooth ball. Divide the dough into 12 equal portions with a bench scraper (for accuracy, weigh with a digital scale if you have one). Form each portion of dough into a smooth ball by pulling the ends of the dough underneath and then rolling between the palms of your hand.

Roll out one ball of dough into a 4-inch round with a dowel rolling pin, thinner on the outside edge and thicker in the middle. Place about 2 teaspoons peanut butter and 1 teaspoon jam in the center of the dough. Bring the edges of the dough up and over the filling and pinch to seal. Repeat with remaining dough, peanut butter, and jam to form 12 buns. Arrange the buns on the lined baking sheets, spacing at least 3 inches apart. Cover with a damp, clean kitchen towel and set aside in a warm spot until doubled in size, 45 minutes to 1 hour.

Preheat the oven to 350°F. Just before baking, whisk together the egg and cream in a small bowl. Brush the egg wash over the buns and then sprinkle each bun with chopped peanuts and flaky salt.

Bake the buns until golden brown, 18 to 20 minutes. Transfer the baking sheets to a wire rack. Let the buns cool on the baking sheet for 5 minutes, then transfer to the rack to cool. Serve warm or at room temperature.

Chocolate Nutella Loaf

MAKES 1 LOAF

This swirly loaf reminds me of architecture school. Unsliced, it looks like a skyscraper I would've been forced to design for my 3D computer modeling class. I hated that class because I have the soul of a grandma and rebelled against anything that took away precious time dedicated to watercolor renderings and building models with cardboard. In the spectrum of designers in my architecture class, I was definitely more analog than the rest and brushed off technology as often as I could. I was known as that girl in the studio who would make you dinner if you'd been living off of potato chips for days, or who would pop into the studio with a tray of freshly baked blueberry muffins at 2:00 a.m. the night before a big critique. I also would most likely keep a jar of Nutella and some sliced bread as my official desk snack, while everyone else had shots of 5-hour Energy. So this chocolate Nutella Loaf is an ode to my late-night and Nutella bread–fueled architecture school days. Twenty-year-old Kristina would have loved the double-chocolate action in this bread. It probably wouldn't have lasted more than two days in her desk locker.

Mother of All Milk Bread Dough, chocolate variation (page 6), made through step 4

All-purpose flour, for dusting

1/2 cup Nutella

After the first proof, transfer the dough to a lightly floured surface. Roll out the dough into a roughly 10 x 18-inch rectangle. With an offset spatula, spread the Nutella over the dough, leaving a 1/2-inch border around the edges. Roll up the dough lengthwise to form a tight roll, pinching the seam to seal. Place the dough seam-side down on the work surface, then slice into six equal portions with a sharp knife.

Line the bottom and sides of a 9 x 5-inch loaf pan with parchment paper, leaving a 2-inch overhang. (If using a pullman pan, no need to line with parchment paper.) Arrange the dough slices, cut sides up, in the pan, in two rows of three. Cover with a damp, clean kitchen towel and set aside in a warm spot until it reaches just above the rim of the pan (just below the rim for a pullman loaf pan), 60 to 90 minutes.

Preheat the oven to 350°F. Bake loaf until slightly darkened around the edges and cooked through, 30 to 33 minutes. Transfer to a wire rack and let the bread cool in the pan for 10 minutes. Using the paper overhang, lift the loaf out and onto the wire rack to cool completely before slicing.

The bread can be stored in a resealable bag at room temperature for up to 4 days. Slices of bread can be stored in a resealable bag in the freezer for up to 3 months. Reheat frozen bread in a toaster or 350°F oven until warmed through, 10 to 12 minutes.

Asian Pear Turnovers with Miso Glaze

MAKES 6

Asian pears are the only pears worth eating, in my opinion. Unlike Bartlett and Anjou pears, the many varieties of Asian pears are crisp, refreshing, and super juicy. They come in a color spectrum of warm tan to slightly green, are spotted with light freckles, and will most likely be shrouded in a foam mesh to protect from bruising because the skin is sensitive. You've gotta protect the good stuff! In my household, serving a small plate of sliced Asian pears whenever they're in season is a sign of love.

Eating the pears fresh is always preferable, but they also bake as well as their apple cousins. I give them the turnover treatment, wrapping them in a blanket of Chinese puff pastry, and dressing them with brown sugar and a pinch of Chinese five-spice. That stuff is potent, so a little goes a long way. Since the pears are high in moisture, you do need to compensate, with the help of cornstarch. The juices thicken and melt into the butter and sugar to make a cozy and warm caramel-like sauce. The final drizzle of miso glaze gives each bite a salty-sweet finish.

For the Turnovers

1 large Asian pear, cored and cut into 1/2-inch cubes

3 tablespoons brown sugar

1 tablespoon unsalted butter, melted

1 1/2 teaspoons cornstarch

1/4 teaspoon Chinese five-spice powder

1/2 teaspoon pure vanilla extract

1/4 teaspoon coarse salt

Chinese Puff Pastry (page 157)

1 large egg

For the Glaze

1 tablespoon unsalted butter, melted

2 teaspoon white miso

1/2 cup confectioners' sugar

1 tablespoon milk

Line a large rimmed baking sheet with parchment paper.

Make the turnovers: In a medium bowl, combine the pear, brown sugar, butter, cornstarch, five-spice, vanilla, and salt, tossing until evenly combined.

On a lightly floured work surface, roll out the puff pastry to an 11 x 16-inch rectangle. Trim 1/2 inch off the edges and then cut into six 5-inch squares.

Top each square with 2 heaping tablespoons filling. In a small bowl, whisk the egg and then brush the beaten egg lightly over the edges of the pastry. Fold the pastry over the filling diagonally, pressing down on the edges and then crimping with a fork to seal. Arrange the pastry on the prepared sheet, spacing 2 inches apart. Freeze until firm, at least 20 minutes or overnight.

Preheat the oven to 425°F. Brush the remaining egg wash over the pastry. Cut a few slits into the pastry with a paring knife to allow steam to vent. Bake until the pastries are golden brown and crisp, 25 to 28 minutes. Transfer the sheet to a wire rack and let the turnovers cool on the sheet for 5 minutes. Transfer turnovers to the wire rack to cool completely.

Make the glaze: In a small bowl, combine the melted butter and miso, whisking until combined. Add the confectioners' sugar and milk, whisking until thick and smooth. Drizzle the glaze over the cooled turnovers. Serve warm or at room temperature.

Sweet Potato and Brown Sugar Mantou

MAKES 12

Mantou are simply unstuffed steamed buns. They are inexplicably tasty, without all the frills of glazes, toppings, and fillings. Consider plain mantou as "bread for the table," or the carb on the side of your main meal to dip into soup or sop up whatever sauce lingers on your plate. Some mornings, my parents would reheat a bag of frozen mantou, serve it with sweetened condensed milk for dipping, and call that breakfast. It was such a treat!

As much as I love the pure flavor of plain mantou and how it goes with any meal, the dough takes well to all kinds of flavorings. I especially love mixing two types of dough, swirling them together into beautiful pinwheel buns. Think chocolate and vanilla. Black sesame and matcha. Sweet potato and brown sugar!

Sweet potato and brown sugar is a cozy, autumn-inspired flavor combo that brightens up any table, especially when rolled up to form rosettes instead of the standard pinwheels. The flavors can lean savory or sweet. Whenever I make them, I can't help but dip a few in sweetened condensed milk, for old time's sake.

For the Sweet Potato Dough

150g (1 ¼ cups) all-purpose flour, plus more for dusting the work surface

25g (2 tablespoons) granulated sugar

½ teaspoon instant yeast

¼ teaspoon baking powder

¼ teaspoon coarse salt

¼ cup sweet potato puree

56g (¼ cup) warm water (110°F)

½ teaspoon canola oil or other neutral-flavored oil, for brushing

For the Brown Sugar Dough

150g (1 ¼ cups) all-purpose flour, plus more for dusting the work surface

30g (3 tablespoons) brown sugar

½ teaspoon instant yeast

¼ teaspoon baking powder

¼ teaspoon coarse salt

56g (¼ cup) warm water (110°F)

½ teaspoon canola oil or other neutral-flavored oil, for brushing

Make the sweet potato dough: In the bowl of an electric mixer fitted with a dough hook, whisk to combine the flour, granulated sugar, yeast, baking powder, and salt. Add the sweet potato puree. With the mixer on low, pour in the warm water and mix to form a shaggy dough, 1 minute. Increase the speed to medium-high and knead until smooth and tacky, another 7 to 8 minutes. (Alternatively, you can knead the dough by hand until smooth, 10 to 12 minutes.) Transfer the dough to a lightly floured work surface. Pinch and pull the ends of the dough into a smooth ball. Lightly brush a medium bowl with the oil and add the dough to the bowl, turn to coat. Cover the bowl with plastic wrap or a damp, clean kitchen towel. Allow the dough to proof in a warm spot until doubled in size, 1 to 1 ½ hours, or in the refrigerator for at least 6 hours or overnight.

Make the brown sugar dough: In the bowl of an electric mixer fitted with a dough hook, whisk to combine the flour, brown sugar, yeast, baking powder, and salt. With the mixer on low, pour in the warm water and mix to form a shaggy dough, 1 minute. Increase speed to medium-high and knead until smooth and tacky, another 7 to 8 minutes. (Alternatively, you can knead the dough by hand until smooth, 10 to 12 minutes.) Transfer the dough to a lightly floured work surface. Pinch and pull the ends of the dough into a smooth ball. Lightly brush a medium bowl with the oil and add the dough to the bowl, toss to coat. Cover the bowl with plastic wrap or a damp, clean kitchen towel. Allow the dough to proof in a warm spot until 1 ½ times larger, 30 to 45 minutes.

Cut twelve 4-inch squares of parchment paper.

Punch down both doughs to deflate them and transfer the doughs to a lightly floured surface, then pinch and pull the ends to form two smooth balls.

Divide both balls into 12 equal portions with a bench scraper (for accuracy, weigh with a digital scale if you have one). Form each portion of dough into a smooth ball by pulling the ends of the dough underneath and then rolling between the palms of your hand. On a lightly floured surface, roll out each ball into a 3-inch round. Keep the rounds of dough covered with a clean kitchen towel as you continue rolling out the dough.

Form the rosettes: Arrange two sweet potato dough rounds and two brown sugar dough rounds in a straight line, alternating and overlapping the edges by 1/2 inch. Cut arrangement in half lengthwise. Roll up each half into a tight roll to form rosettes. Arrange rosettes on the parchment paper squares. Repeat with the remaining rounds of dough to form more rosettes.

Place the formed rosettes and parchment paper on a large rimmed baking sheet and cover with a damp, clean kitchen towel. Set aside in a warm spot until they are 1 1/2 times larger, 30 to 45 minutes.

Prepare your steamer setup (page xxviii) and bring water to a boil. Working in batches if necessary, arrange buns in the bamboo steamer baskets, spacing 2 inches apart. Steam over boiling water for 10 minutes. Turn off the heat and leave the buns in the covered steamer for 5 more minutes to prevent collapsing. Remove the buns from the steamer and allow them to cool for 5 minutes before serving.

Buns can be kept in an airtight container (a resealable bag works great) at room temperature for up to 4 days or in the freezer for up to 3 months. Room temperature buns can be reheated in the microwave for 15 to 20 seconds or steamed for about 2 minutes, until soft and warmed through. Reheat frozen buns by steaming until soft and warmed through, 10 to 15 minutes.

Rhubarb and Cream Cheese Buns

MAKES 12

For the Filling

8 ounces cream cheese, softened

$1/4$ cup granulated sugar

1 large egg

1 teaspoon finely grated lemon zest

$1/2$ teaspoon pure vanilla extract

For the Buns

Mother of All Milk Bread Dough (page 6), made through step 4

All-purpose flour, for dusting the work surface

1 $1/2$ cups $3/4$-inch sliced rhubarb (about 2 stalks)

For the Egg Wash

1 large egg

1 tablespoon milk or heavy cream

$1/4$ cup pearl sugar (optional)

Beyond buns that are stuffed, scored, and twisted into all sorts of shapes and designs, one of my favorite ways to decorate buns is the open-faced style. It is incredibly easy and straightforward, and feels like assembling a bunch of personal pizzas. Nothing unexpected is hiding inside—you know exactly what you're getting in each bite. These cheesy rhubarb buns are definitely inspired by my obsession with cheese Danishes. To be completely honest, I would eat just about anything covered in cream cheese.

The rich and lemony cream-cheese filling weighs down the center of the bun and acts as the perfect bed for the bright, tart rhubarb. You can top these buns with almost any fruit, but the rhubarb patch at our community garden looks especially stunning each spring, and I have to snag a few stalks for these buns.

Line two large rimmed baking sheets with parchment paper.

Make the filling: In a medium bowl, combine the cream cheese, granulated sugar, egg, zest, and vanilla with a flexible spatula until smooth. Set aside until ready to top the buns.

Make the buns: After the first proof, punch down to deflate the dough and transfer it to a lightly floured surface. Pinch and pull the ends of the dough into a smooth ball. Divide the dough into 12 equal portions with a bench scraper (for accuracy, weigh with a digital scale if you have one). Form each portion of dough into a smooth ball by pulling the ends of the dough underneath and then rolling between the palms of your hand. Flatten and roll out each portion into a 4-inch round with a dowel rolling pin. Arrange the rounds on the lined baking sheets, spacing at least 3 inches apart. Top each bun with 2 tablespoons cream cheese mixture, leaving a 1-inch border of dough, and three rhubarb slices. Cover with a damp, clean kitchen towel and set aside in a warm spot until doubled in size, 45 minutes to 1 hour.

Preheat the oven to 350°F.

Right before baking, make the egg wash: In a small bowl, whisk together the egg and cream. Brush the egg wash over the edges of the buns, and sprinkle pearl sugar over the edges if you like.

Bake the buns until golden brown, 18 to 20 minutes. Transfer the baking sheets to a wire rack. Let the buns cool on the baking sheet for 5 minutes, then transfer to the rack to cool. Serve warm or at room temperature.

Buns can be kept in an airtight container (a resealable bag works great) in the fridge for up to 4 days or in the freezer for up to 3 months. Chilled buns can be reheated in the microwave for 15 to 20 seconds, until soft and warmed through. Reheat frozen buns on a baking sheet in a 350°F oven until soft and warmed through, 10 to 12 minutes.

Milk Bread Doughnuts with Salted Egg Yolk Cream

MAKES 12

Is there anything milk bread can't do? Deep frying seems to make everything better, and milk bread doughnuts are no exception. In doughnut form, milk bread reaches new heights of pillowy softness. Because it cooks so quickly in the hot oil, the interior crumb expands into an incredibly airy and delicate structure, creating a cushy home for salted egg yolk pastry cream.

Salted egg yolks are often used in both sweet and savory Asian dishes. They are coveted, especially in mooncakes (page 173), for their creamy texture and salty bite. Since pastry cream naturally leans heavily on eggs for its custardy texture and flavor, the addition of salted egg yolks just makes sense here and creates a wonderful sweet and salty balance.

2 large eggs

50g (¼ cup) sugar, plus additional for dusting the doughnuts

20g (2 tablespoons) cornstarch

¼ teaspoon coarse salt

340g (1 ½ cups) milk

1 teaspoon pure vanilla extract

28g (2 tablespoons) unsalted butter

2 Salted Egg Yolks (page 73)

Mother of All Milk Bread Dough (page 6), made through step 4

Canola or other neutral-flavored oil, for frying

Make the filling: In a medium bowl, whisk to combine the eggs, sugar, cornstarch, and salt until smooth. In a small saucepan, whisk together the milk and vanilla. Heat over medium-low heat, whisking constantly, just until simmering. Immediately turn off the heat. Pour the hot milk mixture into the egg mixture in a thin, steady stream, whisking constantly. Pour the mixture back into the saucepan and heat over medium heat, whisking constantly, until the pastry cream is thickened and the whisk leaves a trail, 3 to 4 minutes. Turn off the heat and whisk in the butter, one tablespoon at a time, until melted and fully incorporated into the cream. Finely grate the salted egg yolks into the pastry cream and mix until combined. Transfer to a bowl and press the surface of the cream with plastic wrap (to prevent a skin from forming). Cover the bowl and chill in the refrigerator for at least 2 hours or overnight. (The cream will thicken as it cools.)

Make the doughnuts: Cut twelve 4-inch squares of parchment paper. After the dough has proofed, transfer it to a lightly floured surface. Roll out the dough until it is ½ inch thick. Using a 3-inch round cookie cutter, cut out rounds and place each on a square of parchment paper. Knead the scraps and cut out more rounds to make 12 total. Cover the dough rounds with a damp, clean kitchen towel and set aside until doubled in size, 45 minutes to 1 hour.

Line a large rimmed baking sheet with paper towels and set a wire rack on top. In a large heavy-bottomed pot, heat 3 inches of oil until it registers 360°F on a deep-fat thermometer.

Working in batches of two or three, use the parchment paper to carefully lower the doughnuts into the oil, removing the paper from the oil. Fry doughnuts until one side is golden brown, 1 ½ to 2 minutes. Flip the doughnuts and fry the until other side is golden brown, 1 1/2 to 2 minutes. Place the doughnuts on the prepared wire rack to cool. Fry the remaining doughnuts, allowing time between each batch for the oil temperature to return to 360°F. While the doughnuts are still warm, toss them in sugar until fully coated. Place them back on the wire rack to cool completely before filling.

With a paring knife, cut a small slit (just big enough to fit a piping tip) through the side of each doughnut, wiggling the blade back and forth to make room for the pastry cream. Place the cream in a pastry bag fitted with a medium round top and fill each doughnut with pastry cream.

Salted Egg Yolks

MAKES 6

Whole salted eggs and individual salted egg yolks are easily found in Chinese grocery stores. The traditional method of salting eggs requires covering either whole duck or chicken eggs in a mixture of mud and salt. My pau pau salts her own eggs in large batches by submerging them in a salt brine. In both methods, the mud and brine protects the egg from bacteria, while the salt draws out the moisture from the egg over the course of a few weeks. The yolks are prized for their golden color and flavor.

My process of salting egg yolks at home is much more streamlined and doesn't require any mud or brine, but you will still need plenty of salt. Egg yolks are directly submerged in salt (for a few days rather than a few weeks) and then slowly dried out in the oven at a low temperature. This is a great use for any leftover yolks from Sesame Crisps (page 211) or a batch of French macarons.

2 cups coarse salt

6 large raw egg yolks

Pour half of the salt into a medium container with a tight-fitting lid. Gently place the egg yolks on the salt, spacing at least 1/2 inch apart. Cover the egg yolks with the remaining salt and cover with the lid. Refrigerate the egg yolks for at least 3 days or up to 5 days.

Preheat the oven to 200°F. Remove the yolks from the salt and rinse under cold water. Pat each yolk dry with a paper towel. Set dry yolks on a wire rack set over a large rimmed baking sheet and bake until dried and firm, 90 minutes.

Allow the yolks to cool and then refrigerate in a small airtight container until ready to use (up to 1 month).

Taro Leaf Buns

MAKES 8

Taro is one of those elusive flavors that's difficult to describe to someone who has never tried it. The starchy root vegetable has a coarse, "hairy" exterior. Not your typical ingredient in a dessert, it's sometimes confused with purple yams or *ube* (a purple yam from the Philippines). You can add taro to soups and stir-fries, or fry thin slices into chips. Here, it's blended into a purple paste that adds subtly sweet flavor and a lovely creaminess to a filling for buns and cookies.

I'm not a fan of taro powder or store-bought taro paste. My biggest qualm with most commercial pastes is that they're either cloyingly sweet or unnaturally purple. Fresh taro is a pale lavender shade. So when I make taro paste, I like to add a little purple sweet potato as a natural way to bump up that color without diluting the taro flavor. While the leaf-shaped buns don't look exactly like the taro leaf specifically, it is still a really gorgeous and simple way to twist dough.

Mother of All Milk Bread Dough (page 6), made through step 4

All-purpose flour, for dusting the work surface

3/4 cup Taro Paste (page 77)

1 large egg

1 tablespoon heavy cream or milk

1/4 cup water

1/4 cup sugar

Line a large rimmed baking sheet with parchment paper.

After the first proof, transfer the dough to a lightly floured surface. Roll out the dough into a roughly 12 x 16-inch rectangle, with the long side facing you. With an offset spatula, spread the taro paste over the top half of the dough, up to the edges. Fold the dough in half lengthwise, pressing the dough down with your hands to press out any air. Cut the dough into eight 3 x 4-inch rectangles.

Working with one piece at a time, cut a slit down the center length of the dough, leaving the last 1/2 inch of one end intact. Hold on to both segments of dough and twist them toward each other 3 times. Pinch the ends of the dough together to create a point at both ends. (See leaf buns diagram on page 49.) Repeat with remaining dough to form eight buns.

Arrange the buns on the prepared baking sheet, spacing at least 3 inches apart. Cover with a damp, clean kitchen towel and set aside in a warm spot to rest until doubled in size, 45 minutes to 1 hour.

Preheat the oven to 350°F. Just before baking, make the egg wash by whisking together the egg and cream in a small bowl. Brush the egg wash over the buns.

Bake the buns until golden brown, 18 to 20 minutes.

Meanwhile, combine the water and sugar in a small saucepan over medium heat. Bring to a simmer and cook until the sugar is dissolved and glaze has thickened, 1 to 2 minutes.

Transfer the baking sheets to a wire rack. Immediately brush the hot buns with glaze to cover completely. Let the buns cool on the sheets for 5 minutes, then transfer to the wire rack to cool. Serve warm or at room temperature.

Buns can be kept in an airtight container (a resealable bag works great) at room temperature for up to 2 days or in the freezer for up to 3 months. Room temperature buns can be reheated in the microwave in 15 to 20 seconds or on a baking sheet in a 300°F oven for about 5 minutes, until soft and warmed through. Reheat frozen buns on a baking sheet in a 350°F oven until soft and warmed through, 10 to 15 minutes.

Taro Paste

MAKES 3 CUPS

250g taro, peeled and cut into 1-inch cubes (about 2 cups)

100g purple sweet potato, peeled and cut into 1-inch cubes (about 3/4 cup)

50g (1/4 cup) sugar

Bring a large pot of water to a boil. Using a spider, carefully lower the cubed taro and sweet potato into the boiling water. Boil until tender, about 20 minutes.

Drain in a colander and rinse under cold water. In the bowl of a food processor, blend taro, sweet potato, and sugar until smooth and thick (the texture will firm up as it cools). Store the paste in an airtight container and chill for at least 1 hour before using. Paste can be refrigerated in an airtight container for up to 2 weeks or frozen for up to 3 months.

Very Chill Jam Buns

MAKES 12

Nonstick cooking spray

Mother of All Milk Bread Dough (page 6), made through step 4

All-purpose flour, for dusting the work surface

1 cup fruit jam or preserves

1 large egg

1 tablespoon heavy cream or milk

2 tablespoons confectioners' sugar, for dusting the buns (optional)

So, you've made it through all the sweet bun recipes, and you may be feeling a little overwhelmed with all the filling combinations and my gentle nudges to develop your origami skills. I totally get it. Though I enjoy a big baking project, I often want a bun without having to think too much—and without a big pile of dishes to wash at the end. If you have some jam and a muffin tin, you can casually craft these Very Chill Jam Buns. Once you've made the milk bread dough, roll out the dough to a large rectangle, spread your favorite jam over the top, roll up the whole thing into a big log, cut it into cinnamon roll–like slices, pop them into a muffin tin, give them a quick egg wash, and bake. That's it! If you want to dust them with confectioners' sugar, you can do that, but no pressure—these are chill buns.

Spray the 12 cups of a standard cupcake tin with nonstick spray.

After the first proof, transfer the dough to a lightly floured surface. Roll out the dough to a roughly 10 x 18-inch rectangle. Using an offset spatula, spread the jam over the dough, leaving a 1/2-inch border around the edges. Roll up the dough lengthwise to form a tight roll. Pinch the seam of the dough to seal. Place the dough seam-side down on the work surface. Trim 1 inch off the ends of the roll and then cut into 12 equal portions with a sharp knife. Place slices in the cups of the tin, cut sides up, and cover with a damp, clean kitchen towel. Set aside in a warm spot until buns are doubled in size, 45 minutes to 1 hour.

Preheat the oven to 350°F. Just before baking, make egg wash by whisking together the egg and cream in a small bowl. Brush the egg wash over the buns.

Bake the buns until golden brown, 18 to 20 minutes. Transfer the tin to a wire rack and let the buns cool in the tin for 5 minutes. Transfer the buns to the rack to cool completely. Dust with confectioners' sugar, if you wish, just before serving.

Buns can be kept in an airtight container (a resealable bag works great) at room temperature for up to 4 days or in the freezer for up to 3 months. Room temperature buns can be reheated in the microwave for 15 to 20 seconds or on a baking sheet in a 300°F oven for about 5 minutes, until soft and warmed through. Reheat frozen buns on a baking sheet in a 350°F oven until soft and warmed through, 10 to 15 minutes.

Keeping Tradition with Auntie Lydia

Cleveland Chinatown is a small enough community that everyone knows everyone . . . or at least everyone knows *of* everyone. My grandparents' generation was especially close-knit, since there weren't quite as many familiar faces in the 1960s. On Sunday mornings, while my family filled their bellies with dim sum and hailed down pushcarts stacked high with their favorite steamers at Li Wai (the local dim sum restaurant), a handful of people would stop by our table with a cheerful "Jo san!," which is "Good morning" in Cantonese. My grandparents were always delighted to see old friends and discuss the achievements of their respective children and grandchildren. The exchange would normally end with the friends being astonished by how much my brother and I have grown since the last time they saw us.

I endearingly refer to these old friends as Aunties and Uncles. They aren't blood-related aunts and uncles, but they're constant fixtures at the small and big moments of my family's lives. One of the Aunties I recall most vividly is Auntie Lydia. She's been a family friend for fifty years, and my mom remembers meeting her as a child. At the time, Lydia was a young woman whose family had just moved to Cleveland from Hong Kong, a few years after she herself had relocated. Over the years, Lydia became one of my pau pau's dearest friends and an unofficial community pillar. She has a deep knowledge of Taoist (a religion many people in the community practice, including my grandparents) rituals and traditions, so I'd always see her at weddings and funerals, facilitating the families. (Here, she's presiding over the tea ceremony at my [actual] aunt's wedding!) Lydia also had a reputation of being an incredible homecook and baker. She was the one who first taught my pau pau how to make steamed cakes with the ingredients they could find at the local grocery stores, as well as other sweets you can't find in bakeries.

Auntie Lydia's journey from Hong Kong to Cleveland was quite similar to my grandparents'. Lydia was a schoolteacher (she'd actually studied at the same school as my goong goong, although a few years after him) and a young mom of two when she left Hong Kong for America. Her own family had settled in San Francisco, but she followed her husband's family to Cleveland. When she first arrived, she desperately wanted to go to school to learn English, but she was a mom with little money. Instead of school, she tried to get a waitressing job, but everyone told her she was too skinny to carry a tray. So she got a job at a factory.

Lydia considers herself a city girl, having spent most of her upbringing in Hong Kong, a major city with every convenience within reach. Before coming to America, she'd never cooked because food was always readily available or prepared for her. Life in Cleveland was quite the opposite. Chinese restaurants and grocery stores were scarce, so if you wanted to eat something authentic, you had to make it yourself. Thankfully for her, her in-laws were incredibly skillful in the kitchen. Her father-in-law was a master at making White Pizza (page 132) and Thousand Layer Cake (a glutinous brown sugar cake made around Chinese New Year), and her mother-in-law knew everything about making steamed cakes, joong (sticky rice wrapped in bamboo leaves made for Dragon Boat Festival), and the crispiest roast pork. Between working, caring for her family, and adjusting to a new country, Lydia found herself learning old-world recipes and traditions from her in-laws. She was a natural student, and since she didn't have the opportunity to study English in America,

Hi, Auntie Lydia!

she focused her attention on absorbing all the knowledge and techniques of this old world of cooking.

Like many strong friendships, food is the reason my pau pau connected with Lydia. She'd befriended Lydia's mother-in-law first because she, too, wanted to learn the old-world techniques. Pau Pau was raised on a farm, where they grew their own food and cooked everything from scratch with whatever resources were available. After living in Hong Kong and immigrating to Cleveland, she hung on tightly to the practices she'd learned from her own family and found Lydia's mother-in-law's food comforting and familiar. Over decades, the three of them bonded in the kitchen as they gossiped, swapped recipes, and made enough food to feed their loved ones and more.

I owe a lot to Auntie Lydia. Without her, I might not have the recipes for Pau Pau's Steamed Cupcakes and White Pizza to share. She also was the person who tipped off my grandparents that a big house on East 31st Street and Payne was for sale, so otherwise, who knows where we would have had weekly family dinners? I'm thankful that someone like her exists in our small Chinese community and continues to carry on the history, culture, and recipes for future generations. It's not only the bakeries and restaurants carrying on our food traditions—it's also the quiet homecooks and Auntie Lydias of the world.

pork buns and beyond

Chapter 3

For many people, barbecue pork buns, or *char siu bao*, are the gateway bite into dim sum and Chinese bakeries. When I ask bakery owners what their top sellers are among non-Asian customers, the unanimous answer is "char siu bao!" Maybe it's the similar flavors of American barbecue sauce, or the fact that straight-up pork isn't as intimidating as pork "floss" (shredded pork dried into fine, fluffy strands). Barbecue pork has crossover appeal. Combine bits of succulent roast pork with a thick, sweet-and-salty barbecue sauce, tender onions, and a squishy bun, and you've got yourself a comforting, savory snack.

I love a freshly steamed pork bun as much as the next person, but I was also a huge fan of Chinese bakery–style hot dog buns as a kid. It's another Chinese bakery favorite, not to be confused with the ballpark variety, though hot dogs wrapped in dough seem to transcend cultural borders. However, the Chinese bakery repertoire of savory buns isn't limited to barbecue buns and hot dogs. Ingredients like seaweed and curry chicken are just as prevalent. Expand your definition of savory buns further with such nontraditional fillings as tuna, miso corn, Chinese broccoli (*gai lan*), and Thanksgiving leftovers. This chapter isn't called "Pork Buns and Beyond" for nothing!

Char Siu Bao
(BBQ Pork Buns)

The smell of *char siu* (Chinese BBQ pork) wafting through the kitchen is pure nostalgia for me. Growing up, I spent most of my weekends and afternoons at "the restaurant." Our family's restaurant was our home away from home. Everyone in the family had a role there, even while holding down full-time jobs elsewhere or studying in college. When I wasn't working on my multiplication tables or watching *Pokémon*, I was the occasional carry-out runner. My goong goong constantly moved from one kitchen task to the next. One minute he was wielding a giant, fiery wok, and the next he was rolling up egg rolls at lightning speed. I loved sneaking into the kitchen for a quick snack. Sometimes I would even convince someone to fry up a fresh egg roll for me, with a side of sweet-and-sour sauce.

It's been almost twenty years since I've been in that kitchen, but I remember it vividly. The wall lined with wok stations loudly clanging, and bits of rice, noodles, and vegetables jumping out of the hot woks. The chilly walk-ins my little brother and I dashed into for a popsicle or a brief respite from the Midwestern summer heat. I was always hoping that a fresh slab of char siu would emerge from the standup BBQ ovens, and someone would slice off a piece or two for me.

Char siu is essentially candied pork. My family's recipe requires a good cut of pork shoulder or pork butt. It is then marinated in a blend of hoisin, oyster sauce, honey, Chinese cooking wine, and a touch of Chinese five-spice powder, to achieve all those sweet, salty, and spice notes. The characteristic red color comes from food coloring or fermented red tofu. Not everyone can get their hands on fermented red tofu, however, and some people prefer to skip food coloring altogether, so the color enhancement is optional. The pork is cooked at a high temperature and requires a few glazes to achieve that perfect caramelized lacquer.

This recipe makes more char siu than you need for steamed buns, and that is intentional. The pork is wonderful sliced and served over steamed rice or a bowl of noodles, diced and tossed into fried rice, or simply as a meaty snack. You'll thank me later. Just remember to save some for your buns!

Char Siu Bao (BBQ Pork Buns)

MAKES 12

For the Char Siu Filling

12 ounces (1 1/2 cups) Char Siu Pork (page 87), chilled

2 tablespoons canola or other neutral-flavored oil

1/2 cup minced onion

1/3 cup water

2 tablespoons cornstarch

1 tablespoon honey

1 tablespoon oyster sauce

1 tablespoon dark soy sauce

1/2 teaspoon coarse salt

1/4 teaspoon ground white pepper

For the Buns

Fluffy Steamed Bun Dough (page 17), made through step 2

All-purpose flour, for dusting

Make the filling: Chop the pork into 1/2-inch pieces and transfer to a mixing bowl.

In a medium skillet, heat the canola oil over medium-high heat until shimmery. Add the onion and cook, stirring frequently, until tender and brown around the edges, 3 to 4 minutes. Transfer to the bowl with the pork.

In a small saucepan, whisk to combine the water, cornstarch, honey, oyster sauce, soy sauce, salt, and white pepper until smooth. Bring to a boil over medium heat. Reduce to a simmer and cook, whisking constantly, until thickened, about 1 minute. Pour over the pork mixture and toss until combined. Cover the bowl with plastic wrap and refrigerate until the mixture is firm but scoopable, at least 1 hour or up to overnight.

Cut twelve 4-inch squares of parchment paper.

Make the buns: After the first proof, punch down to deflate the dough and transfer it to a lightly floured surface. Pinch and pull the ends of the dough into a smooth ball. Divide the dough into 12 equal portions with a bench scraper (for accuracy, weigh with a digital scale if you have one). Form each portion of dough into a smooth ball by pulling the ends of the dough underneath and then rolling between the palms of your hand.

Roll each ball into a 4-inch round with a dowel rolling pin, with thinner edges and a thicker middle. Working with one piece at a time, place a heaping tablespoon of filling in the center. Pull up the edges of the dough and pinch together to seal the bun. Place pleat-side up or pleat-side down on a square of parchment paper. Repeat with remaining rounds and filling to form 12 buns. If it's taking you a long time to form the buns, cover formed buns with a kitchen towel and refrigerate to prevent overproofing. Otherwise, cover the buns with a damp, clean kitchen towel and let them rest in a warm spot until they are 1 1/2 times larger, 30 to 45 minutes.

Prepare your steamer setup (page xxviii) and bring water to a boil. Place buns in the steamer baskets, allowing at least 2 inches between each bun. If you can't fit them all, steam in batches and keep remaining buns in the fridge, to prevent overproofing. Once boiling, steam each batch for 10 minutes, then turn off the heat and leave the buns in the covered steamer for 5 more minutes to prevent collapsing. Carefully remove the buns from the steamer and allow them to cool for 5 minutes before serving.

Buns can be kept in an airtight container (a resealable bag works great) in the refrigerator for up to 4 days, or the freezer for up to 3 months. Refrigerated buns can be reheated in the microwave for 30 to 45 seconds or steamed for about 2 minutes, until soft and warmed through. Reheat frozen buns by steaming until soft and warmed through, 10 to 12 minutes.

Char Siu Pork

SERVES 4 TO 6

3 pounds boneless pork shoulder or pork butt, trimmed of excess fat

$1/2$ cup honey

$1/4$ cup hoisin sauce

$1/4$ cup oyster sauce

$1/4$ cup Shaoxing cooking wine

1 teaspoon Chinese five-spice powder

1 teaspoon coarse salt

$1/2$ teaspoon ground white pepper

$1/2$ teaspoon red food coloring (gel paste or liquid; optional)

$1/4$ cup ketchup

Cut the pork lengthwise into 1 $1/2$-inch-wide planks (you should get three or four), and transfer to a large resealable plastic bag.

In a medium bowl, whisk to combine the honey, hoisin, oyster sauce, wine, five-spice, salt, white pepper, and food coloring (if using) until smooth. Place about $2/3$ marinade into the bag with the pork. Seal the bag and toss the pork in the marinade until evenly coated. Place the bag in a bowl, then transfer to the refrigerator and let the pork marinate at least 6 hours or up to overnight.

Whisk the ketchup into the remaining $1/3$ marinade, then transfer to a small bowl. Cover with plastic wrap and refrigerate until you're ready to cook the pork.

Remove the pork from the refrigerator about an hour before cooking and allow it to come to room temperature. Preheat the oven to 400°F. Line a large rimmed baking sheet with aluminum foil and set a wire rack on the baking sheet.

Place the pork strips on the wire rack (discard marinade) and roast for 20 minutes. Remove from the oven, brush the pork with some of the reserved sauce and roast 10 minutes longer. Flip the pork, brush with more sauce, and roast for 10 more minutes. Brush pork with remaining sauce and roast until shiny with slightly burnt edges, 10 minutes. Remove from the oven and allow the pork to rest for 20 minutes before serving or preparing the char siu bao filling.

Pork Floss and Seaweed Pull-Apart Rolls

MAKES 8 LARGE ROLLS

I know it as "pork floss" and others call it "pork sung." I've also heard it called "meat wool," which I find absolutely hilarious. Whatever you call it, these wispy strands of sweet and salty dried pork have an airy, delicate texture that makes floss a flavorful addition to jook (page 230), salads, and yes, buns. The combination of mayo, pork floss, and dried seaweed or furikake is popular in Chinese bakeries. The creamy mayo anchors the saltiness of seaweed and pork floss with a little richness and tartness, while also keeping the buns extremely soft. Just as people fight over the center cinnamon roll, you may have to elbow a few people out of the way to claim the softest-of-soft pork floss buns in the middle.

All-purpose flour, for dusting

Mother of All Milk Bread Dough (page 6), made through step 4

100g (1/2 cup) mayonnaise

1 cup pork floss, plus more for topping

2 tablespoons furikake

1/4 cup finely chopped green onions

Nonstick cooking spray, for pan

1 large egg

1 tablespoon heavy cream or milk

1 teaspoon toasted sesame seeds, for topping

Lightly flour a work surface. After the first proof, transfer the dough to the surface and roll it out into a roughly 10 x 18-inch rectangle. Using an offset spatula, spread the mayonnaise over the dough, leaving 1/2 inch clear around the edges. Sprinkle the pork floss, furikake, and green onions evenly over the surface. Roll up the dough lengthwise to form a tight roll, pinching the seam to seal. Place the dough seam-side down on the work surface. Trim 1 inch off each end of the coil and then slice eight equal portions with a sharp knife.

Coat a 10-inch round cake pan with nonstick spray. Arrange the dough slices cut side up in the pan, with a small gap between each bun. Cover the pan with a damp, clean kitchen towel and set aside in a warm spot until the buns double in size, 60 to 90 minutes.

Just before baking, make the egg wash by whisking together the egg and cream in a small bowl. Brush the egg wash over the buns. Sprinkle sesame seeds evenly over the buns.

Bake until the buns are golden brown, 25 to 28 minutes. Transfer to a wire rack and allow the buns to cool in the pan. Serve warm or completely cooled.

Buns can be kept in an airtight container (a resealable bag works great) in the refrigerator for up to 4 days, or the freezer for up to 3 months. Refrigerated buns can be reheated in the microwave for 30 to 45 seconds or in a 300°F oven for about 5 minutes, until soft and warmed through. Reheat frozen buns on a baking sheet in a 350°F oven until soft and warmed through, 10 to 15 minutes.

Miso Corn Buns

MAKES 12

When the days grow longer and the temperatures start to soar, you'll find ears and ears of corn on my kitchen counter and a container of homemade miso butter waiting to be slathered onto freshly grilled corn kernels. I wanted to represent this favorite seasonal flavor combination in bun form, while also taking inspiration from the cheesy corn-and-ham buns found in Chinese bakeries. Ideally, you'll want to make these buns when corn hits its sweet peak in mid- to late summer, but frozen or canned corn will work in a pinch (in other words, you can enjoy this any time of year). Miso is made from fermented soybeans (and sometimes rice and other grains) ground into a deeply flavorful, slightly salty paste. I keep lighter white miso and a richer red miso in my refrigerator at all times. Here, the sunny corn kernels plump up when cooked in the miso butter, for a sweet-and-savory umami bomb you'll want to eat straight up with a spoon.

Mother of All Milk Bread Dough (page 6), made through step 4

All-purpose flour, for dusting

3 tablespoons unsalted butter

1 1/2 tablespoons white miso

2 cups fresh or frozen corn kernels (or drained canned corn)

1 teaspoon sugar

1/2 teaspoon coarse salt

1 large egg

1 tablespoon heavy cream or milk

2 tablespoons white sesame seeds, toasted

1/3 cup bias-sliced green onions, for topping

Buns can be kept in an airtight container (a resealable bag works great) in the refrigerator for up to 4 days or in the freezer for up to 3 months. Refrigerated buns can be reheated in the microwave for 30 to 45 seconds or in a 300°F oven for about 5 minutes, until soft and warmed through. Reheat frozen buns on a baking sheet in a 350°F oven until soft and warmed through, 10 to 15 minutes.

While the dough is proofing, line two large rimmed baking sheets with parchment paper and lightly flour a work surface.

In a medium pan over medium heat, melt the butter. Add the miso and break up with a flexible spatula. Increase heat to medium-high and add the corn, sugar, and salt. Sauté until the corn is bright yellow and slightly brown around the edges, 6 to 7 minutes. Transfer corn filling to a medium bowl and cool to room temperature.

After the first proof, punch down to deflate the dough and transfer it to the floured surface. Pinch and pull the ends of the dough into a smooth ball. Divide the dough into 12 equal portions with a bench scraper (for accuracy, weigh with a digital scale if you have one). Form each portion of dough into a smooth ball by pulling the ends of the dough underneath and then rolling between the palms of your hand.

Roll out each portion of dough into a 4-inch round with a dowel rolling pin. Place the rounds on the baking sheets, spacing at least 3 inches apart. Top each round with 1 1/2 tablespoons corn topping. Cover the buns with a damp, clean kitchen towel and let them rest in a warm spot until doubled in size, 45 minutes to 1 hour.

Preheat the oven to 350°F. Just before baking, whisk together the egg and cream in a small bowl. Brush the egg wash over the edges of the buns. Sprinkle the sesame seeds over the egg wash and top the corn filling with sliced green onions, dividing evenly.

Bake until buns are golden brown, 18 to 20 minutes. Transfer the sheets to a wire rack. Let the buns cool for 5 minutes on sheets, then transfer to the rack to cool. Serve warm or cooled completely.

Tuna Buns

MAKES 12

Your favorite bun says a lot about you. If your top pick turns out to be this one, I say you're a risk taker, a rebel, someone who doesn't care what other people think—or maybe you just love tuna melts. A bun topped with tuna salad and cheese is a flavorful, satisfying treat that feels more like a meal than other buns do. The tuna is briny, the green onions add freshness, the mayo adds a little creaminess, and mozzarella around the edges adds a subtly crisp texture. You're going to be making these buns at home, so their freshness won't be an issue (you never know how long the ones in Chinese bakery cases have been there). In fact, I doubt you'll have many of these lying around for long.

Mother of All Milk Bread Dough (page 6), made through step 4

All-purpose flour, for dusting

2 (5-ounce) cans tuna (packed in water), drained

1/2 cup mayonnaise

1/4 cup coarsely chopped green onions (whites and greens), plus more for topping

1/4 teaspoon coarse salt

1/2 teaspoon ground white pepper

1 large egg

1 tablespoon heavy cream or milk

1/2 cup shredded mozzarella

While the dough is proofing, line two large rimmed baking sheets with parchment paper and lightly flour a work surface.

Make the topping: Combine the tuna, mayo, green onions, salt, and white pepper in a medium bowl until well mixed. Cover the bowl and refrigerate until ready to top the buns.

After the first proof, punch down to deflate the dough and transfer it to the floured surface. Pinch and pull the ends of the dough into a smooth ball. Divide the dough into 12 equal portions with a bench scraper (for accuracy, weigh with a digital scale if you have one). Form each portion of dough into a smooth ball by pulling the ends of the dough underneath and then rolling between the palms of your hand.

Roll out each ball of dough into a 4-inch round with a dowel rolling pin. Place the rounds on the baking sheets, spacing at least 3 inches apart. Top each round with 2 tablespoons filling. Cover with a damp, clean kitchen towel and let rest in a warm spot until doubled in size, 45 minutes to 1 hour.

Preheat the oven to 350°F. Right before baking, whisk together the egg and cream in a small bowl. Brush the egg wash over the edges of the buns. Sprinkle mozzarella over the edges and top with more chopped green onions.

Bake until buns are golden brown, 18 to 20 minutes. Transfer the sheets to a wire rack. Let the buns cool for 5 minutes on sheets, then transfer to the rack to cool. Serve warm or cooled completely.

Buns can be kept in an airtight container (a resealable bag works great) in the refrigerator for up to 4 days or in the freezer for up to 3 months. Refrigerated buns can be reheated in the microwave for 30 to 45 seconds or in a 300°F oven for about 5 minutes, until soft and warmed through. Reheat frozen buns on a baking sheet in a 350°F oven until soft and warmed through, 10 to 15 minutes.

Hot Dog Flower Buns

MAKES 12

This recipe ignited the idea for this book. A few years ago, I posted Hot Dog Flower Buns on my blog and was inundated with excited comments from readers joyfully nostalgic for the chance to re-create a Chinese bakery favorite at home. I have countless memories of dragging my parents to bakeries and begging them for a hot dog bun, so it was comforting to hear that many others had similar experiences. It encouraged me to explore and share more facets of Chinese baking.

When I was younger and our family would travel to Hong Kong, my dad would wake up much earlier than the rest of us and venture off to the closest bakery, to bring back treats for our first breakfast (our "second breakfast" would most likely be dim sum a few hours later). His bounty always included a hot dog flower bun or two because he knew I loved them so much. I would pluck off each meat-filled petal with a big smile—what's better than vacation, when you can have hot dogs for breakfast? Each "petal" was a perfect bite. It's an inge-nious way to eat a hot dog, really—no chance of your bun splitting in half and watching your hot dog fall to the ground.

Making these buns is not unlike making pigs-in-a-blanket. The hot dogs are wrapped in a cozy blanket of soft milk bread dough and then sliced to form the petals. You arrange the petals in a flower formation, with the rings of dough barely touching one another. As the buns bake in the oven, the bread expands around the hot dog pieces, adhering to the other petals to form one cohesive, floral-shaped bun.

If you want to save a step, the sugar glaze is optional, but it does give the buns that glossy finish you see in bakeries. The sweetness from the glaze also complements the salty, smoky flavor of the hot dogs.

Mother of All Milk Bread Dough (page 6), made through step 4

All-purpose flour, for work surface

12 hot dogs

1 large egg

1 tablespoon heavy cream or milk

2 teaspoons toasted sesame seeds

2 tablespoons chopped green onions, green parts only

1/4 cup water

1/4 cup sugar

While the dough is proofing, line two large rimmed baking sheets with parchment paper.

After the first proof, punch down to deflate the dough and transfer it to a lightly floured surface. Pinch and pull the ends of the dough into a smooth ball. Divide the dough into 12 equal portions with a bench scraper (for accuracy, weigh with a digital scale if you have one). Form each portion of dough into a smooth ball by pulling the ends of the dough underneath and then rolling between the palms of your hand.

On the work surface, roll out a portion of dough into a 3 x 7-inch rectangle (it should be large enough to wrap around a hot dog). Place a hot dog in the center of the dough and pinch the edges of the dough together to seal completely around it. Slice into six equal pieces. Arrange the pieces on the baking sheet, cut sides up, in a flower formation—one in the center with five pieces surrounding

it. Repeat with remaining dough and hot dogs. Space each bun at least 3 inches apart. Cover with a damp, clean kitchen towel and let them rest in a warm spot until doubled in size, 45 minutes to 1 hour.

Preheat the oven to 350°F. Right before baking, whisk together the egg and cream. Brush the egg wash over the buns and sprinkle with the sesame seeds and green onions.

Bake until buns are golden brown, 18 to 20 minutes.

Meanwhile, combine the water and sugar in a small saucepan over medium heat. Bring to a simmer and cook until the sugar is dissolved and the glaze has thickened, 1 to 2 minutes.

Transfer the baking sheets to a wire rack. Immediately brush the hot buns with glaze to cover completely. Let the buns cool for 5 minutes on sheets, then transfer to the rack to cool. Serve warm or cooled completely.

Buns can be kept in an airtight container (a resealable bag works great) in the refrigerator for up to 4 days, or the freezer for up to 3 months. Refrigerated buns can be reheated in the microwave for 30 to 45 seconds or in a 300°F oven for about 5 minutes, until soft and warmed through. Reheat frozen buns on a baking sheet in a 350°F oven until soft and warmed through, 10 to 15 minutes.

Gingery Bok Choy and Gai Lan Steamed Buns

MAKES 12

For the Filling

2 tablespoons canola or other neutral-flavored oil

1/2 cup finely chopped green onions, whites and greens separated

1 tablespoon grated peeled fresh ginger

2 cups coarsely chopped gai lan

4 cups coarsely chopped baby bok choy

1 tablespoon oyster sauce

1 tablespoon sriracha

1 teaspoon sesame oil

1 teaspoon sugar

1 teaspoon coarse salt

1/4 teaspoon ground white pepper

8 ounces marinated baked tofu, cut into 1/4-inch cubes

2 tablespoons cornstarch

Fluffy Steamed Bun Dough (page 17), spinach variation, made through step 2

All-purpose flour, for dusting

If you take a stroll through the produce aisle of any Asian market and see tender leafy greens with labels reading "yu choy," "gai lan," or "tatsoi," grab them. Asian leafy greens are beautiful, nutritious, and just as versatile as kale and broccoli. Some varieties are bitter, while others are more sweet. A few of the greens are incredibly delicate (pea shoots, for example) and barely require cooking; others are heartier and retain a great crunch even after being cooked. You've probably eaten or at least heard of bok choy. It is mild in flavor and has an amazing texture that holds up whether slowly braised or quickly fried in a hot pan.

For these buns, I paired readily available bok choy with *gai lan* (also known as Chinese broccoli). My family cooked gai lan weekly, and I continue that practice. I love it steamed and topped with a drizzle of oyster sauce. Gai lan looks like broccoli rabe, with a hearty stem and leafy ends, but is far less bitter and more tender than conventional broccoli florets. The bok choy and gai lan are cooked with fresh ginger, for a gentle hint of heat, and seasoned with sesame oil, soy sauce, and sriracha for a fiery kick. Marinated baked tofu is extra firm and deeply savory. It adds heartiness and a boost of protein in the filling. If you spot some gorgeous tatsoi or yu choy at the market, it wouldn't hurt to stuff those into the buns instead.

Make the filling: Heat the oil in a large skillet over medium-high. Add the whites of the green onions and the ginger. Cook until brown around the edges, about 2 minutes. Add the gai lan, bok choy, oyster sauce, sriracha, sesame oil, sugar, salt, and pepper. Cook, stirring occasionally, until the vegetables are tender, 5 to 7 minutes. Transfer the vegetables to a medium bowl and add the onion greens, tofu, and cornstarch, mixing with a flexible spatula until evenly combined. Cover the bowl with plastic wrap and refrigerate for at least 1 hour or up to overnight.

Cut twelve 4-inch squares of parchment paper.

After the first proof, punch down to deflate the dough and transfer it to the floured surface. Pinch and pull the ends of the dough into a smooth ball. Divide the dough into 12 equal portions with a bench scraper (for accuracy, weigh with a digital scale if you have one). Form each portion of dough into a smooth ball by pulling the ends of the dough underneath and then rolling between the palms of your hand.

Roll out a portion of dough into a 4-inch round with a dowel rolling pin, with thinner edges and a thicker middle. Place a heaping tablespoon of the filling in the center of the dough. Pull up the edges of the dough and pinch together to seal the bun. Place pleat-side up or pleat-side down on a square of parchment paper. Repeat

with remaining dough and filling. If it's taking you a long time to form the buns, cover formed buns with a kitchen towel and place in the fridge to prevent overproofing. Otherwise, cover the buns with a damp, clean kitchen towel and let them rest in a warm spot until they are 1 ½ times larger, 30 to 45 minutes.

Prepare your steamer setup (page xxviii) and bring water to a boil. Place buns in the bamboo steamer baskets, allowing at least 2 inches between each. If you can't fit them all, steam in batches and keep remaining buns in the fridge to prevent overproofing. Steam for 10 minutes. Turn off the heat and leave the buns in the covered steamer for 5 more minutes to prevent collapsing. Carefully remove the buns from the steamer and cool for 5 minutes before serving.

Buns can be kept in an airtight container (a resealable bag works great) in the refrigerator for up to 4 days, or the freezer for up to 3 months. Refrigerated buns can be reheated on a plate in the microwave for 30 to 45 seconds or steamed for about 2 minutes, until soft and warmed through. Reheat frozen buns by steaming until soft and warmed through, 10 to 15 minutes.

Steamed Spring Chicken Buns

MAKES 12

Surprisingly, it's been hard for me to find a decent steamed chicken bun in a Chinese bakery. Most bakeries hit their char siu bao out of the park, but when it comes to chicken buns, the filling is often disappointingly dense and bland. The best steamed chicken buns I've eaten were in Beijing, at a little stand a block away from my apartment. On my way into work, I would stop and order three steamed buns for the equivalent of one dollar. I didn't know how to speak Mandarin, so I just pointed and hoped for the best. They were always fresh and delicious, especially the chicken buns. They were packed full of vegetables and chives. Vegetables lighten the filling and provide much needed moisture to the chicken filling, which can easily dry out. These buns are filled with fresh spring produce, like garlic chives, green peas, and carrots for a (more than) decent steamed chicken bun. Sometimes, I'll even lightly pan-fry my steamed buns in a hot pan for extra texture and toasty flavor (see step 6).

2 tablespoons canola or other neutral-flavored oil

1/2 cup grated carrot

1/2 cup frozen peas

2 tablespoons oyster sauce

1/2 teaspoon coarse salt

1/2 teaspoon ground white pepper

10 ounces (3 to 4) boneless skinless chicken thighs, cut into 1/2-inch cubes

2/3 cup chopped Chinese garlic chives or green onions

2 tablespoons cornstarch

Fluffy Steamed Bun Dough (page 17), made through step 2

All-purpose flour, for dusting

Make the filling: Heat the oil in a small skillet over medium. Add carrot, peas, oyster sauce, salt, and pepper. Cook, stirring occasionally, until the vegetables are tender and brown around the edges, 5 minutes. Add the chicken and cook, stirring occasionally, until cooked through, 8 to 10 minutes. Transfer the filling to a medium bowl. Add the garlic chives and cornstarch and mix until combined. Cover the bowl with plastic wrap and refrigerate until chilled, at least 1 hour or up to overnight.

Cut twelve 4-inch squares of parchment paper.

After the first proof, punch down to deflate the dough and transfer it to the floured surface. Pinch and pull the ends of the dough into a smooth ball. Divide the dough into 12 equal portions with a bench scraper (for accuracy, weigh with a digital scale if you have one). Form each portion of dough into a smooth ball by pulling the ends of the dough underneath and then rolling between the palms of your hand.

Roll out a dough ball into a 4-inch round with a dowel rolling pin, with thinner edges and a thicker middle. Place a heaping tablespoon of the filling in the center of the dough. Pull up the edges of the dough and pinch together to seal the bun. Place pleat-side up or pleat-side down on a square of parchment paper. Repeat with remaining dough and filling. If it's taking you a long time to form the buns, cover formed buns with a kitchen towel and place in the fridge to prevent overproofing. Otherwise, cover the buns with a damp, clean kitchen towel and let them rest in a warm spot until they are 1 1/2 times larger, 30 to 45 minutes.

Prepare your steamer setup (page xxviii) and bring water to a boil. Place buns in the bamboo steamer baskets, spacing at least 2 inches apart. If you can't fit them all, steam in batches and keep remaining buns in the fridge to prevent overproofing. Cover and steam buns over boiling water, 10 minutes. Turn off the heat and leave buns in the covered steamer for 5 more minutes to prevent collapsing. Remove buns from the steamer and allow to cool for 5 minutes before serving.

As an additional step, to toast the buns, heat a pan over medium heat. Once hot, add a few buns to the pan and toast until golden brown, 90 seconds to 2 minutes.

Buns can be kept in an airtight container (a resealable bag works great) in the refrigerator for up to 4 days, or the freezer for up to 3 months. Refrigerated buns can be reheated in the microwave for 30 to 45 seconds or steamed for about 2 minutes, until soft and warmed through. Reheat frozen buns by steaming until soft and warmed through, 10 to 12 minutes.

Mushroom Mushroom Buns

MAKES 10

Mushroom buns that actually look like mushrooms are elusive (and usually gone by the time the dim sum cart reaches my table), so I wanted to learn how to make them on my own. A deep dive online revealed that the crackly brown mushroom-like topping is made with a paste of cocoa powder and water, which is brushed onto the buns before they proof. As each bun proofs and eventually steams in the oven, its topping cracks and mimics the appearance of a shiitake mushroom cap. I reserve some of the bun dough to make little stems for each bun, to really drive home the mushroom aesthetic! But feel free to omit the stems and make twelve stemless mushroom mushroom buns instead.

If you're skeptical about the mushroom/cocoa powder flavor pairing, don't worry: you barely taste the cocoa powder. I add a dash of cayenne for a little heat; the flavors blend well with the earthy mushrooms. Use a blend of quality mushrooms; not all mushrooms provide the same flavors and textures. I recommend a mix of shiitake, which have a ton of flavor, and trumpet mushrooms, which provide a meaty texture and don't cook down to tiny bites of mushroom.

For the Filling

2 tablespoons olive oil

1/2 medium onion, coarsely chopped

10 ounces mushrooms (including stems), blend of shiitake and trumpet, cleaned and coarsely chopped

1 tablespoon dark soy sauce

2 teaspoons sugar

3/4 teaspoon coarse salt

1/2 teaspoon ground white pepper

2 tablespoons cornstarch

For the Topping

1 tablespoon cocoa powder

1/4 teaspoon cayenne powder

2 teaspoons water

Fluffy Steamed Bun Dough (page 17), made through step 2

All-purpose flour, for dusting

Make the filling: Heat the olive oil in a medium skillet over medium-high. Add the onion and sauté until slightly tender and brown around the edges, 3 to 4 minutes. Add the mushrooms, soy sauce, sugar, salt, and pepper. Cook, stirring occasionally, until the mushrooms are tender, 8 to 9 minutes. Transfer to a medium bowl, add the cornstarch, and mix until combined. Cover the bowl with plastic wrap and refrigerate for at least 1 hour or up to overnight.

Make the topping: Whisk to combine the cocoa powder, cayenne, and water in a small bowl until smooth.

Cut ten 4-inch squares of parchment paper and a larger sheet for the stems.

After the first proof, punch down to deflate the dough and transfer it to the floured surface. Pinch and pull the ends of the dough into a smooth ball. Divide the dough into 12 equal portions with a bench scraper (for accuracy, weigh with a digital scale if you have one). Form each portion of dough into a smooth ball by pulling the ends of the dough underneath and then rolling between the palms of your hand. Divide two balls into ten smaller balls, for the mushroom stems. Roll the small portions of dough into balls and set on the larger sheet of parchment paper.

Roll out a larger portion of dough into a 4-inch round with a dowel rolling pin, with thinner edges and a thicker middle. Place a heaping tablespoon of the filling in the center of the dough. Pull

up the edges of the dough and pinch together to seal the bun. Place seam-side down on a square of parchment paper. Using a pastry brush, brush the top of the bun with the cocoa paste. Repeat with remaining dough and filling. If it's taking you a long time to form the buns, place in the fridge uncovered to prevent overproofing. Otherwise, leave the buns uncovered so the cocoa paste can dry out and let them rest in a warm spot until they are 1 1/2 times larger, 30 to 45 minutes.

Prepare your steamer setup (page xxviii) and bring water to a boil. Place the buns and the stems in the bamboo steamer baskets, allowing at least 2 inches between each. If you can't fit them all, steam in batches and keep the remaining buns in the fridge to prevent overproofing. Steam for 10 minutes. Turn off the heat and leave the buns in the covered steamer for 5 more minutes to prevent collapsing. Carefully remove the buns from the steamer and allow to cool for an additional 5 minutes. Pair each mushroom top with a stem and stack the bun on top of the stem to make a full mushroom.

Buns can be kept in an airtight container (a resealable bag works great) in the refrigerator for up to 4 days or in the freezer for up to 3 months. Refrigerated buns can be reheated on a plate in the microwave for 30 to 45 seconds or steamed for about 2 minutes, until soft and warmed through. Reheat frozen buns by steaming until soft and warmed through, 10 to 15 minutes.

Crispy Panko Pork Chop Sandwiches

MAKES 8

When my dad talks about the pork chop sandwiches he would order in Hong Kong, I can almost see him salivating midsentence. The sandwich is a true mash-up of all the cultural influences in Hong Kong. It first originated in nearby Macau, which was under Portuguese rule for a long time, so the sandwich was typically served on a slightly crusty Portuguese bread roll. As the popularity of the fried pork chop sandwich grew, more Hong Kong–style diners (*cha chaan tengs*) and street food stalls started to serve them.

The combination of crispy, crunchy fried pork and squishy buns is such a satisfying textural experience. The more elusive variety is the pork chop *bo lo bao*, where the regular buns are swapped out for sweet pineapple buns (page 45). Try it: you may think it's going to taste weird, but it's nothing short of magical, akin to the flavor combination of fried chicken and waffles. Pre-pork chop bo lo bao, you might not have enjoyed eating a cookie-topped bun and a fried pork chop in a single bite, but after you've tried it, you won't be able to stop dreaming about it.

This recipe can easily be halved if you don't want to make a lot of sandwiches.

For the Buns

Mother of All Milk Bread Dough (page 6), made through step 4

All-purpose flour, for dusting

1 large egg

1 tablespoon heavy cream or milk

2 tablespoons furikake

For the Pork Chops

4 medium (4-ounce) boneless pork chops

3/4 cup all-purpose flour

1/2 teaspoon garlic powder

2 large eggs

1 1/2 cups panko bread crumbs

1 teaspoon coarse salt, plus more for sprinkling

Canola or other neutral-flavored oil, for frying

For the Sandwiches

1/2 cup ketchup

1 teaspoon curry powder

1/2 cup mayonnaise

3 cups finely shredded napa or green cabbage

Make the buns: While the dough is proofing, line a large rimmed baking sheet with parchment paper and lightly dust a work surface with flour.

After the first proof, punch down the dough to deflate it and transfer to the floured surface. Pinch and pull the ends of the dough into a smooth ball. Divide the dough into eight equal portions with a bench scraper (for accuracy, weigh with a digital scale if you have one). Shape each portion of dough into a smooth ball by tucking the ends underneath and then roll each ball between your hands to form a football-shaped bun.

Place the buns on the baking sheets, spacing at least 2 inches apart. Cover with a damp, clean kitchen towel and let rest in a warm spot until doubled in size, 45 minutes to 1 hour.

Preheat the oven to 350°F. Right before baking, make the egg wash by whisking together the egg and cream in a small bowl. Brush the egg wash over the buns and sprinkle evenly with furikake.

Bake until buns are golden brown, 18 to 20 minutes. Transfer the baking sheet to a wire rack and allow the buns to cool on the sheet for 5 minutes. Transfer to a wire rack to cool completely.

Make the pork chops: With your knife parallel to the cutting board, slice each chop in half so that they are thin. Place the flour and garlic powder in a shallow dish, the eggs in a second shallow dish, and panko and salt in a third shallow dish. Whisk the eggs and toss the panko and salt to combine. Dip each split pork chop in the flour to coat completely, then in the egg wash (letting excess drip back into the bowl), and finally in the panko (shaking off any extra). Make sure to cover all sides during each coating, and place each coated chop on a plate while you coat the rest.

Heat 1 inch of canola oil in a cast-iron skillet or heavy-bottomed pan until it registers 360°F on a deep-fry thermometer. If you don't have a thermometer, the oil should be hot but not smoking. Test the temperature by throwing a few pieces of panko into the oil; if they turn golden brown in about 30 seconds, it's ready.

Carefully lay two (or however many fit in a single layer) pork chops at a time in the hot oil. Fry on one side until golden brown, about 2 minutes, then flip and fry the other side until golden brown, 90 seconds to 2 minutes. Transfer the pork chops to a wire rack set over a baking sheet. Sprinkle with salt and then repeat to fry the remaining pork chops.

Assemble the sandwiches: Mix the ketchup and curry powder together in a small bowl. Slice all the buns in half lengthwise. Spread curry ketchup on one side of each bun and mayonnaise on the other half. Layer a crispy panko pork chop on the bottom bun, add finely shredded cabbage, and top with the top bun. Serve immediately.

Thanksgiving Leftover Gua Bao

MAKES 8

I think we can all agree that the best part of Thanksgiving is the leftovers. Why else cook a feast large enough to feed double your guest list, if you're not planning to have pie for breakfast several days in a row? I've carried on my mom's tradition of making a giant pot of turkey jook with the remains of our turkey and, of course, assembling glorious leftover turkey sandwiches piled high with all the side dish leftovers. I have to admit that I'm one of those people who will order the Thanksgiving leftover sandwich at a diner in the middle of July. I'm a huge fan of cold, thick-sliced turkey (I'm known in my family as the only one who enjoys roast turkey), tangy cranberry sauce, and starchy sides tucked between two thick slices of bread.

Each year, I like to play around with ways to reimagine Thanksgiving leftovers. Instead of stacking everything between sliced bread, stuffing it inside a steamed bun makes sense. I almost always have leftover mashed or roasted sweet potatoes, which makes them perfect for sweet potato steamed bun dough! They give the buns a bright orange color and a wonderfully soft and almost creamy texture. Making gua bao–style buns with the dough is like making a bunch of mini Thanksgiving leftover sandwiches! I've shared my favorite leftover combination, which absolutely requires crispy onions for texture, but feel free to stuff your buns with any of your favorite leftovers.

1/3 cup cranberry sauce

1/4 cup hoisin sauce

8 Fluffy Steamed Buns (Gua Bao, page 17), sweet potato variation

1 large leftover turkey breast, cut into 1/4-inch slices, cold or reheated in the oven

1 cup roasted Brussels sprouts, cold or reheated in the oven

1/2 cup crispy fried onions (from a green bean casserole or a can)

To assemble the gua bao, smear a little bit of cranberry sauce and hoisin inside each bun. Add a few slices of turkey and Brussels sprouts and top with crispy fried onions.

Sambal and Parmesan Buns

MAKES 12

Here is a great example of how you can get creative with fillings and flavors without having to spend extra time making components from scratch. All you need is a jar of *sambal oelek* (an Indonesian chili paste) and some Parmesan cheese—ingredients I always have in my refrigerator. Sambal oelek is quite hot so you don't need much for a kick of spice. A sprinkle of Parmesan adds a salty and cheesy layer. The score-and-roll method showcased in this bun is one of my favorite styles. It's very easy to do, and the results are impressive—a win-win in my book.

Mother of All Milk Bread Dough (page 6), made through step 4

All-purpose flour, for dusting

¼ cup sambal oelek

½ cup finely grated Parmesan, plus more for topping

1 large egg

1 tablespoon heavy cream or milk

While the dough is proofing, line two baking sheets with parchment paper and lightly flour a work surface with flour.

After the first proof, punch down the dough to deflate it and transfer to the floured surface. Pinch and pull the ends of the dough into a smooth ball. Divide the dough into 12 equal portions with a bench scraper (for accuracy, weigh with a digital scale if you have one). Form each portion of dough into a smooth ball by pulling the ends of the dough underneath and then rolling between the palms of your hand.

Roll out a portion of dough into a roughly 3 x 5-inch oval. Cut vertical slits, ¼ inch apart, over the top half of the dough. Spread 1 teaspoon sambal oelek on the lower (uncut) half of the dough, then sprinkle with 2 teaspoons of Parmesan. Gently roll up the dough, starting from the covered end and working toward the cut end to form a tight roll (the sambal oelek should be visible between the slits of the dough). Place the buns seam-side down on the baking sheets, spacing at least 3 inches apart. Cover with a damp, clean kitchen towel and let rest in a warm spot until the buns are doubled in size, 45 minutes to 1 hour.

Preheat the oven to 350°F. Right before baking, whisk together the egg and cream. Brush the egg wash over the buns and sprinkle with Parmesan.

Bake until buns are golden brown, 18 to 20 minutes. Allow the buns to cool on the baking sheet for 5 minutes, then transfer to a wire rack to continue cooling. Serve warm or completely cooled.

Buns can be kept in an airtight container (a resealable bag works great) at room temperature for up to 4 days, or the freezer for up to 3 months. Room temperature buns can be reheated on a plate in the microwave for 15 to 20 seconds or on a baking sheet in a 300°F oven for about 5 minutes, until soft and warmed through. Reheat frozen buns on a baking sheet in a 350°F oven until soft and warmed through, 10 to 15 minutes.

Curry Chicken Puffs

MAKES 9

The term "curry chicken" is pretty vague, because so many different cultures have their own versions. For me, the Cantonese-style curry chicken that was on the weekly dinner rotation in my house comes immediately to mind. You could smell the curry wafting through the hallway, signaling our appetites to get ready for dinner. My mom makes hers with chicken wings and generous cubes of hearty potatoes, both swimming in an ocher-hued sauce made with a yellow curry powder that was a touch sweet and mildly spicy. She served it over a heaping bowl of jasmine rice. My favorite (admittedly odd) thing to do was squish the potatoes and rice together with a fork to create a double-starch curry mash-up. It was excellent.

The flavors of curry chicken taste simply of home. I'll occasionally indulge in a curry chicken puff if I spot a fresh, crisp-looking one at a bakery, but they never quite taste how I want them to. I miss the sweetness and the potato chunks. In these puffs, I essentially packaged my mom's weeknight meal into a pastry shell. The buttery pastry adds a much more exciting textural experience than rice but still delivers on the double-carb mash-up. The sad thing about curry chicken puffs is that they are gone in a few bites. But the wonderful thing about making them yourself is that they're all yours, and you'll have at least a few more to enjoy later.

For the Filling

2 tablespoon canola or other neutral-flavored oil

1/4 cup coarsely chopped onion

1 medium yellow potato, such as Yukon gold, chopped into 1/4-inch pieces

6 ounces (about 2) boneless skinless chicken thigh, cut into 1/2-inch pieces

1/4 cup canned coconut milk

1 tablespoon cornstarch

1 1/2 teaspoons curry powder

1 teaspoon sugar

1/2 teaspoon coarse salt

1/4 teaspoon ground white pepper

For the Puffs

All-purpose flour, for dusting

Chinese Puff Pastry (page 157)

1 large egg, lightly beaten

Sesame seeds, for topping

Make the filling: In a medium skillet, heat the oil over medium heat. Add the onion and cook, stirring occasionally, until brown around the edges, 3 to 4 minutes. Add the potato and cook, stirring occasionally, until tender and browned, 8 to 10 minutes. Remove from the heat.

In a medium mixing bowl, combine the chicken, coconut milk, cornstarch, curry powder, sugar, salt, and pepper. Add the onion and potato and mix until combined. Cover the bowl with plastic wrap and refrigerate until chilled, at least 1 hour or up to overnight.

Line a large rimmed baking sheet with parchment paper.

Make the puffs: On a lightly floured surface, roll out the sheet of puff pastry into a 16 x 16-inch square. Using a 4-inch cookie cutter, cut out 18 pastry rounds. Arrange nine pastry rounds on the prepared baking sheet, spacing at least 2 inches apart. Brush the beaten egg onto the edges of each round. Top each round with 1 heaping tablespoon filling. Top with the remaining pastry rounds, pressing down around the edges to seal. Freeze filled pastry (still on baking sheet) until firm, 15 to 30 minutes. Preheat the oven to 450°F.

Just before baking, brush the tops with beaten egg and cut slits into the top with a sharp paring knife, to allow steam to vent. Sprinkle sesames over the tops.

Bake the puffs until golden brown and crisp, 20 to 24 minutes. Transfer baking sheets to a wire rack and let puffs cool for 5 minutes. Transfer puffs to the rack to cool 10 minutes longer before serving.

Puffs can be kept in an airtight container (a resealable bag works great) in the refrigerator for up to 4 days or in the freezer for up to 3 months. Reheat puffs on a baking sheet in a 350°F oven until crisp and warmed through, 8 to 10 minutes for refrigerated, or 15 to 18 minutes for frozen.

pork buns and beyond 113

Everything Bagel Bao

MAKES 12

Mother of All Milk Bread Dough
(page 6), made through step 4

All-purpose flour, for dusting

For the Filling

12 ounces cream cheese,
softened

4 green onions, whites and
greens, finely chopped

1/2 teaspoon coarse salt

1/4 teaspoon ground white
pepper

For the Topping

1 tablespoon white sesame seeds

1 tablespoon black sesame seeds

1 tablespoon dried garlic or
onion flakes

1 teaspoon poppy seeds

1 teaspoon flaky sea salt

For the Egg Wash

1 large egg

1 tablespoon heavy cream or
milk

My partner, Reuben, hails from the great state of New Jersey. Over the years, he's introduced me to the wonders of Jewish cooking, "pork roll, egg, and cheese," appropriate pasta portions, and, most importantly, the best bagels in the world. Hightstown Hot Bagels is located a few minutes from Reuben's parents' house, and for us, they're the gold standard in bagels. Grabbing a baker's dozen is always the first thing we do after we touch down at the airport, and I try my hardest to save some room in my luggage to bring a few bagels home with me after our visit. They are soft, chewy, and always fresh and warm. With the exception of a small handful of spots, most bagels in the Bay Area are tough—it hurts your jaw to eat one. So I satisfy bagel cravings by sprinkling my own homemade "everything bagel" seasoning on things like biscuits and milk bread and pretend that I'm in the parking lot of Hightstown Hot Bagels.

Making decent bagels is a work in progress for me. But these Everything Bagel Bao more than hit the spot. The buns are stuffed with green-onion cream cheese, which gets warm and melty in the oven, and topped with the flavor bomb that is everything bagel seasoning. I tend to make my own filling and topping mix, but you can use your favorite packaged cream cheese or top it with a store-bought everything bagel seasoning, white sesame seeds, Asiago cheese, or any other favorite bagel toppings. Sneaking in some lox would also be a smart move.

While the dough is proofing, line two baking sheets with parchment paper and lightly dust a work surface with flour.

Make the filling: Combine the cream cheese, green onions, coarse salt, and white pepper in a medium bowl, mixing with a flexible spatula until smooth.

After the first proof, punch down the dough to deflate it and transfer to the floured surface. Pinch and pull the ends of the dough into a smooth ball. Divide the dough into 12 equal portions with a bench scraper (for accuracy, weigh with a digital scale if you have one). Form each portion of dough into a smooth ball by pulling the ends of the dough underneath and then rolling between the palms of your hand.

Roll out a portion of dough into a 4-inch round with a dowel rolling pin. Place 1 tablespoon filling in the center of the round. Pull up the edges of the dough and pinch together to seal the bun. Repeat with remaining dough and filling, placing the buns seam-side down on the baking sheets and spacing at least 3 inches apart. Cover with a damp, clean kitchen towel and let rest in a warm spot until buns are doubled in size, 45 minutes to 1 hour.

Make the topping: Combine both sesame seeds, the dried garlic, poppy seeds, and sea salt in a small bowl.

Preheat the oven to 350°F. Make the egg wash: Whisk together the egg and cream in a small bowl. Brush the egg wash over the buns and sprinkle evenly with the topping.

Bake until buns are golden brown, 18 to 20 minutes. Transfer the baking sheet to a wire rack and allow the buns to cool on the sheet for 5 minutes. Transfer to the rack to continue cooling. Serve warm or completely cooled.

Buns can be kept in an airtight container (a resealable bag works great) in the refrigerator for up to 4 days, or the freezer for up to 3 months. Refrigerated buns can be reheated on a plate in the microwave for 30 to 45 seconds or on a baking sheet in a 300°F oven for about 5 minutes, until soft and warmed through. Reheat frozen buns on a baking sheet in a 350°F oven until soft and warmed through, 10 to 15 minutes.

Garlic and Chive Whole-Wheat Flower Buns

MAKES 8

Steamed "flower buns," or huā juǎn, are a step between mantou and your typical stuffed bun. Traditional huā juǎn are filled with sesame oil, chopped green onions, and maybe a sprinkling of white pepper or Sichuan peppercorns. Instead of being "stuffed," the ingredients are spread out onto steamed bun dough, folded into layers, cut into strips, and then twisted into elegant blossoms. It's meditative to watch someone make them and even more so to twist the dough yourself.

I love using whole-wheat bun dough in this recipe because it provides a nutty, earthy backdrop for the strong aromatics. I've altered the fillings to include crispy garlic and chives, for an allium-forward bun. These are wonderful to eat on their own or dipped into chili oil. They are also reminiscent of garlic knots found in pizza parlors, a very good thing.

1/4 cup extra virgin olive oil

1/4 cup minced garlic (8 to 10 cloves)

Fluffy Steamed Bun Dough (page 17), whole-wheat variation, made through step 2

All-purpose flour, for dusting

1/3 cup finely chopped fresh chives

1/2 teaspoon flaky salt

Heat the oil in a saucepan over medium-low heat. Add the garlic and cook, stirring occasionally, until lightly golden brown and crisp, 4 to 5 minutes. Strain the oil through a fine mesh sieve to remove the crisp garlic. Reserve the garlic and 2 tablespoons of the oil separately for the buns.

Cut eight 4-inch squares of parchment paper.

After the first proof, transfer the dough to a lightly floured surface. Roll out the dough to a roughly 10 x 16-inch rectangle. Brush the dough with the garlic oil and sprinkle the crisp garlic, chives, and salt evenly over the surface. Fold the dough into thirds, like a letter. Flatten and roll out the dough with a rolling pin into a roughly 10 x 16-inch rectangle. Cover the dough with a clean kitchen towel and let rest for 15 minutes. (Don't be tempted to skip this step, as the dough will not stretch out as easily without a proper rest.)

Cut the dough into eight equal-width strips (1 1/2 x 10 inches), then cut in half into 1 1/2 x 5-inch strips. Stack two strips of dough on top of each other and press lengthwise down the center of the dough with a chopstick. Pinch the two short ends of the dough with either hand, gently lengthen and stretch the dough, then twist the dough into a spiral. While securely holding onto one end, twist the dough around the pinching fingers, then pinch to secure the other end to the dough (see photos). Place the formed bun on a square of parchment paper. Cover with a damp, clean kitchen towel and let rest in a warm spot until they are 1 1/2 times larger, 30 to 45 minutes.

Prepare your steamer setup (page xxviii) and bring water to a boil. Place buns in the bamboo steamer baskets, spacing at least 2 inches apart. If you can't fit them all, steam in batches and keep

remaining buns in the fridge to prevent overproofing. Steam for 10 minutes. Turn off the heat and leave the buns in the covered steamer for 5 more minutes. Carefully remove the buns from the steamer and cool for 5 minutes before serving.

Buns can be kept in an airtight container (a resealable bag works great) at room temperature for up to 4 days or in the freezer for up to 3 months. Room temperature buns can be reheated on a plate in the microwave for 15 to 25 seconds or steamed for about 2 minutes, until soft and warmed through. Reheat frozen buns by steaming until soft and warmed through, 10 to 15 minutes.

Deep-Dish Pepperoni Bread

MAKES 1 LOAF

I grew up eating pepperoni bread at my neighbors' houses, school fundraisers, and graduation parties. It's an Ohio delicacy (with Appalachian roots, supposedly) that I never really loved but ate anyway, because there isn't a bottom on bread and cured meat. The bread encasing the presliced pepperoni was often dry, and it confounded me that there was never any cheese inside the bread. I had completely forgotten about this lackluster culinary experience until I had the idea to stuff milk bread with quality pepperoni and fresh tomato sauce, and sprinkle cheese inside *and* outside. Those memories of disappointing pepperoni bread came flooding back—and I vowed not to repeat them.

My version of pepperoni bread would be right at home at your local school fundraiser or graduation party, but it's so good it could even pass as an impressive appetizer at your next dinner party or game night. Ideally, use pepperoni you slice yourself, and fresh tomato sauce. But whether you're making the sauce or using your favorite jarred variety, reduce it to a thick paste so that it's easier and neater to assemble the bread. Here, the pepperoni, tomato sauce, and a melty mozzarella are tucked into layers of soft milk bread. I sprinkle cheese around the edges of the cast-iron skillet to add another layer of Midwestern-ness, à la Detroit-style pizza.

1 ½ cups tomato sauce (homemade or your favorite store-bought variety)

2 tablespoons extra virgin olive oil

2 cups shredded mozzarella

Mother of All Milk Bread Dough (page 6), made through step 4

All-purpose flour, for dusting

½ cup (about 5 ounces) sliced pepperoni

1 large egg

1 tablespoon heavy cream or milk

Bring the tomato sauce to a simmer in a small saucepan over medium heat. Cook until reduced by half, 10 to 15 minutes. Allow the sauce to cool to room temperature.

Brush a 10-inch cast-iron skillet or round cake pan with the olive oil and sprinkle 1 cup of the shredded mozzarella around the edge of the pan.

After the first proof, transfer the dough to a lightly floured surface. Roll out the dough to a roughly 10 x 18-inch rectangle. Using an offset spatula, spread the reduced sauce over the dough, leaving a ½-inch border around the edges. Sprinkle the remaining mozzarella and the sliced pepperoni over the tomato sauce. Roll up the dough lengthwise to form a tight roll, pinching the seam to seal. Place the dough seam-side down on the work surface. Cut the roll in half lengthwise with a sharp knife. Arrange the halves of the dough parallel to each other. Pinch one end of each roll half together and then begin crisscrossing the two rolls to form a twisted braid. Carefully transfer the braided loaf to the cast-iron skillet and bring the two ends of the twisted dough together to form a round loaf. Cover with a damp, clean kitchen towel and let the loaf rest in a warm spot until doubled in size, 60 to 90 minutes.

Preheat the oven to 375°F. Right before baking, make the egg wash by whisking together the egg and cream in a small bowl. Brush the egg wash over the loaf, focusing on the areas not covered in sauce.

Bake until loaf is golden brown, 40 to 45 minutes. Allow the bread to cool in the pan for 15 minutes before slicing and serving. Serve the bread directly from the cast iron or transfer to a plate.

Bread can be kept in an airtight container (a resealable bag works great) in the refrigerator for up to 4 days, or the freezer for up to 3 months. Refrigerated bread can be reheated in the microwave for 30 to 45 seconds or in a 300°F oven for about 5 minutes, until soft and warmed through. Reheat frozen bread on a baking sheet in a 350°F oven until soft and warmed through, 10 to 15 minutes.

Eastern Bakery

Walking through San Francisco's Chinatown is especially magical during Chinese New Year. Markets are crowded with shoppers buying everything they need for the family feast, the grannies are chattering a little louder than usual, and bakeries showcase their best seasonal cakes and bakes in honor of the holiday. On the corner of Grant Avenue and Commercial Street, smack-dab in the middle of Chinatown, a big neon sign reads EASTERN BAKERY, CHINESE & AMERICAN FOOD. The oldest Chinese bakery in San Francisco is particularly busy, and a happy bunch of visitors and locals press their faces to window displays of crispy bow tie cookies and golden-crusted mooncakes.

Open since 1924, Eastern Bakery is the perfect place to purchase a bite of Chinatown nostalgia. Originally serving American diner fare and Chinese baked goods, it now focuses mainly on Chinese-style baked goods. Individually wrapped mooncakes line the counters, and cookies, candies, and decorated cakes fill display cases. Mementos from its nearly century-old history adorn the walls. Bay Area families have been visiting the bakery for decades, sharing their love for the freshly baked treats and a time-travel immersion in Chinatown of old.

Owner Orlando Kuan, a constant fixture floating between the front register and the kitchen, purchased the bakery from the original owners in 1985. Several bakers the original owners hired still work here—one has been baking at Eastern for more than forty years! Like many, Kuan has a unique immigrant story. Hailing from Peru, Kuan's parents owned a wholesale bakery that catered to the local tastes. As Kuan explained, "Baking is almost universal, so we made a few Chinese items, such as breads, butterfly cookies, and cakes."

While Chinese bakes fill Eastern's display cases, Kuan is most proud of his Coffee Crunch Cake, a bouncy vanilla sponge cake popularized by San Francisco's revered Blum's Bakery, which shuttered for good in 1974. However, long-committed patrons of Eastern Bakery have disputed this and say that Eastern Bakery's employees delivered their coffee crunch cakes to Blum's Bakery to sell. The Coffee Crunch Cake has been preserved and perfected as a beloved necessity for birthdays, Mother's Day, and any other reason to celebrate. The roasted-coffee whipped cream and crunchy crumbled toffee create an incredibly satisfying bite. I devoured a slice of the famous cake in about five seconds—it lives up to the hype.

Depending on the time of day or day of the week, Eastern Bakery might be filled with families picking up after-school treats or hordes of people trying to place cake or mooncake orders for Lunar New Year or Harvest Moon celebrations. It's hard to find a bakery that makes mooncakes from scratch, and most only do during the weeks around the Harvest Moon Festival in September. Eastern Bakery makes fresh mooncakes (including the fillings) year-round (Bill Clinton even stopped by in 1995 for a White Lotus Mooncake). The freshness of those mooncakes has a lot to do with their popularity, as do using high-quality ingredients and following a secret Chinese recipe—which, Kuan said with a smile, he isn't able to divulge. Buying a mooncake prepackaged in a tin can't compare—you're buying a product that's "at least a month old, shipped by boat from China, and typically full of preservatives," said Kuan. As with many things in life, the fresher the mooncake, the better.

I'm just one of many who have fallen under Eastern Bakery's spell. Every time I walk through those doors, I can't resist a cocktail bun that's still warm from the oven or a slice of that inexplicably good Coffee Crunch Cake. Chatting with Orlando and enjoying the hum and history of Chinatown make the experience even sweeter.

gao (cakes + tarts)

Chapter 4

The Chinese Lunar calendar is filled with plenty of occasions to celebrate. Rich, dense mooncakes stuffed with a variety of sweet pastes help celebrate the Mid-Autumn Festival, typically held in mid- to late September (specifically, the 15th day of the 8th month on the Lunar calendar, during a full moon). The biggest holiday of the year, Chinese New Year, is the time when families reunite, cook a large feast, and admire a new year's moon. We enjoy my pau pau's steamed cakes, their tops bursting to signify the luck and prosperity you hope for in the year ahead.

Being Asian American and having a foot in two cultures means double the reasons to bake something festive throughout the year. Instead of Christmas bûche de noël (yule log), for example, we might celebrate with tender Swiss rolls flavored with tea or a wintery cheesecake dusted with snowy confectioners' sugar. Birthdays, weddings, and graduations are celebrated with layers of sponge cake adorned with whipped cream and glossy fruit. Countless mini tarts honor all the big and small moments in between.

Pau Pau's Steamed Cupcakes (Fa Gao)

MAKES 10

I called these Pau Pau's Cupcakes growing up. She only makes them for Chinese New Year, but I look forward to the tall, blossoming cake all year long. *Fa gao* is also sometimes called "prosperity cake," because the bigger and taller the cake tops bloom, the more prosperous your new year promises to be. Unlike what most people would consider a cupcake, fa gao isn't frosted or decorated in any way. It is an unassuming cake, with a bloomed top that gives it a little flair.

As a kid, I had a particular way of eating Pau Pau's cupcakes. First, I'd pluck off each petal and eat them one by one, and then I'd smash the base of the cupcake into a dense little pancake to munch on. (Please tell me someone else ate them this way?) Perhaps I subconsciously picked up on the pancake-like flavor as a kid—flavor that comes, literally, from pancake mix. Yep, there's Bisquick in Pau Pau's recipe! Back in Hong Kong, Pau Pau used a self-rising flour that's made specifically for fa gao. When the family immigrated to the United States, she had to work with the ingredients she could readily access at the local markets in downtown Cleveland. It turns out that self-rising flour and Bisquick have virtually the same ingredients: all-purpose flour, baking powder, and salt. Only the addition of hydrogenated vegetable shortening in Bisquick sets them apart.

It cracks me up that Bisquick has been Pau Pau's secret ingredient all these years. Say what you will about boxed mixes, but after fifty years of using Bisquick, it has become essential to the soft texture of her fa gao.

150g (1 ¼ cups) pancake mix, such as Bisquick

150g (1 ¼ cups) all-purpose flour

130g (⅔ cup) firmly packed dark brown sugar

300g (1 ⅓ cups) water

Prepare your steamer setup (page xxviii) and bring water to a rapid boil. Line ten individual 3-inch cupcake molds with paper liners and arrange in two bamboo steamers.

In a medium mixing bowl, whisk to combine the pancake mix, flour, brown sugar, and water until smooth. (The batter should be thick but runny.)

Divide the batter evenly between the molds, filling each about three-quarters full. Stack the bamboo steamers and cover with a lid. Steam for 15 minutes. Lift the lid, remove the steamers, and allow the cupcakes to cool for 5 minutes. Serve warm or at room temperature.

Specialty equipment: *This recipe requires individual 3-inch cupcake/ tart molds (page xxix).*

Cupcakes can be stored in an airtight container (a resealable bag works great) at room temperature for up to 4 days.

Malay Cake (Ma Lai Gao)

MAKES 1 CAKE

My world changed when I stepped into Xiao Long Bao, one of my favorite dumpling shops in San Francisco, and ordered *ma lai gao*. Until then, I had never tasted a swoon-worthy Malay cake and usually passed it over on dim sum carts in favor of egg tarts, and in bakery cases in favor of more enticing buns. The Malay cake at Xiao Long Bao changed all of that. I ordered it on a whim and realized it's one of the best snack cakes. The bouncy, airy texture and custardy, caramelly flavor make it impossible to eat just one slice.

As cakes go, ma lai gao is unusual. For starters, it's steamed instead of baked. Old-school Malay cakes, like the one at Xiao Long Bao, are leavened using a starter like a levain. You can tell which cakes are made using a starter: if the crumb is full of long, streaky air holes. A lot of bakeries have taken to using chemical leaveners, like baking powder and baking soda, to save time and yield just as delectable and airy cakes. This recipe takes that same chemical leavener route, relying on baking powder, baking soda, and eggs for its lift. Allowing the batter to rest might seem untraditional, but what's happening during this time is that the batter is hydrating, and the chemical leaveners are activating. Baking powder is double acting, meaning it starts to activate when it comes into contact with a liquid and again when it's introduced to heat. When the batter is rested properly, it will be frothy and light, and the result will be a tender and bouncy cake.

115g (1 cup) cake flour (not self-rising)

10g (1 tablespoon) cornstarch

1 tablespoon baking powder

1/2 teaspoon baking soda

1/4 teaspoon coarse salt

65g (1/3 cup) canola or other neutral-flavored oil

80g (1/3 cup) evaporated milk

1 teaspoon pure vanilla extract

4 large eggs

100g (1/2 cup) granulated sugar

50g (1/4 cup) firmly packed dark brown sugar

Sift the flour, cornstarch, baking powder, baking soda, and salt through a fine mesh sieve into a medium bowl to remove any clumps. In a small bowl or liquid measuring cup, whisk to combine the oil, evaporated milk, and vanilla.

In the bowl of a stand mixer fitted with the whisk attachment, beat the eggs on medium until light and foamy, 3 minutes. Increase the mixer to medium-high, gradually add the granulated sugar and mix until fluffy and tripled in size, 6 to 8 minutes. Add the brown sugar, mixing until incorporated, 1 minute. Pour the milk mixture into the batter and mix on medium-high until well incorporated, 1 minute.

Sift the dry ingredients into the egg mixture, using a whisk to incorporate just until mixture is smooth and no streaks of dry flour remain. Cover the bowl with plastic wrap and rest at room temperature for 1 hour. (The batter will be airy with lots of small bubbles on the surface.)

Prepare your steamer setup (page xxviii), using a basket big enough to fit an 8-inch cake pan, and bring water to a boil. Cut a round of parchment paper to line the bottom of an 8-inch cake pan. Pour the batter into the pan and set into the steamer. Cover with

a lid and place on top of the steamer setup. Steam until the center of the cake is set and puffy, 25 to 28 minutes. Lift the lid, remove the steamer, and allow the cake to cool for 15 minutes in the pan. To release the cake, run a small offset spatula around the edge and carefully tip the cake out. Slice, and serve the cake warm or at room temperature.

Cake can be stored in an airtight container at room temperature for up to 4 days.

White Pizza (White Sugar Cake, Bai Tang Gao)

MAKES ONE 8-INCH PIZZA . . . UH, CAKE

No, you didn't skip a page and start a new chapter about Chinese pizza, minus the red sauce—although that does sound temping! "White pizza" is what my brother and I called Pau Pau's white sugar cake. We called it that because it was round, and when Pau Pau dabbed at the tops, using a chopstick dipped in red food coloring, the dots looked like pepperoni slices, and the cake was cut into wedges. The name stuck; now everyone in our family refers to it as white pizza. To the rest of the world it's known as white sugar cake or *bai tang gao*, a steamed dessert made of rice flour, sugar, water, and yeast.

The way my pau pau makes white pizza requires a few days of prep and a detailed and well-timed schedule for each step. Her process is meticulous, but it's worth every step.

Day 1

In the afternoon, rinse dry white rice and soak in water for 6 hours.

Blend softened rice in a blender into a thick slurry.

Around 10:00 p.m., add yeast and allow the rice batter to ferment for 6 to 7 hours.

Day 2

Wake up at the crack of dawn.

Add a little more water, sugar, and baking powder to the batter and let it rest for another hour.

Prepare the steamer setup and grease all the cake pans in your possession.

Steam a dozen white pizzas.

Once cool, decorate with red spots by dipping the end of a straw in red food coloring.

Call all your children and grandchildren over to claim their white pizzas while the cakes are fresh.

First of all, she is making white pizza the traditional way, by soaking and grinding up grains of rice, and making a huge quantity to feed her extended family (she makes enough batter to fill a giant stock pot). I've tirelessly studied her system and managed to streamline the process and quantity to produce one single white pizza. I saved an entire day of work (and gained a few extra hours of sleep) by using finely ground rice flour instead of blending whole grains of softened rice. When making one pizza, the process is much shorter, but you still need a little patience to allow the cake batter to ferment. Letting the cake batter rest allows the yeast to feast on the sugar in the batter, which produces a ton of tiny air bubbles when the cake is steamed. White sugar cake is sweet, with a subtle fermented tang and a chewy rice-cake texture. It is best enjoyed warm or at room temperature—but hold the tomato sauce.

I asked Pau Pau why she dots the tops of the white pizza with red dye, thinking there would be some tradition or history behind it. She said it's purely because she thought it was cute!

130g (1 cup) white rice flour

3/4 teaspoon instant yeast

100g (1/2 cup) granulated sugar, plus a pinch

283g (1 1/4 cups) warm water (110°F), divided

1/2 teaspoon baking powder

Nonstick cooking spray

In a medium mixing bowl, whisk to combine the rice flour, yeast, and a pinch of sugar. Add 227g (1 cup) of the warm water and whisk until smooth. Cover the bowl with plastic wrap and allow the batter to rest at room temperature for 2 hours. (The surface will be covered in small bubbles.)

In a small bowl, whisk to combine the 100g (1/2 cup) sugar, remaining 56g (1/4 cup) warm water, and the baking powder. Add the sugar mixture to the rice batter, whisking to combine. Cover the bowl with plastic wrap and allow the batter to proof at room temperature for 1 hour. (The surface will be covered in small bubbles.)

Prepare your steamer setup (page xxviii) and bring water to a boil. Coat an 8-inch cake pan with nonstick spray. Give the batter a mix, as the rice flour tends to sink to the bottom. Pour the batter into the cake pan and set the pan in the bamboo steamer. Steam for 20 minutes.

Lift the lid, remove the steamer, and allow the cake to cool for 15 minutes in the pan. The cake will start to pull away from the sides of the pan. Carefully remove the cake from the pan by sliding it onto a cutting board or plate. Cut the cake into 8 slices and serve.

The cake can be stored in an airtight container at room temperature for a day.

To dot the top of the cake with red spots, mix a tiny drop of red food coloring with 1 tablespoon of water. Dip the end of a straw into the red water and press the straw tip gently on to the cooled white pizza.

Chinese Celebration Calendar

Lantern Festival

15th day of the 1st lunar month (February)

This signifies the end of Lunar New Year celebrations. It involves the lighting of lanterns, lots of firecrackers, high-energy lion dances, and eating more food.

Lunar New Year

1st day of the 1st lunar month (January)

My favorite holiday of the year! Families reunite and celebrate the beginning of the new year. Dining tables are filled with special dishes that symbolize wealth, health, and prosperity. Homes are cleaned and then decorated with red and gold. Kids are gifted red envelopes filled with money.

Qingming Festival (Tomb Sweeping Day)

15 days after Spring Equinox (April)

A day to pay respects to your ancestors. Families clean the burial sites of their loved ones, bring them flowers and their favorite foods, and burn incense and ghost money. This day always coincided with my family's annual road trip to Chicago, where my great-grandfather is buried.

Dragon Boat Festival

5th day of the 5th lunar month (May)

There's a superstition that the fifth month of the year is quite unlucky, so this is an opportunity to ward off negative energy, with a more festive spirit. Of course, there's dragon boat racing, but I've always known of this festival as the time of year my pau pau makes enough *joong* or *zhongzi* (sticky rice stuffed into lotus leaves) to feed our whole family.

Harvest Moon Festival

15th day of the 8th lunar month (September)

Mooncake season! Well, more like another time for family to gather over a lot of food and admire the full moon together. It's a time of reflection and thankfulness. The timing is right before traditional harvest season, so admiring the moon, being together, and especially sharing mooncakes set you up for a prosperous season ahead.

Qixi Festival
(Chinese Valentine's Day)

7th day of the 7th lunar month (August)

Based on the folktale of "The Cowherd and The Weaver Girl," a classic tale of star-crossed lovers, separated by the heavenly river (the Milky Way). But every year on the seventh day of the seventh month, a flock of birds forms a bridge over the river, and the lovers can reunite. To be honest, I've never celebrated Chinese Valentine's Day, but the story was just too sweet for me to not include it on the calendar.

Winter Solstice

(December)

Winter is coming! This day celebrates the arrival of winter. To prepare for the colder, harsher months ahead, families typically eat warming foods, such as dumplings heavy on the ginger and medicinal soups, so they stay healthy and strong. Eating *tang yuan* (a sweet soup with glutinous rice balls filled with red bean or black sesame) is also commonly eaten on this day because it represents family and togetherness. If you haven't noticed already, those two things are a pretty big deal during most holidays.

Chinese Sponge Cake

MAKES ONE TWO-LAYER 8-INCH
CAKE

Are you wondering when we're actually going to *bake* a cake? Preheat your oven! Sponge cake is the base for most baked Chinese cakes, such as Paper Cupcakes (see variation below), Swiss rolls (pages 147 and 149), and Shiny Fruit Cream Cakes (page 141). This vanilla sponge, similar to a French genoise or American chiffon cake, is tender and light as air. It's delightful enjoyed as is, with a cup of Hong Kong Milk Tea (page 255). The cake is incredibly versatile, taking well to all kinds of flavor additives, like citrus zest, matcha, and cocoa powder. Once you're familiar with the sponge cake, you can get creative with infinite combinations.

100g (¾ cup plus 2 tablespoons) cake flour (not self-rising)

20g (2 tablespoons) cornstarch

1 teaspoon baking powder

Pinch of coarse salt

6 large eggs, whites and yolks separated

100g (½ cup) sugar, divided

¼ teaspoon cream of tartar

65g (⅓ cup) canola or other neutral-flavored oil

1 teaspoon pure vanilla extract

Flavor Variations

Matcha Sponge Cake: Add 10g (2 tablespoons) food-grade matcha powder to the dry ingredients.

Chocolate Sponge Cake: Add 16g (3 tablespoons) cocoa powder to the dry ingredients.

Lemon Sponge Cake: Add the zest of one lemon to the egg yolks.

Preheat the oven to 350°F. Cut rounds of parchment paper to line the bottom of two 8-inch round cake pans.

In a medium bowl, whisk to combine the cake flour, cornstarch, baking powder, and salt.

Place the egg whites in the bowl of an electric mixer fitted with the whisk attachment. Place the egg yolks in a separate large mixing bowl. Whisk the egg whites on medium speed until foamy, 1 to 2 minutes. Add 50g (¼ cup) of the sugar and the cream of tartar, increase the speed to medium-high, and whisk until stiff peaks form, 5 to 7 minutes.

To the yolks, add the remaining 50g (¼ cup) sugar, the canola oil, and vanilla. Vigorously whisk until pale and smooth, about 3 minutes. Using a flexible spatula, scoop 1 cup egg white mixture and fold into the egg yolk mixture until fully incorporated. Fold the remaining egg white mixture into the yolk mixture in three additions, alternating each addition with half the flour mixture and reaching to the bottom and around the sides of the bowl as you fold so that no traces of flour remain. Take care not to deflate the beaten egg whites too much as you fold.

Divide the batter evenly between the prepared cake pans. Bake until the tops of the cakes are lightly golden brown, 23 to 25 minutes (for 9-inch round cake pans, bake for 3 to 5 minutes less). Transfer the pans to a wire rack and let the cakes cool for 5 minutes. (The cakes will deflate slightly as they cool.) Invert the cake pans onto the wire rack to completely cool (this will prevent the cakes from deflating too much). To release the cakes, run a small offset spatula around the edges, and carefully tip the cake layer out. Peel off the parchment paper. To decorate the cake, see page 142 for design inspiration.

Make sure no yolk gets into your egg whites. The presence of any fat in the egg whites will prevent them from whipping up properly.

Variation: Paper Cupcakes

MAKES 12 CUPCAKES

Preheat the oven to 400°F. Line a standard muffin tin with 12 tulip paper liners. Prepare the sponge cake batter as directed. Pour the batter into the liners, dividing evenly. Place the tin in the oven and immediately reduce the temperature to 350°F. Bake until the cupcake tops are lightly golden brown, 23 to 25 minutes. Transfer the pan to a wire rack and let cupcakes cool. Serve warm or at room temperature. Makes 12 cupcakes.

Tulip paper liners are easily available for purchase or you can make them yourself: Cut twelve 6-inch squares of parchment paper. Place a parchment paper square over a muffin tin and press down with a cup to push the paper to the sides of the tin, forming a cup. Repeat with remaining liners.

Shiny Fruit Cream Cake

MAKES ONE LAYERED 8-INCH CAKE

Most of my childhood birthday cakes came from Giant Eagle, the main grocery store chain in the Cleveland area. Each year the cakes were decorated with my favorite cartoon characters or adorned with perfectly piped lavender buttercream flowers—my favorite color for the greater part of the '90s and early 2000s. To the dismay of the adults in my family, these Giant Eagle sheet cakes were heavy on the frosting and *very* sweet. I asked for them because it's what all the other kids in my class had at their birthday parties. Today, the very thought of those birthday cakes gives me a toothache. (I still have a lot of love for Giant Eagle though.) I finally understand the appeal of the borderline-gaudy, fruit-topped cakes I see in every Chinese bakery. These cakes are light and frosted with whipped cream instead of buttercream, and the glistening fruits (often lacquered in syrup) impart natural sweetness and pops of color.

Fruit options are endless, but a Cho family favorite is a simple vanilla sponge cake with whipped cream and ripe strawberries.

For the Cake

2 (8-inch) layers Chinese Sponge Cake (page 138)

A combination of fresh fruits including sliced kiwis, strawberries, and blueberries

Sugar Glaze (page 142), optional

Stabilized Whipped Cream

1 teaspoon gelatin powder

1 tablespoon water

3 cups heavy cream, chilled

1/4 cup plus 2 tablespoons confectioners' sugar

2 teaspoons pure vanilla extract

Make the stabilized whipped cream: Whisk to combine the gelatin powder and water in a small, microwave-safe bowl, then set aside to allow the gelatin to bloom for 5 minutes. Cook the mixture in the microwave on high until it's back to a liquid state, about 10 seconds. (Alternatively, heat the mixture in a small saucepan over low heat until liquid.)

In the bowl of a stand mixer fitted with the whisk attachment, beat the cream on low speed for 1 minute. Add the sugar and vanilla. Increase the speed to medium and beat until soft peaks form, about 3 minutes. Add the gelatin mixture and beat until stiff peaks form, 2 to 3 minutes more. Store the whipped cream in the fridge until ready to assemble the cake.

Assemble the cake: Place one cake layer on a cake board or plate. Top with a thick (1/2-inch) layer of whipped cream and then place the remaining cake layer on top. Cover the sides and top of the cake with more whipped cream and smooth the edges using a bench scraper or offset spatula.

Decorate the cake top with fruit (see page 142 for design inspiration). For an optional detail, fit a piping bag with a star tip, fill with the remaining whipped cream, and pipe tiny stars along the edges of the cake.

If you like, brush the glaze onto the fruit using a pastry brush.

Adding gelatin to the whipped cream stabilizes it, helping it hold its shape when used to decorate a cake, especially if it's piped. If you're not too concerned about the piping details of your cake, simply omit the gelatin.

Cake Styles

1 **Full Fruit:** Start by placing a larger piece of fruit (like a strawberry) in the middle. Arrange concentric circles of sliced fruit, working from the center outward, until the top is fully covered in fruit. A cookie cutter comes in handy to create crisp shapes out of sliced fruit.

2 **Minimal:** To create the grooves in the cream, gently press the tip of an offset spatula into the center of the cake and rotate the cake (on a rotating cake stand) while slowly pulling the spatula out toward the edge. Slice a small apple or stone fruit into thin slices and arrange them on top of the cake like the hour markers of a clock. Accent with mint leaves.

3 **Petal:** Place a few berries in the very center of the cake. Fill a piping bag fitted with a large St. Honore piping tip (or a tapered tip) and pipe large, dramatic petals from the center outward, around the cluster of fruit so it looks like a large sunflower.

4 **Crescent Wreath:** Arrange small berries, seeds, and sprigs of rosemary or mint in a crescent form for a modern wreath aesthetic.

Sugar Glaze

57g (¼ cup) water

50g (¼ cup) granulated sugar

Whisk to combine the water and sugar in a small saucepan. Bring to a simmer over medium heat and cook until the mixture has thickened and sugar has dissolved, 5 minutes. Allow the mixture to cool to room temperature.

1

2

3

4

Matcha and Jasmine Swiss Roll

MAKES 1 CAKE

Jasmine Whipped Cream (page 57)

Ingredients for Chinese Sponge Cake, matcha variation (page 138)

Though it has its origins in Europe, the Swiss roll has become a swirly fixture in Chinese bakeries. The classic vanilla variety can be found next to rolls flavored with matcha, pandan, mango, and lychee. I love grabbing a slice and slowly peeling back the spiral, eating it bite by bite, until I reach the center, with the maximum whipped cream-to-cake ratio.

Once you've nailed the sponge cake recipe, consider yourself ready to make your first Swiss roll. Let yourself go wild with cake and whipped-cream flavor combinations. I love infusing tea flavors into cakes and creams. Matcha, when used sparingly, gives Swiss rolls a lovely flavor and naturally adds a vibrant green color. Steeping jasmine tea in the heavy cream gives it a beautiful floral flavor that balances the matcha's earthiness.

Preheat the oven to 350°F and line a large rimmed baking sheet with parchment paper.

Prepare the cake batter as directed on page 138 through step 4, adding the matcha powder to the dry ingredients in step 2.

Transfer the batter to the prepared baking sheet and smooth the top using an offset spatula. Make sure the batter is even and reaches the edges of the sheet. Bake until the center is set and the top is lightly golden brown, 10 to 12 minutes.

Transfer the baking sheet to a wire cooling rack and allow the cake to cool for 10 minutes. Run an offset spatula around the edges of the pan to help release the cake. Starting from one short side, carefully roll up the cake into a log, using the parchment paper to assist you. Once rolled, allow the cake to cool for 10 more minutes. Unroll the cake and allow it to cool completely.

Spread the whipped cream on the cake in an even layer, Starting from a short side, carefully and tightly roll up the cake. Set the cake seam-side down, wrap in parchment paper or plastic wrap. Chill in the fridge for at least 1 hour, or up to overnight, to set. Slice with a sharp knife and serve.

Wrap the roll in plastic wrap and store in the refrigerator for up to 4 days.

Coffee Crunch Swiss Roll

MAKES 1 CAKE

This variation on a classic Swiss roll was absolutely inspired by the splendor of Eastern Bakery's Coffee Crunch Cake. But instead of re-creating Eastern's layered cake, I've adapted the flavors and texture into a rolled cake. A sweet vanilla sponge cake base is rolled around a coffee-infused cream filling. For a final touch, the cake is topped with bits of salty toffee, which gives it its signature crunch. It's a wonderful slice of cake, perfect for breakfast, as a midday pick-me-up, after-dinner dessert, or late-night snack—any time of day!

For the Coffee Filling

2 tablespoons coarsely ground coffee

2 cups heavy cream

1/4 cup confectioners' sugar

Pinch of salt

For the Toffee Topping

4 tablespoons unsalted butter, chilled and cubed

1/2 cup granulated sugar

1/2 teaspoon coarse salt

For the Cake Roll

Ingredients for Chinese Sponge Cake (page 138)

Make the filling: Combine the coffee and cream in a medium saucepan. Bring to a gentle simmer over medium heat, then immediately turn off heat. Cover with a lid and steep for 10 minutes. Strain through a fine-mesh sieve set over a medium bowl; discard coffee grounds. Cover the bowl and refrigerate until cool, at least 1 hour or up to overnight.

In the bowl of an electric mixer fitted with the whisk attachment, combine the coffee-infused cream, confectioners' sugar, and salt. Beat until medium-stiff peaks form. Refrigerate the whipped cream in an airtight container until ready to assemble the cake (up to 3 days).

Make the topping: Line a large rimmed baking sheet with a silicone baking mat. In a medium saucepan, combine the butter, granulated sugar, and salt. Heat over medium heat, stirring with a flexible spatula to combine as the butter melts and mixture comes to a boil. Continue to boil, stirring occasionally, until the mixture deepens in color and reaches 285°F on an instant thermometer, 7 to 8 minutes. (The mixture will bubble up as it boils.) Be careful as you make caramel, as you can easily burn yourself. Pour the caramel onto the prepared baking sheet and spread into an even layer with a flexible spatula. Let the toffee harden at room temperature, 30 to 45 minutes, then break it up into little pieces. Store in an airtight container until ready to assemble the cake (up to 1 month).

Make the cake roll: Preheat the oven to 350°F and line a large rimmed baking sheet with a sheet of parchment paper.

Prepare the sponge cake batter as directed on page 138 through step 4. Transfer the batter to the prepared baking sheet and smooth the top using an offset spatula. Make sure the batter is even and reaches the edges of the sheet. Bake until the center is set and the top is lightly golden brown, 10 to 12 minutes.

Transfer the baking sheet to a wire rack and allow the cake to cool for 10 minutes. Run an offset spatula around the edges of the pan to help release the cake. Starting from a short side, gently roll up the cake into a log, using the parchment paper to assist you. Allow the rolled cake to cool for 10 more minutes. Unroll the cake and allow it to cool completely.

Using an offset spatula, spread about 2/3 filling on the cake in an even layer. Tightly roll up the cake, starting from a short side. Set the cake seam-side down, wrap in parchment paper or plastic wrap, and refrigerate until firm, 1 hour or overnight. Frost the surface of the cake with the remaining whipped cream and sprinkle with toffee pieces. Slice with a sharp knife and serve.

Cover the roll in plastic wrap and store in the refrigerator for up to 4 days.

Black Sesame Soufflé Cheesecake

MAKES ONE TALL 7-INCH CAKE

In my family, cheesecakes are reserved for the holidays. There's something about whipping up a cheesecake while the snow is falling outside that feels so cozy and familiar. For a long time, my uncle was on cheesecake duty and always brought a frozen classic New York–style cheesecake from Costco to the family holiday gathering. I still have a sweet spot for those cheesecakes, but in recent years I've taken over cheesecake duty, with my homemade versions. I love to experiment with different techniques and flavors. The most formidable recipe I've ever attempted was the Japanese soufflé cheesecake. It has a quintessential jiggle and tastes like a cloud of sweet, tangy, fluffy cream cheese. This style of cheesecake was popularized in Japanese bakeries, but Chinese bakeries have adopted it for its irresistible texture and gentle sweetness.

Some bakers are intimidated at mention of the word "soufflé" because of the fear that the soufflé will suddenly collapse if your footsteps are too heavy or you bump into the oven. But soufflés are a lot more resilient than you might think. The rise and airy texture of this cheesecake is completely reliant on whipped egg whites, while egg yolks lend richness and creaminess when blended smooth with the cream cheese. For everything to incorporate smoothly, I highly recommend making sure all the ingredients are at room temperature. The process of making the batter and then baking the cheesecake low and slow definitely requires some patience, but you'll be rewarded with the fluffiest cheesecake.

I love the addition of black sesame paste—it's a little smoky and very nutty, and it gives the cheesecake an austere aesthetic. But this recipe is highly adaptable, flavor-wise. You can omit the sesame paste, for pure cheesecake flavor, substitute an equal amount of tahini, add a tablespoon of matcha powder, or opt for bright citrus flavors, with a tablespoon of lemon or lime zest.

226g (8 ounces) cream cheese, cubed, softened

30g (2 tablespoons) unsalted butter, softened

50g (¼ cup) heavy cream, room temperature

40g (2 tablespoons) Black Sesame Paste (page 14)

40g (⅓ cup) cake flour (not self-rising)

6 large eggs, whites and yolks separated, room temperature

¼ teaspoon cream of tartar

100g (½ cup) sugar

Preheat the oven to 350°F. Line the bottom of a tall 7-inch round cake pan (with 3-inch sides and a removable bottom) with parchment paper. Wrap the exterior base with aluminum foil. Bring a kettle of water to a boil (you will need it when baking the cheesecake).

Place the cream cheese and butter in a large bowl set over a double boiler with simmering water and stir with a flexible spatula until smooth and combined. Remove the bowl from the heat. Add the cream, sesame paste, and flour and mix until smooth. Add the egg yolks, one at a time, mixing until smooth before adding the next.

In the bowl of an electric mixer fitted with the whisk attachment, beat the egg whites on low speed until foamy, around 1 minute. Add the cream of tartar and sugar and increase speed to medium. Whisk until medium peaks form, 5 to 6 minutes.

Add a quarter of the whipped egg whites to the cream cheese mixture, folding it in with a flexible spatula. Avoid deflating the egg whites too much by gently scraping the sides and bottom of the bowl with the flexible spatula as you work your way around it. Add the remaining egg whites in three additions, folding in each before adding the next, until no streaks of egg remain.

Transfer the mixture to the prepared cake pan and smooth the top with an offset spatula. Place the cake pan in a larger Dutch oven or another deep, oven-safe pan or baking dish. Carefully fill the larger pan with enough boiling water to come halfway up the side of the cake pan.

Bake for 20 minutes. Open the oven door for a few seconds to release some steam and then reduce the temperature to 300°F. Continue to bake until the cake is set and lightly golden brown on top, 55 to 60 minutes (it's okay if a few cracks appear on the surface).

Remove the larger pan with the cake pan still inside of it from the oven, and allow the cheesecake to cool in the water for 1 hour. Transfer the cake pan to a wire cooling rack and allow it to cool completely, about 1 hour longer. To release the cheesecake, run a small offset spatula around the sides. Carefully lift the cake out of the pan by pressing the removable bottom upwards. Serve cheesecake at room temperature or refrigerate until ready to serve.

Special equipment: *This recipe is best made in a 7-inch round cake pan with 3-inch sides and a removable bottom, a very specific pan size. Otherwise, you can bake the cheesecake in a regular 8-inch round cake pan, but it won't be as tall or jiggly.*

The cheesecake can be refrigerated, covered, for up to 3 days.

Mango Mousse Cake

MAKES ONE 8-INCH CAKE

This cake relies heavily on the sweetness and ripeness of in-season mangoes for its refreshingly ethereal bite. If your mangoes aren't super sweet, you can add 1/4 cup confectioners' sugar to the whipped cream. My favorite mangoes are the Champagne, or Ataulfo, varieties from Mexico, and Manila mangoes from the Philippines. These are small, juicy, less fibrous, and very sweet when ripe. To make the creamy and bright mousse, mango puree is folded into whipped cream set with a little gelatin. To let the mango shine, some mousse is sandwiched between layers of simple vanilla sponge cake, and the rest is topped with toasted shredded coconut for texture, and thinly sliced mango for a graceful decorative detail.

The mark of any good mousse cake is being able to see all the distinctive layers. Take advantage of a cake ring to cut clean edges off the cake layers, then use the ring as a frame when stacking the layers. A film of acetate will keep everything nice and neat. The moment the cake is finally set, and you pull back the acetate, is incredibly satisfying.

For the Mousse

230g (1 cup) heavy cream

1/2 teaspoon ground turmeric, to color the mousse (optional)

285g (2 cups) cubed mango (from about 2 ripe mangoes)

1 tablespoon unflavored powdered gelatin

1/4 cup water

1 1/2 cups shredded unsweetened coconut

2 (9-inch) layers Chinese Sponge Cake (page 138)

1 large mango, peeled, pitted, and thinly sliced

Make the mousse: In the bowl of an electric mixer fitted with the whisk attachment, whisk the cream and turmeric (if using) until stiff peaks form.

In the bowl of a food processor, puree the mango until smooth.

In a small heatproof bowl, combine the gelatin and water. Allow the gelatin to bloom for 5 minutes. Return the gelatin back to a liquid state by microwaving for 10 seconds.

In a medium mixing bowl, combine the mango puree and gelatin, stirring with a flexible spatula until the mixture is smooth. Fold the mango puree into the whipped cream until light and smooth. Keep the mousse at room temperature until ready to assemble the cake (up to 1 hour).

Toast the coconut in a skillet over medium-low heat, stirring occasionally, until lightly golden brown, 3 to 4 minutes. Transfer to a small bowl and allow to completely cool.

Working with one cake layer at a time, press an 8-inch cake ring into the cake to trim off the edges. Discard the edges (or save for a snack).

To assemble the cake, line the 8-inch cake ring with a strip of acetate, tape the ends to secure, and place on a cake board or large serving platter. Place one cake layer inside the cake ring. Add 2/3 mousse and spread into an even layer with an offset spatula, all the way to the edges. Top with the remaining cake layer, gently pressing down. Spread the remaining mango mousse in an even layer over the cake, all the way to the edges. Sprinkle with toasted coconut and decorate with the mango slices. Cover the cake (over the ring of acetate) with plastic wrap and refrigerate until the mousse sets, at least 4 hours before serving, or overnight. Remove the cake ring and acetate before serving.

Special equipment: *This recipe requires an 8-inch cake ring and acetate strips.*

Once covered, the cake can be refrigerated for up to 4 days.

Chinese Puff Pastry

MAKES ABOUT 1 ½ POUNDS
PASTRY (ENOUGH FOR 12 TO 18
TART ROUNDS)

Chinese puff pastry is similar to French puff pastry, with laminated layers of butter and flour that add up to one delightfully flaky dough. The differences between the French and Chinese varieties are subtle: the Chinese puff is slightly less buttery (don't worry—there is still plenty of butter) and a tad more crisp. Use this as the base recipe for egg tarts (page 161), Curry Chicken Puffs (page 112), turnovers (page 64), and Pistachio Palmiers (page 203), to name a few favorite applications.

For the Butter Block

227g (1 cup; 2 sticks) unsalted butter, chilled

150g (1 ¼ cups) all-purpose flour

For the Flour Dough

210g (1 ⅔ cups) all-purpose flour, plus more for rolling

1 large egg

½ teaspoon coarse salt

75g (⅓ cup) ice water

Make the butter block: Cut the butter into 1-inch cubes and place in the bowl of a food processor. Add the flour and pulse until smooth (it will be crumbly at first). Transfer the butter mixture to a sheet of plastic wrap. Fold the plastic over the butter mixture and then press to form a roughly 5-inch square. Refrigerate until firm but still somewhat pliable, 30 to 35 minutes.

Make the flour dough: Place the flour, egg, salt, and ice water in the clean bowl of the food processor. Pulse just until a smooth ball of dough forms. Transfer the dough to a lightly floured surface and slightly flatten into a disk. Wrap the dough in plastic wrap and refrigerate until chilled, 30 to 35 minutes.

Unwrap both the dough and butter block. Lightly dust a clean work surface with flour and roll out the flour dough with a large rolling pin into a 7 x 10-inch rectangle. Place the butter block in the center of the dough and fold the edges of the dough over the butter block so that it is tightly wrapped. Flip over the pastry dough so it is seam-side down. Continue to lightly dust the work surface if the dough starts to stick. With the rolling pin, firmly press down on the dough to thin it out (this should prevent it from tearing). Roll out the dough into a 6 x 12-inch rectangle. Fold the dough into thirds, like a letter, and press it down with the rolling pin again to flatten. Roll the dough into a 6 x 12-inch rectangle and repeat the process of folding the dough into thirds like a letter one more time. Flatten and roll the dough into an 8 x 12-inch rectangle and wrap tightly with plastic wrap.

Refrigerate the dough for at least 30 minutes before working it again. At this point, the puff pastry can be either frozen or refrigerated for future use.

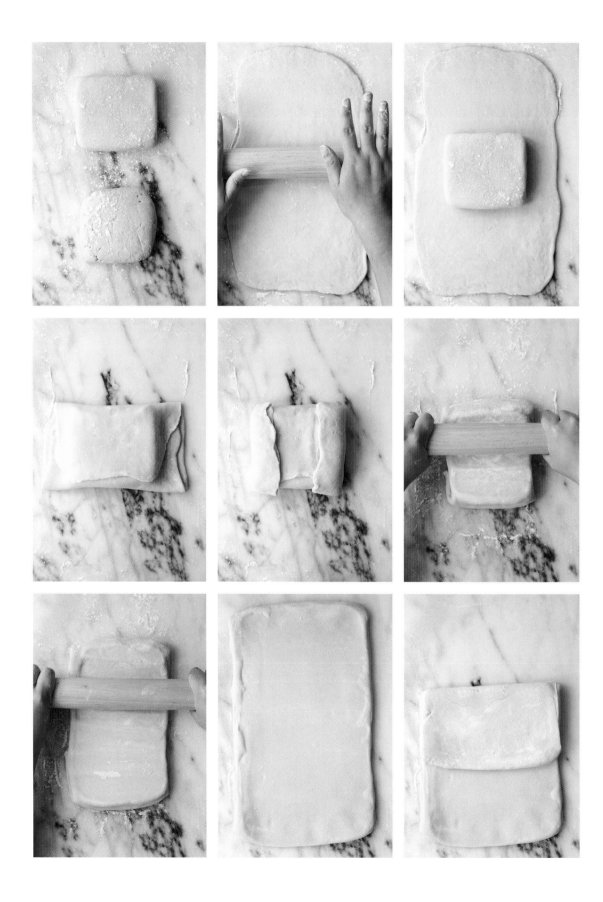

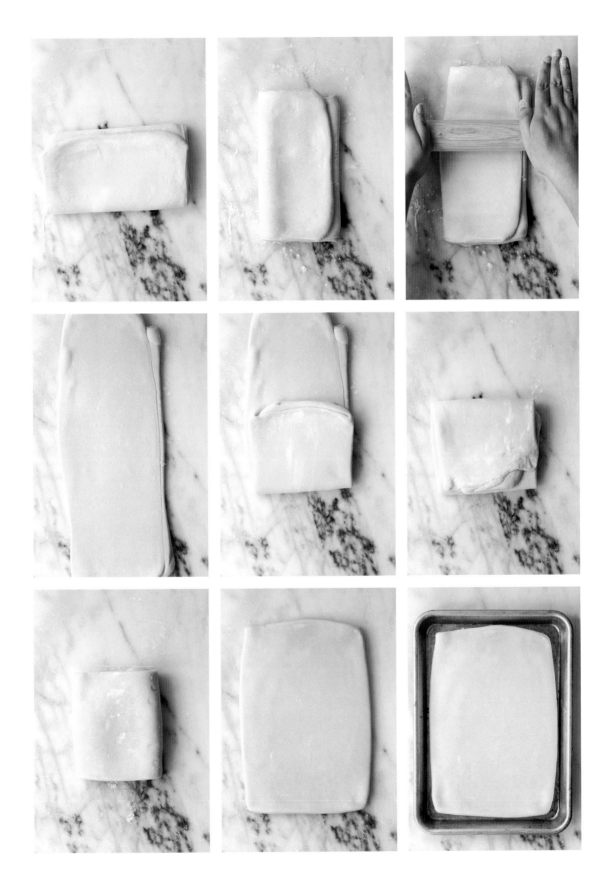

Classic Egg Tarts (Dan Tat)

MAKES 12

She's beauty and she's grace. She's the most popular Chinese pastry in the United States. Egg tarts are buttery and flaky, and their resemblance to little sunbursts makes you smile just looking at them. At the end of every dim sum feast, after we've eaten our fill of *cheung fun* and dumplings, my mom would track down the cart full of golden egg tarts. If she couldn't find the cart, she'd flag down a waiter to put in a special order for at least two dozen freshly baked egg tarts, enough for each of us to inhale a pastry or two at the table and a few extra to take home and enjoy later.

Egg tarts are a perfect example of the European influence in Chinese culture. Pastry chefs in Hong Kong utilized the techniques and ingredients that were accessible to them, including lard instead of butter and evaporated milk as a substitute for fresh cream or milk. Like those chefs, I use what is most commonly found in my local grocery stores. So while this recipe uses butter, by all means use lard, if you can find it.

There are three different types of egg tarts: with a puff pastry base, with a shortcrust base, and Macau style (page 164), featuring a laminated base and a caramelized custard filling. A crisp pastry base and a smooth, sweet filling is essential, but I like the variety you get with the Chinese puff pastry base, featured here. The texture of flaky pastry, shattering into a field of crumbs and juxtaposed with the rich eggy filling, is one of the most satisfying bites.

If you prefer egg tarts with shortcrust instead, swap out the puff pastry for the shortcrust pastry in the Lemon Coconut Tart recipe (page 167).

For the Filling

100g (1/2 cup) sugar

150g (2/3 cup) water

2 large eggs plus 1 large egg yolk

90g (1/4 cup plus 2 tablespoons) milk

1/2 teaspoon pure vanilla extract

Chinese Puff Pastry (page 157, or see recipe notes on page 162)

All-purpose flour, for rolling

Make the filling: In a small saucepan, combine the sugar and water. Swirl the saucepan and bring the mixture to a boil over medium heat. Boil until the sugar has dissolved and the mixture has thickened, 3 to 4 minutes. Remove the saucepan from the heat and allow the syrup to cool for 10 minutes.

In a medium mixing bowl, whisk to combine the eggs and egg yolk, milk, and vanilla. Pour the syrup into the egg mixture, whisking until smooth. (As an extra step to ensure a really smooth custard, you can strain the egg mixture through a fine mesh sieve to remove any bits of egg that didn't fully incorporate.)

On a lightly floured surface, roll the pastry into a roughly 12 x 16-inch rectangle. Using a fluted 4-inch cookie cutter, cut out 12 rounds.

Gently press the rounds into twelve 3-inch tart molds, pressing against the bottom and sides to prevent air pockets. The pastry should extend about 1/4 inch above the rims. Arrange the pastry molds on a plate or medium rimmed baking sheet and refrigerate until firm, at least 20 minutes or overnight (cover with plastic wrap if chilling overnight).

Preheat the oven to 400°F.

Place the tart shells on a large rimmed baking sheet, spaced 2 inches apart. Fill each tart shell with the filling, up to 1/4 inch below the edge of the pastry. Bake for 15 minutes. Reduce the heat to 350°F and bake until the filling is set but still has a slight jiggle in the center, 20 to 24 more minutes.

Transfer the baking sheet to a wire rack and let the tarts cool on the sheet for 10 minutes. Remove the egg tarts from the tart molds and serve warm or at room temperature.

Special equipment: *This recipe requires 12 individual 3-inch metal tart or cupcake molds (page xxix).*

The tarts can be refrigerated in an airtight container (a resealable bag works great) for up to 4 days (or frozen for up to 3 months). Reheat in a 350°F oven on a baking sheet until crisp and warmed through, 8 to 10 minutes (or a few minutes longer if they're frozen).

Store-bought puff pastry is totally acceptable, but I encourage you to try making the Chinese Puff Pastry for the true dim sum taste.

You will most likely have a decent amount of puff pastry left over, which is the nature of making neat pastry. Instead of discarding it, cut the scraps into roughly 3-inch pieces and bake in a 400°F oven until golden brown, 20 to 25 minutes. Once cooled, dust with a little confectioners' sugar or cinnamon. Scraps also can be stored in the freezer for up to 3 months.

Macau-Style Egg Tarts (Po Tat)

MAKES 18

The small country of Macau, just a short ferry ride from Hong Kong, was a Portuguese colony for more than four hundred years. Thus, the food is notable for its Portuguese influences. One of the most famous Macanese pastries is a variation of the egg tart, or *po tat:* the Portuguese *pastéis de nata*. These creamy little tarts are filled with custard, flavored with a hint of cinnamon, and baked at a much higher temperature than classic Cantonese egg tarts. The most distinctive difference between the two styles of egg tarts are the dark brown, caramelized spots on the Macau-style tarts.

Traditionally, the characteristic spiraled, flaky layers are made by rolling out really thin, almost see-through layers of pastry, brushing them with softened butter, rolling the layers up, and finally, cutting them into slices. I took the nontraditional route, however, opting instead to roll up my puff pastry into a log and then slicing it into rounds of pastry destined for little tart molds. I find my method of rolling up puff pastry just as effective as the classic technique, but it's a much quicker and cleaner process that takes advantage of the Chinese puff pastry in another way.

Chinese Puff Pastry (page 157)

For the Custard

287g (1 ¼ cups) milk

140g (²/3 cup) heavy cream

¾ teaspoon pure vanilla extract

4 large egg yolks

100g (½ cup) sugar

20g (2 tablespoons) flour

½ teaspoon ground cinnamon, preferably Saigon

½ teaspoon coarse salt

On a lightly floured surface, roll the pastry into a roughly 12 x 18-inch rectangle, then trim off the edges. From a long side, roll up the pastry into a log. Using a sharp knife, trim 1 inch off each end, then cut into 18 equal pieces. Place one slice, cut side up, into eighteen 3-inch tart molds. Lightly dust your thumbs with flour and press the pastry into the molds: First, press directly down into the bottom of the mold and then around the sides. The pastry should be thinner at the bottom and extend at least ¼ inch above the rim of the mold. If you're finding the pastry hard to stretch out, let it warm up for a few minutes. Arrange the pastry molds on a plate or medium rimmed baking sheet and refrigerate until firm, at least 20 minutes or overnight (cover with plastic wrap if chilling overnight).

Make the custard: In a medium saucepan, whisk to combine the milk, cream, and vanilla. Bring to a simmer over medium heat, then immediately turn off the heat. Allow the mixture to cool until warm, about 10 minutes.

In a medium mixing bowl, whisk to combine the egg yolks, sugar, flour, cinnamon, and salt into a thick paste. Whisking constantly, pour the warm milk mixture into the egg mixture. Whisk until smooth. Refrigerate the custard until chilled, at least 30 minutes or when ready to fill the tarts (up to overnight). Stir the custard again before filling the tarts.

Preheat the oven to 500°F and line a large rimmed baking sheet with foil.

Dividing evenly, fill the tart shells with custard, up to ¼ inch below the edge of the pastry. Arrange on the prepared baking sheet, spacing 2 inches apart. Bake until the pastry is deeply golden brown and the custard is covered with dark brown spots, 15 to 18 minutes.

Transfer the baking sheet to a wire rack. Allow the tarts to cool in the molds for 10 minutes and then carefully remove them. Serve tarts warm or at room temperature.

Special equipment: This recipe requires eighteen 3-inch metal tart or cupcake molds (page xxix).

The tarts can be refrigerated in an airtight container for up to 4 days (or frozen for up to 3 months). Reheat in a 350°F oven on a baking sheet until crisp and warmed through, 8 to 10 minutes (or a few minutes longer if they're frozen).

Lemon Coconut Tarts

MAKES 12

Coconut tarts are sort of like the Chinese version of the English Bakewell tart. Both have a crisp shortcrust base and a sweet, cakey filling. Bakewells feature almonds, and these tarts have shredded coconut. Despite their popularity, I was never a fan of coconut tarts because of their tendency to dry out. That changed once I started to bake them myself and developed the tender, buttery filling of my dreams. Imagine the best coconut macaroon ever, sitting pretty inside a buttery pie crust. A touch of lemon zest and juice brightens up the otherwise rich and decadent dessert.

For the Shortcrust Pastry

170g (^{3}/4 cup; 1 ^{1}/2 sticks) unsalted butter, chilled

38g (3 tablespoons) sugar

45g (3 tablespoons) water

220g (1 ^{3}/4 cups) all-purpose flour, plus more for dusting

For the Filling

56g (4 tablespoons) unsalted butter, softened

100g (^{1}/2 cup) sugar

1 large egg

160g (2 cups) shredded unsweetened coconut

20g (2 tablespoons) all-purpose flour

1 teaspoon baking powder

^{1}/4 teaspoon coarse salt

Grated zest and juice of 1 lemon

56g (^{1}/4 cup) milk

75g (^{1}/4 cup) sweetened condensed milk

1 ^{1}/2 teaspoons pure vanilla extract

Make the pastry: Cut the butter into 1-inch cubes. Place the butter, sugar, water, and all-purpose flour in the bowl of a food processor. Pulse just until crumbly. Transfer the dough to a lightly floured surface and knead just until combined. Form the dough into a 1-inch-thick disc and wrap in plastic wrap. Freeze until firm but still somewhat pliable, 30 to 35 minutes (or refrigerate for 45 to 60 minutes).

Meanwhile, make the filling: In a medium bowl using a flexible spatula, cream the butter and sugar until light and smooth, 1 minute. Add the egg and mix until well blended, then fold in the coconut, flour, baking powder, salt, lemon zest and juice, milk, condensed milk, and vanilla until just combined.

Preheat the oven to 400°F.

On a lightly floured surface, roll out the dough until it's ^{1}/8 inch thick. With a 4-inch cookie cutter, cut out rounds, then knead the scraps and roll out again to cut more until you have 12 rounds. Press each round into a 3-inch tart mold. The pastry should extend ^{1}/4 inch above the rim of the molds.

Arrange the tarts on the prepared baking sheet, spacing 2 inches apart. Dividing evenly, fill each pastry shell ^{3}/4 full (a little less than 2 tablespoons each).

Bake until tarts are golden brown, 24 to 26 minutes. Transfer the sheet to a wire rack and allow the tarts to cool for 10 minutes before removing from the molds. Serve warm or at room temperature.

Special equipment: This recipe requires 12 individual 3-inch metal tart or cupcake molds (page xxix). If you have smaller, 2 ^{3}/4-inch fluted tart molds, the recipe will make about 16 tarts. Cut the pastry into 3 ^{1}/2-inch rounds instead.

The tarts can be stored in an airtight container at room temperature for up to 4 days or frozen for up to 3 months. Reheat frozen tarts in a 350°F oven until warmed through and crisp, 10 to 15 minutes.

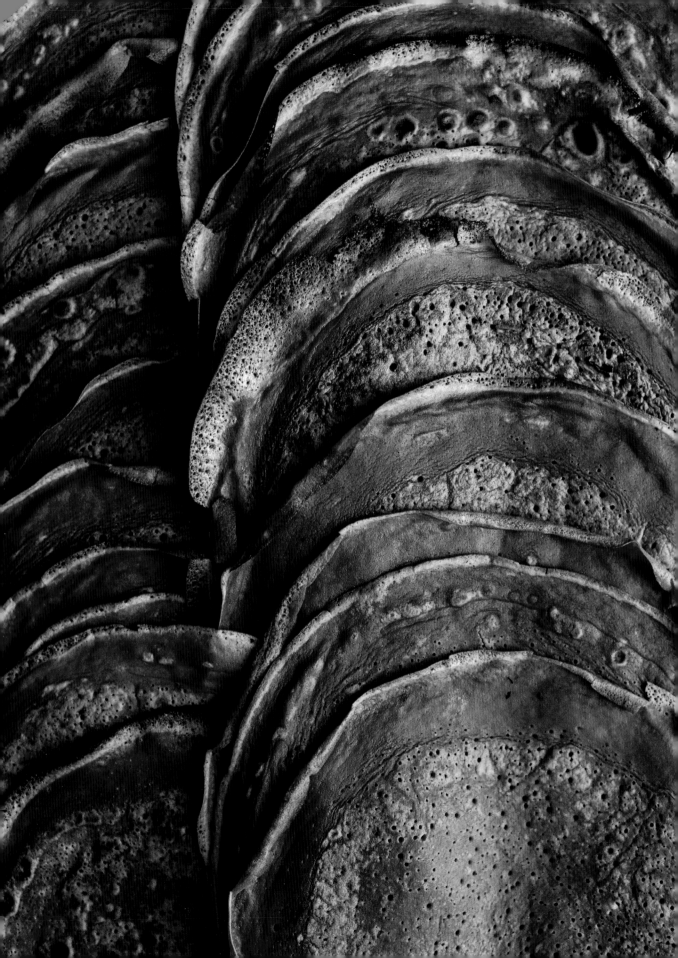

Chocolate and Salted Peanut Crepe Cake

MAKES ONE 6-INCH CAKE

If you're someone who finds decorating a cake and cutting fruit into dainty pieces to be your worst nightmare, this crepe cake will be right up your alley. Crepe cakes are deceptively easy to make, but look extra impressive with minimal effort because the lacy ruffled edges form naturally! Once you get into the rhythm of cooking the thin crepes, the process starts to feel meditative. This is a great time to put on an episode of your favorite podcast or a playlist of cheerful French bistro music.

I love how most Chinese bakeries portion out slices of crepe cake for purchase, so you can try a few different flavors. This chocolate-peanut version is a new favorite. The crepe layers are nice and spongy, with crisp edges, and taste just like the leftover milk from a bowl of Cocoa Krispies. You'll want to put the salted peanut whipped cream on everything—it's a nice balance of sweet and salty and provides a nutty layer of flavor.

For the Crepes

500g (2 ¼ cups) milk

227g (1 cup) water

50g (¼ cup) sugar

3 large eggs

20g (2 tablespoons) canola or other neutral oil

1 teaspoon pure vanilla extract

300g (2 ½ cups) cake flour (not self-rising)

25g (¼ cup) unsweetened cocoa powder

1 ½ teaspoons baking powder

¼ teaspoon coarse salt

Salted Peanut Whipped Cream (page 171)

Make the crepes: In a large mixing bowl, whisk to combine the milk, water, sugar, eggs, canola oil, and vanilla until smooth.

In a medium mixing bowl, whisk to combine the flour, cocoa powder, baking powder, and salt. Add the dry mixture to the wet mixture and whisk until smooth. Cover the bowl with plastic wrap and allow the batter to rest at room temperature for 1 hour (or refrigerate up to overnight).

Heat an 8-inch nonstick skillet over medium heat. Pour ¼ cup batter into the pan, gently swirling it around to evenly coat the surface. Cook until the crepe is set and the edges are crisp and starting to release from the pan, 1 to 2 minutes. Slide a spatula underneath the crepe and flip. Cook on the other side for 1 minute. Transfer the crepe to a wire rack to cool. Repeat with remaining crepe batter to make about 25 crepes. It's okay to slightly lay one crepe over another (like shingles) as they cool. Allow all the crepes to completely cool.

To assemble the cake, place one crepe on a serving plate or cake board. With an offset spatula, spread a thin layer of whipped cream over the crepe. Repeat layering and filling the cake with the remaining crepes and whipped cream.

Serve the crepe cake immediately, or cover and refrigerate until ready to serve (up to 3 days).

For a shorter 8-inch crepe cake, cook about ⅓ cup of batter at a time in a 10-inch nonstick skillet to make about 18 crepes.

Cover the cake in plastic wrap and store in the refrigerator for up to 3 days.

Salted Peanut Whipped Cream

MAKES ABOUT 4 CUPS

2 cups heavy cream

1/4 cup creamy peanut butter

1/2 cup confectioners' sugar

3/4 teaspoon coarse salt

In the bowl of an electric mixer fitted with the whisk attachment, combine the cream, peanut butter, sugar, and salt. Start beating on low speed and then increase to medium, until medium peaks form, about 5 minutes. Set aside or cover and chill until ready to assemble the crepe cake (up to 3 days).

The Art of Mooncakes

The symbol of Mid-Autumn Festival is, without a doubt, mooncakes. Starting in early September and ending around early October, Chinese bakeries and markets are packed with mooncakes in varying sizes, shapes, and patterns, and with multiple fillings. The styles vary from region to region. I grew up eating Cantonese-style mooncakes, debatably the most common iteration. These cakes are filled with sweet pastes, nuts, and salted yolks, all shrouded in a soft, thick pastry crust. They're meant to represent the moon and are often embossed with characters representing wishes for health and longevity or simply reflecting the filling inside. Each mooncake is cut into little wedges to be shared among family. You rarely eat an entire mooncake on your own (unless it's a mini mooncake)—these cakes are *dense*.

When I asked my pau pau if she'd ever attempted to make mooncakes at home or knew anyone who did, she couldn't fathom the concept. "They are only made by a true master," she said, "with decades of experience." That didn't exactly instill a lot of confidence in me. But I always appreciate a kitchen challenge—and these were definitely a challenge at first. Mooncakes are a labor of love, and as with any process-driven kitchen project, it's best to understand all the components and have them prepped for assembly before you begin.

Crust

The crust of traditional Cantonese mooncakes is made with flour, oil (or lard), golden syrup, and alkaline water. I realize that the last two ingredients may be unlikely pantry staples for most people, but both are available at specialty food stores and from online sellers. Golden syrup is not regular simple syrup. It's technically an inverted sugar syrup, made by heating up sugar, water, and an acid. It prevents sugar from crystallizing and yields a soft and tender texture in baked goods. It's an essential ingredient in achieving classic mooncake pastry texture. (I suggest saving yourself the trouble of making your own and instead using Lyle's Golden Syrup, a common ingredient in British baking, available online and at specialty food stores.) The addition of alkaline water (also known as lye water or *kansui*, which can be found at Asian markets) gives the crust its golden-brown color and distinctive chewiness.

Filling

Procuring ingredients for mooncake fillings is a bit easier to manage. Classic fillings include red bean paste, white lotus seed paste, mixed nuts, and salted egg yolks. My favorite is red bean paste (page 53) with a salted egg yolk (page 73). Premade fillings can be found at Asian markets, but I prefer the flavor of homemade pastes.

Mooncake Molds

Forming the mooncakes, using either a traditional wooden mold or a modern, plastic plunger-style mold, requires some practice. The wooden molds have a lovely, old-school feel, but I'm here to tell you: Using the plastic plunger-style mold will save you a lot of heartache. It's much easier to work with and will make releasing the actual mooncake a million times easier. Your first few mooncakes might look a tad irregular, but I promise you'll get the hang of it.

A lot of people feel apprehensive about purchasing a mold solely for making mooncakes once a year. I like to run my kitchen pretty lean and try to not purchase tools that have one specific purpose. So instead of thinking of the molds solely for mooncakes, consider using them as an all-purpose cookie stamp. You can use the molds to make Macau-style cookies (page 212) and pressed shortbread or gingerbread tiles. Many cultures have their own version of stamped cookies, like Lebanese *ma'amoul* and German *springerle*. Get creative, and you'll find more than a few reasons to bust out the mooncake mold year-round.

Twice Baking

Once you've formed a few mooncakes, the baking part is, well, a piece of cake. Mooncakes are baked twice, sort of like biscotti. The first session in the oven is to set the delicate pattern in place, and the second time is to fully cook the mooncake and develop its beautiful, deep golden-brown color. After the first bake, brush the mooncakes with a light coating of thin egg wash. A natural-bristle pastry brush works best here, rather than a silicone brush. The egg wash should be thin, so it doesn't gunk up the intricate valleys and impressions from the mold. If you see that there's a little too much egg wash, dab the surface of the mooncake where there is too much egg wash with a paper towel. When fresh out of the oven, the pattern of the mooncakes might look a bit distorted, but don't be disappointed. As the mooncakes cool, the pattern will start to look more defined. You'll also want to "age" your mooncakes in an airtight container at room temperature for one or two days, to allow the crust to soften and get a nice shine. (It's perfectly okay to sample a few mooncakes fresh from the oven, though.)

My pau pau wasn't wrong when she said that mooncakes are generally made by true masters. It's an art form, but one that can be learned. You need patience, determination, and a few modern inventions, like the plunger-style mold. Once you're comfortable with the classic Cantonese-style mooncake, making the variations will feel like a cake walk.

Red Bean and Salted Egg Yolk Mooncakes

MAKES 12 SMALL MOONCAKES

In recent years, mooncake makers have taken their creations to new heights, using filling flavors like vanilla latte and rose jam. All are fun and delicious, but I always come back to the traditional flavors, including my favorite mooncake, which has a salted egg yolk inside. The savory yolk is at once creamy and crumbly, and pairs so well with the sweet dough surrounding it. If you're lucky, you'll find mooncakes with an egg yolk or two, which means there's more of the best part to share with your family. I also love the sweet-and-salty contrast of a mooncake filled with rich and nutty red bean paste.

For the Dough

300g (2 ½ cups) all-purpose flour, plus more for dusting

110g (½ cup) canola or other neutral-flavored oil

160g (½ cup) golden syrup (like Lyle's Golden Syrup)

8g (1 teaspoon) alkaline water

For the Filling

250g (¾ cup) red bean paste (page 53)

6 Salted Egg Yolks (page 73), cut in half

For the Egg Wash

1 large egg

2 tablespoons tap water

Specialty equipment: This recipe requires a 50g mooncake mold for small mooncakes (page xxix). You can also use a 100g mooncake mold for larger mooncakes.

This recipe will make 6 large mooncakes (one salted egg yolk in each) with a 100g mooncake mold.

Make the dough: In a large mixing bowl, combine the flour, oil, golden syrup, and alkaline water. Using a flexible spatula, mix to form a shaggy dough, then knead with your hands to form a smooth, cohesive dough. Form the dough into a thick disc, wrap in plastic, and allow it to rest at room temperature for 45 minutes.

Preheat the oven to 350°F and line a large rimmed baking sheet with parchment paper.

On a lightly dusted work surface, divide the dough into 12 equal portions with a bench scraper (for accuracy, weigh with a digital scale if you have one). Roll each piece into a smooth ball. Working with one piece of dough at a time, flatten with your palm, then roll out dough into a 4-inch round with a dowel rolling pin. Continue to lightly dust with flour if sticking. Use a bench scraper to help lift up the dough. Top the round with ½ tablespoon bean paste, then half a salted egg yolk, and top with another ½ tablespoon paste. Bring the edges of the dough up around the filling. The dough won't initially cover all of the filling; just pinch it together until it completely wraps the filling. Pinch together any cracks that form and roll into a smooth ball.

As you form the balls, arrange them on the prepared baking sheet, spacing at least 2 inches apart. Lightly dust the mooncake mold with flour. Place one ball in the mold and press the plunger down to apply pressure, but take care not to press too hard. Gently release from the mold and return to the baking sheet. Repeat with remaining dough and filling to form all 12 mooncakes.

Bake the mooncakes until the edges are lightly golden brown, 9 to 11 minutes. Remove the sheet from the oven and allow the cakes to cool on the sheet for 10 minutes.

In a small bowl, mix together the egg and water. With a pastry brush, lightly coat the mooncakes (top and sides) with egg wash. Return to the oven and bake until deep golden brown, 10 minutes. Transfer the baking sheet to a wire rack and allow the mooncakes to cool completely on the sheet. Before serving, store mooncakes in an airtight container at room temperature for 1 to 2 days to allow the dough to soften.

Mooncakes can be stored in an airtight container (a resealable bag works great) at room temperature or the refrigerator for up to 5 days.

If you want to omit the salted egg yolk, fill each mooncake with about 1 1/2 tablespoons red bean paste.

Honey Pistachio Mooncakes

MAKES 12 SMALL MOONCAKES

A lot of the conversations I have with my mom revolve around brainstorming recipe ideas, or my taking detailed notes about how she makes her famous spring rolls or fried chicken. I asked for her help in creating a fuss-free mooncake flavor, with a filling that was easy to make and didn't require a special trip to the Asian market. Our inspiration was the traditional and decisive mixed nuts and ham mooncake, a flavor that never seemed to make it onto our mooncake plate at home. The filling actually isn't bad: sweet nuts are mixed with bits of salty cured pork. Our version focuses on the mixed nut portion and omits the pork. Pistachios are blended with honey (orange blossom honey is a good choice), coconut oil, and a generous amount of salt. The filling tastes like a candy bar (minus the chocolate) and is delicious enough to eat with a spoon.

The biggest challenge of making a mooncake filling is ensuring that it's firm enough to keep the mooncakes from deflating in the oven. This filling can be pressed into a ball and withstand the weight of the mooncake pastry. Pistachio, or any nut really, is perfect for that very reason, but it also happens to be my mom's favorite. This recipe is dedicated to (and inspired by) her.

For the Dough

300g (2 ¹/2 cups) all-purpose flour, plus more for dusting

110g (¹/2 cup) canola or other neutral-flavored oil

160g (¹/2 cup) golden syrup (like Lyle's Golden Syrup)

8g (1 teaspoon) alkaline water

For the Filling

200g (1 ¹/2 cups) roasted unsalted pistachios

80g (¹/4 cup) honey

25g (2 tablespoons) coconut oil

10g (1 tablespoon) cornstarch

1 teaspoon coarse salt

For the Egg Wash

1 large egg

2 tablespoons tap water

Make the dough: In a large mixing bowl, combine the flour, canola oil, golden syrup, and alkaline water. Using a flexible spatula, mix to form a shaggy dough, then knead with your hands to form a smooth, cohesive dough. Form the dough into a thick disc, wrap in plastic, and allow it to rest at room temperature for 45 minutes.

Preheat the oven to 350°F and line a large rimmed baking sheet with parchment paper.

Make the filling: In the bowl of a food processor, pulse the pistachios until coarsely ground. Add the honey, coconut oil, cornstarch, and salt and continue to pulse a few more times. The filling should be a little crumbly but stick together when pressed. (Avoid overprocessing, so you don't end up with pistachio butter.) Divide the filling into 12 equal portions (for accuracy, weigh with a digital scale if you have one) and shape each piece into a ball.

Divide the disc of dough into 12 equal pieces with a bench scraper (for accuracy, use a digital scale). Roll each piece into a smooth ball. Working with one piece at a time, flatten a dough ball with your palm and roll out into a 4-inch round. Continue to lightly dust with flour if sticking. Use a bench scraper to help lift up the dough. Center a ball of filling on the round. Bring the edges of the dough up around the filling. The dough won't initially cover all of the filling; just pinch it together until it completely wraps the filling. Pinch together any cracks that form and roll into a smooth ball.

As you form the balls, arrange them on the prepared baking sheet, spacing at least 2 inches apart. Lightly dust the mooncake mold with flour. Place a ball in the mold and press the plunger down to apply pressure, but take care not to press too hard. Gently release from the mold and return to the baking sheet. Repeat with remaining dough and filling to form all 12 mooncakes.

Bake mooncakes until the edges are lightly golden brown, 9 to 11 minutes. Remove the sheet from the oven and allow the cakes to cool on the sheet for 10 minutes. In a small bowl, mix together the egg and tap water. With a pastry brush, lightly coat the mooncakes with egg wash. Return to the oven and bake until deep golden brown, 10 minutes. Transfer the baking sheet to a wire rack and allow the mooncakes to completely cool on the sheet. Before serving, store mooncakes in an airtight container (a resealable bag works great) at room temperature for 1 to 2 days to allow the exterior dough to soften.

Specialty equipment: This recipe requires a 50g mooncake mold for small mooncakes (page xxix). You can also use a 100g mooncake mold for larger mooncakes.

This recipe will make 6 large mooncakes with a 100g mooncake mold.

Mooncakes can be stored in an airtight container at room temperature or the refrigerator for up to 5 days.

No Mooncake Mold?
No Problem.

I think it's worth it to own a mooncake mold, but if you don't have one, you can still join in on the fun. A lot of bakeries sell adorable animal-shaped mooncakes. Thanks to the bulbous shapes of mooncakes, the animals are typically round and plump. My mom has loved the pig-shaped mooncakes since she was a little girl. You can also make turtles, goofy rabbits, bears, and more. (This is a great time to dust off your Play-Doh sculpting skills.) Once you've filled the mooncake with your favorite filling, use bits of dough to form their features, like noses, ears, and feet. It's pretty hilarious to see all the personalities the animal-shaped mooncakes take on from your expert sculpting skills.

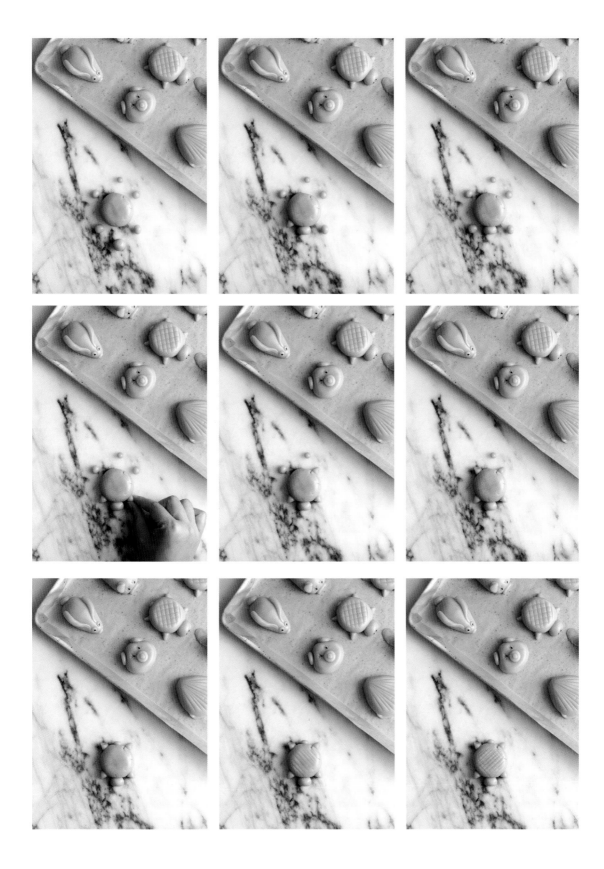

Thousand Layer Mooncakes with White Lotus Seed Paste

Every region in China has its own style of mooncake. Other Asian countries celebrating the Mid-Autumn Festival also have distinct mooncake styles. Suzhou-style mooncakes have a light and flaky crust and are filled with savory pork. Yunnan-style mooncakes have a bready, crusty exterior. These spiral mooncakes are Chaoshan-style mooncakes, aka Thousand Layer Mooncakes. The pastry is similar to puff pastry and is made by laminating a water-based dough (water dough) with a shortening or lard-based dough (oil dough), then stuffing it with either a sweet or savory filling. The spirals are hypnotizing and made even more distinct with the addition of a little matcha in the water dough. Omit the matcha if you prefer a beautifully golden-brown mooncake.

MAKES 6

For the Filling

180g (1/2 cup) White Lotus Seed Paste (page 187)

For the Water Dough

125g (1 cup plus) all-purpose flour

12g (1 tablespoon) sugar

30g (3 tablespoons) vegetable shortening, cubed

55g (1/2 cup) water

4g (2 teaspoons) food-grade matcha powder (optional)

For the Oil Dough

100g (3/4 cup plus 1 tablespoon) all-purpose flour

60g (1/4 cup plus 2 tablespoons) vegetable shortening, cubed

Line a medium plate with parchment paper. Using a 1 1/2-tablespoon cookie scoop, portion out six scoops of white lotus paste and drop onto the parchment paper. Freeze the paste until solid, at least 45 minutes or overnight (cover if freezing overnight).

Make the water dough: In a medium mixing bowl, whisk to combine the flour, sugar, and matcha powder (if using). Add the shortening and water, breaking up the shortening with your fingers and kneading the dough until smooth, 3 to 4 minutes. Pat the dough into a thick disc, wrap in plastic, and refrigerate for 30 minutes.

Make the oil dough: In a medium mixing bowl, combine the flour and shortening, breaking up the shortening with your fingers and kneading until smooth, 1 to 2 minutes. Pat the dough into a thick disc, wrap in plastic, and refrigerate for 30 minutes.

Preheat the oven to 400°F and line a large rimmed baking sheet with parchment paper.

Divide both the water and oil doughs into three equal pieces (six pieces total) with a bench scraper (for accuracy, weigh with a digital scale if you have one). On a lightly floured surface, roll each portion of the oil dough into a smooth ball. Roll out the water dough into 4-inch rounds. Working with one pair at a time, center a ball of oil dough ball on a water-dough round, pull up the edges, and pinch together to cover completely. Place the ball seam-side down and flatten with your palm. Continue to dust with flour if sticking. Roll out the dough into a long oval, about 8 inches long, then roll up into a roll, starting with a short edge. Flatten the dough with your palm again and roll out into an 8-inch long oval. Roll up the dough, starting with a short edge. Cut the dough in half crosswise with a sharp knife. Place one piece of dough cut-side up, and flatten with your palm. Roll out into a 4-inch round, flip so

that the prettier side of the dough is facing the bottom, and place the filling in the center. Pull up the edges of the dough and pinch together to fully seal. Place the mooncake on the prepared baking sheet and repeat with remaining doughs and filling to make six mooncakes, spacing each at least 2 inches apart.

Bake until mooncakes are flaky and slightly golden, 25 to 28 minutes. Transfer the baking sheet to a wire rack and allow the mooncakes to cool on the sheet. Serve warm or at room temperature.

Mooncakes can be stored in an airtight container at room temperature or in the refrigerator for up to 5 days.

White Lotus Seed Paste

MAKES 2 ½ CUPS

100g (1 cup) dried lotus seeds

50g (¼ cup) sugar

45g (¼ cup) oil

Soak the seeds in water for 8 hours or overnight. Drain and rinse the seeds. Some of the seeds might have small green sprouts inside, try your best to remove as many of these as you can.

In a medium saucepan, combine soaked seeds and enough water to cover the seeds by 2 inches. Bring the water to a simmer and continue to simmer until the seeds are tender, 45 minutes to 1 hour. Drain the seeds and rinse under cold water.

In the bowl of a food processor, combine seeds and sugar. Blend until smooth. In a medium nonstick frying pan over medium-low heat, add the puree and canola oil. Stir constantly with a flexible spatula until the oil is blended in and the color deepens, 8 to 10 minutes. Transfer the white lotus seed paste to a heat proof container and allow to cool.

Store in an airtight container in the fridge for up to 2 weeks or the freezer for up to 3 months.

Snow Skin Ice Cream Mooncakes

MAKES 6

Snow skin mooncakes, made popular in Hong Kong, are a colorful, modern interpretation of traditional baked mooncakes. Instead of a cakey pastry dough, these have a mochi-like exterior and are served cold or even frozen, which is how the name was derived. Standard fillings include red bean paste and custard, but I find the soft-on-soft texture combo less than desirable for my tastes. That's where ice cream comes in. Taking inspiration from one of my favorite summer treats, mochi ice cream, I stuff my snow skin mooncakes with my favorite ice cream. The dough stays firm yet chewy, and contrasts beautifully with the texture of a good-quality ice cream. Don't limit yourself to making these only during mooncake season. Ice cream is a necessity year-round.

1/2 cup ice cream (your favorite flavor)

For the Snow Skin Dough

90g (1/2 cup) glutinous rice flour

30g (3 tablespoons) wheat starch, plus more for dusting

50g (1/4 cup) sugar

113g (1/2 cup) milk

12g (1 tablespoon) canola or other neutral-flavored oil

Tiny drop of food coloring (color is up to you)

Specialty equipment: This recipe requires a 50g mooncake mold for small mooncakes (page xxix).

Leave the ice cream out at room temperature for a few minutes to soften. Line a small rimmed baking sheet or plate with parchment paper. Scoop 6 heaping tablespoons (a 1 1/2-tablespoon cookie scoop comes in handy here) ice cream onto the parchment paper, spacing them 1 inch apart. Freeze until solid, at least several hours or preferably overnight (cover with plastic wrap if freezing overnight).

Make the dough: In a medium saucepan (preferably nonstick for easier cleanup), whisk to combine the rice flour, wheat starch, and sugar. Add the milk, oil, and food coloring until smooth. Heat over medium heat. Using a flexible spatula, continue to stir and scrape the sides and bottom of the pan until the batter transforms into a cohesive dough (it should resemble Play-Doh) and pulls cleanly away from the sides, 3 to 4 minutes.

Transfer the dough to a work surface lightly dusted with wheat starch and allow to cool completely. Dust the surface of the dough with a little wheat starch and knead until smooth, 1 minute. Divide the dough into six equal pieces with a bench scraper (for accuracy, weigh with a digital scale if you have one). Roll the pieces into smooth balls and then flatten with your hands into 4-inch rounds. Continue to dust with wheat starch as needed. Set the dough rounds on a plate and cover loosely with plastic wrap. Refrigerate until cool to the touch, at least 30 minutes or up to 2 hours (any longer, it will be too firm to assemble) before filling the mooncakes.

Line another small rimmed baking sheet with parchment paper. Working quickly and with one piece of dough at a time, place a scoop of ice cream in the center of the dough and bring up the edges of the dough together to encase it. Keep pinching the dough close together until the ice cream is fully wrapped. Dust the dough with wheat starch and insert into the mooncake mold, seam-side facing the work surface, and press down on the plunger. Immediately place the mooncake on the baking sheet or directly into the freezer. Continue to form more cakes with the remaining ice cream and dough. Before serving, freeze the mooncakes until solid, at least 1 hour.

Use ice cream that freezes very hard. (Häagen-Dazs works well). Stay away from anything that says, "slow churned." And sorbet is out of the question.

When chilling the individual components, don't rush the process. Be methodical and make sure both the ice cream and the dough are portioned out and chilled long enough (the ice cream should *very* firm) before you try to assemble them.

This is not a recipe to attempt on the hottest day of the year. Either turn the air-conditioning on high or wait for a breezy day or cool night.

Work close to your freezer, so you can quickly pop things back in to firm up when needed.

no fortune cookies

Chapter 5

The most recognizable "Chinese" cookie undoubtedly is the fortune cookie. I've eaten my fair share of fortune cookies, each one containing a tiny piece of paper inside offering all sorts of information: new phrases in Chinese, auspicious lottery numbers, and predictions that true love is right around the corner. But as this chapter title says, you won't find any fortune cookie recipes here. Fortune cookies happily cap off most meals at Chinese American restaurants; at our restaurant, my family served them with a scoop of ice cream. But as much as I enjoy the tuile-like cookies, I'm not going to suggest you make them at home, since they're not worth the time and effort (in my opinion), and never quite as snappy as the restaurant ones. You're better off picking up a few at your favorite Chinese restaurant or planning a trip to San Francisco's Chinatown and picking up a bag from Golden Gate Fortune Cookie Factory.

Instead, this chapter shines a spotlight on other notable Chinese cookies and small treats, like my beloved Goong Goong's Almond Cookies, Taiwanese Pineapple Cakes, and intricately stamped and tender Chocolate-Hazelnut Macau-Style Cookies. Some cookies are speckled with seeds rather than the usual chocolate, and others are more crisp than gooey. Be assured, however, that these cookies are no less delicious than your favorites. There's still plenty of butter and sugar to satisfy any sweet tooth, and lots of delightfully chewy and crunchy texture combos to keep things interesting.

Goong Goong's Almond Cookies

My goong goong always wanted to be a baker. I didn't know this until I started writing this book, but I did know about his famous almond cookies. They were praised for their soft, chewy centers and crisp edges—very different from the crunchy, crumbly variety found in stores and bakeries. According to my mom, when Goong Goong first moved to America from Hong Kong in the late 1960s, his first restaurant job was as a cookie baker, a station step just above dishwasher. It also was a rare station, because few Chinese restaurants served desserts beyond fortune cookies and sliced oranges. He spent day after day making endless trays of his golden, almond-studded cookies. I like to imagine that's when he started dreaming of becoming a baker.

After a few years working in restaurants and climbing his way up from cookie baker, Goong Goong was ready to strike out on his own. He tried to teach himself how to make buns and bread but, according to Pau Pau, they always turned out like bricks. So he stuck with Chinese American food and opened his first restaurant. Its success propelled him to open more throughout his long career. For a few years, he kept alive the practice of making almond cookies, but finally succumbed to the growing demands of running restaurants. He retired the baking sheets for good, instead serving commercially made fortune cookies with ice cream.

I only got to enjoy Goong Goong's almond cookies once. It was the summer before I left for college—and decades since the last time he'd made them. I wanted to spend an afternoon in the kitchen with him before I moved hours away. On a worn little piece of paper neatly notated in Chinese characters and numbers, he had outlined the materials and steps needed to create the famous almond cookies. I'm sure he'd never baked these outside of a commercial kitchen, so he had to do some quick math to scale it down for our regular oven. We fumbled through the recipe and eventually had a tray of warm, heavenly, almond-scented cookies to show for it. I loved them, but to my goong goong and my mom, they weren't quite the same. Maybe it was decades of anticipation or memories clouded by time, but to them they were good but not great. We still devoured way too many of them while sitting around the dining table.

This memory is very precious to me because it is one of the few that I have of baking with my family. It would also be the last time I spent time in the kitchen with Goong Goong before he passed away. I have bittersweet emotions revisiting this recipe, and try to make it as perfect as his was back in the day. Whenever I bake these cookies, I think of his laugh and the way he would sing my Chinese name, *Yee Yee*. I also like to think that my making his cookies and writing a cookbook about Chinese baking would have made him incredibly proud, and in some way fulfilled that dream he had of becoming a baker.

These cookies are soft in the center, crisp around the edges, and perfectly sweet, with just enough almond flavor to fill your kitchen with the intoxicating scent of buttery almonds. Better yet, they have the seal of approval from my mom and the rest of my family, which is all I really needed. I hope Goong Goong's beloved cookies find a home in your own family's kitchen too.

Goong Goong's
Almond Cookies

MAKES 15

125g (1 cup) all-purpose flour

1/4 teaspoon baking soda

1/2 teaspoon coarse salt

113g (1/2 cup; 1 stick) unsalted
butter, softened

130g (2/3 cup) sugar

1 large egg

3/4 teaspoon pure almond extract

1 large egg yolk

12 sliced almonds

Flaky salt, for topping

In a medium bowl, whisk to combine the flour, baking soda, and salt.

In another medium bowl, mix to combine the butter and sugar with a flexible spatula until smooth. Add the egg and almond extract and continue to mix until fully incorporated. Add the dry ingredients and mix until a thick dough is formed (it will be sticky). Cover the bowl with plastic wrap and chill until slightly firm but scoopable, about 1 hour.

Preheat the oven to 350°F and line two large rimmed baking sheets with parchment paper.

Using a 1 1/2-tablespoon cookie scoop, measure out 1 1/2 tablespoons of dough and place on the prepared sheet. (Or use a spoon to scoop and roll the dough into a smooth ball, wetting your hands if the dough is still sticky.) Repeat with remaining dough, spacing them 3 inches apart. Wet your fingers with water to prevent dough from sticking and gently press down on the dough balls with your fingers until they are 1/2 inch thick.

In a small bowl, whisk the egg yolk and use to lightly brush the tops of the cookies. Place an almond slice on each cookie.

Bake until cookies are golden brown and crisp around the edges, 16 to 18 minutes. Transfer the sheets to a wire rack, sprinkle with flaky salt, and allow cookies to cool on the sheets for 5 minutes. Transfer cookies to the rack to cool. Serve warm or at room temperature.

Cookies can be stored in an airtight container (a resealable bag works great) at room temperature for up to 5 days.

If the cookies come out of the oven looking less than perfectly round, don't fret! The moment you transfer the sheet to a cooling rack (this only works when the cookies are still warm), grab a round cutter or glass that's slightly larger than the cookies, place it directly over a cookie and gently swirl the cutter or cup in one direction. The cookie will bump around and gradually take on a rounder shape!

Coconut and Peanut Mochi Balls

MAKES 20

For the Mochi

1 (13.5-ounce) can full-fat coconut milk

225g (1 ½ cups) glutinous rice flour

200g (1 cup) sugar

4 tablespoons cornstarch, for dusting

For the Filling

1 cup roasted unsalted peanuts

¼ cup peanut butter

2 tablespoons honey

½ teaspoon coarse salt

¾ cup finely shredded unsweetened coconut, for topping

I could eat these snowball-like confections by the handful. They're also one of the few gluten-free Chinese bakery options, thanks to glutinous rice flour. Think of them as sweet dumplings: chewy mochi is stuffed with crunchy roasted peanuts mixed with honey, some peanut butter, and a generous pinch of salt. It's the satisfying amalgamation of chewy and crunchy that makes the treats so popular. My filling deviates slightly from tradition—the addition of peanut butter and honey provides a little moisture, which helps the filling stick together better. The filling is plenty sweet, but the salt gives it that sweet-salty contrast I love.

Make the mochi: In a medium saucepan (preferably nonstick for easier cleanup), whisk to combine the coconut milk, rice flour, and sugar until smooth. Heat over medium heat, stirring continually with a flexible spatula until the batter transforms into a cohesive dough (it should resemble a slightly sticky Play-Doh) and pulls cleanly away from the sides, 6 to 7 minutes.

Dust a silicone baking mat with 2 tablespoons cornstarch and transfer the hot mochi to the mat. Liberally dust the top of the mochi and a rolling pin with the remaining 2 tablespoons cornstarch, then roll the mochi into a 12 x 15-inch rectangle. Dust with a little more cornstarch, if needed. Allow the mochi to cool completely.

Meanwhile, make the filling: In the bowl of a food processor, pulse the peanuts, peanut butter, honey, and salt until crumbly. When pressed, the filling should stick together.

Cut the cooled mochi into twenty 3-inch squares. Working with one piece at a time, top a mochi square with 1 tablespoon filling (press the filling together with your hand so it is compact). Pull up the edges of the mochi square, pinch together to seal, and roll to form a small ball. Roll the ball in coconut, then place on a plate or small rimmed baking sheet. Repeat the process with the remaining mochi and filling. Serve at room temperature or refrigerate until ready to serve (up to 5 days).

Special equipment: A silicone baking mat is helpful here because the mochi tends to be really sticky.

Mochi balls can be stored in an airtight container (a resealable bag works great) at room temperature or in the refrigerator for up to 5 days.

Taiwanese Pineapple Cakes

MAKES 18

For the Filling

1 (14-ounce) can crushed pineapple, drained

1/2 cup granulated sugar

1/4 teaspoon coarse salt

1/2 teaspoon pure vanilla extract

For the Pastry

150g (1 1/4 cups) all-purpose flour, plus more for dusting

20g (2 tablespoons) confectioners' sugar

20g (2 tablespoons) tapioca starch

1/4 teaspoon coarse salt

113g (1/2 cup; 1 stick) cold unsalted butter, cut into cubes

1 large egg

Special Equipment: *This recipe requires pineapple cake molds (page xxviii).*

Pineapple cakes can be stored in an airtight container (a resealable bag works great) at room temperature for up to 5 days.

My dad tries to visit his family in Hong Kong every other year. If I'm unable to join him, I look forward to seeing what's inside the suitcase of goodies he brings back from the homeland. One of our favorite treats is Taiwanese pineapple cakes, much easier to find in Hong Kong than in the States. The small, rectangular, meticulously wrapped cookies are made of chewy, buttery shortbread filled with a caramelized pineapple jam. The best pineapple cakes come from Taiwan, where they've grown the fruit for centuries. If you can buy some on your next trip to Taiwan, I'm jealous. But you don't have to fly across the world to Taiwan or Hong Kong to savor these fresh, delicious cake-like pineapple cookies. All you need are some pineapple cake molds (available at Asian houseware stores or online) and the recipe below.

Make the filling: In a medium saucepan, combine the pineapple, granulated sugar, salt, and vanilla extract. Cook over medium heat, stirring frequently, until thick and caramelized, 20 to 30 minutes. Transfer the filling to a heat-proof container and allow to cool completely at room temperature (or refrigerate until ready to form the cakes).

Make the pastry: In the bowl of a food processor, pulse to combine the flour, confectioners' sugar, tapioca starch, salt, butter, and egg until a cohesive dough forms.

Transfer the dough to a sheet of plastic wrap, pat into a 1-inch-thick disc, and tightly wrap. Refrigerate the dough until firm but still somewhat pliable, 30 to 45 minutes.

Preheat the oven to 350°F and line a large rimmed baking sheet with parchment paper.

Use a bench scraper to divide the dough into 18 equal-size pieces (use a digital scale if you have one). Working with one piece at a time, roll the dough into a smooth ball. Place the dough ball on a lightly floured work surface, gently flatten with the palm of your hand, and roll out to a 3-inch round with a dowel rolling pin. Place a teaspoon filling in the center of the dough, pull up the edges, and pinch together to seal. Place the filled cake inside the pineapple cake mold, seam side down, and gently press down with the plunger until it evenly fills the mold. Remove the plunger and transfer the pineapple cake, still in the mold, onto the prepared baking sheet. Repeat with the remaining pastry and pineapple filling. If you have a limited number of molds, keep the dough and filling in the refrigerator until ready to form the next batch.

Bake in the molds until the cakes are golden brown, 25 to 27 minutes. Transfer the sheet to a wire rack and allow the cakes to cool on the sheet for 5 minutes. Remove the molds and allow the cakes to cool completely on the rack. Enjoy the cakes fresh or store in an airtight container for 24 hours to allow the shortbread to soften.

Fried Sesame Balls

MAKES 12

145g (1 cup) glutinous rice flour

100g (1/2 cup) sugar

113g (1/2 cup) water

3/4 cup Red Bean Paste (page 53)

4 cups canola or other neutral-flavored oil, for frying

For the Coating

1/2 cup water

1 tablespoon glutinous rice flour

1/3 cup white sesame seeds

1/3 cup black sesame seeds

If you find it difficult to fill the sesame balls, use plastic wrap to assist you: Place a sheet of plastic wrap on your work surface. Place a round of dough on top of the plastic wrap and add the red bean paste. Gather the edges of plastic wrap up to form a tight bundle around the sesame ball, making sure the red bean paste is fully enclosed. Unwrap the plastic, transfer the ball to the baking sheet, and proceed to fill the rest.

I can't resist a plate of piping-hot sesame balls straight from the fryer, deep-fried to golden perfection. Fried sesame balls are similar to the Coconut and Peanut Mochi Balls (page 197), but instead of being covered in coconut and stuffed with peanuts, these balls are filled with sweet red bean paste and rolled in sesame seeds. Other filling possibilities include Taro Paste (page 77) and custard (page 164). You can order sesame balls year-round at dim sum and in bakeries, but as they're considered auspicious, they're often served at home during Chinese New Year, to represent a wish for wealth. Round foods also symbolize the moon and families gathering together. Next Chinese New Year, fry up a platter of sesame balls to share with your friends and family, for good luck's sake!

Place the flour in a medium mixing bowl. In a medium saucepan, combine the sugar and water and bring to a simmer over medium-high heat, stirring occasionally to dissolve the sugar. Remove the pan from the heat and immediately pour the syrup into the bowl of flour. Stir with a flexible spatula to form a shaggy dough. Allow the dough to cool until cool enough to handle, about 10 minutes. Knead with your hands in the bowl to shape it into a smooth dough, 3 to 4 minutes. Cover the bowl with plastic wrap and allow the dough to rest as it cools to room temperature, about 30 minutes.

Use a bench scraper to divide the dough into 12 equal pieces (for accuracy, weigh each piece with a digital scale if you have one). Roll each piece of dough into a smooth ball and cover with a clean kitchen towel to keep from drying out. Working with one piece, flatten the dough into a 3-inch round and top with a tablespoon bean paste. Pull up the edges of the dough and pinch together to seal. Roll the filled dough between your hands to form a smooth ball and place on a plate or small rimmed baking sheet. Repeat with remaining dough and bean paste.

In a medium-deep saucepan or pot, heat the canola oil over medium heat until a deep-fat thermometer registers 360°F.

While the oil is heating, make the coating: Whisk to combine the water and rice flour in a small bowl. (This will help the sesame seeds stick.) In another small bowl, combine the white and black sesame seeds until evenly mixed.

Working with one at a time, dip each ball of dough into the flour and water mixture and then roll in the sesame seeds, shaking off any excess. Place balls on a plate or small rimmed baking sheet.

Working in batches of four or five (to avoid overcrowding the pot), fry the balls, turning frequently, until golden brown all over, 5 minutes. Using a spider, transfer the balls to a wire rack set over a large rimmed baking sheet to cool slightly. Sesame balls are best served immediately, or at least on the same day as frying.

Pistachio Palmiers

MAKES 32

I know what you're thinking: *Palmiers are French!* You're right. But palmiers have somehow found a home in Chinese bakeries under the name "butterfly cookies." A palmier cookie is puff pastry in its purest, most simple form, rolled up with a generous layer of sugar that melts into little pools of caramel as it bakes. You'll find a variety of palmier flavors in Chinese bakery cases, some dipped in chocolate and others that are savory, speckled with cheese and black pepper. They range in size too—I've seen palmiers as big as my face. For this recipe, I opted for a more manageable size—I'd rather have multiple cookies than one giant one. I love the addition of pistachios for extra crunch, and the flavor of the caramelized pistachio sugar is the stuff dreams are made of.

$1/2$ cup sugar

$1/2$ cup roasted pistachios

All-purpose flour, for dusting

Chinese Puff Pastry (page 157)

1 large egg

In the bowl of a food processor, pulse to combine the sugar and pistachios until the mixture has a medium-coarse texture, about 30 seconds.

On a lightly floured work surface, roll out the sheet of puff pastry into a 12 x 16-inch rectangle. In a small bowl, whisk the egg and use a pastry brush to brush egg onto the surface of the puff pastry, all the way to the edges. Sprinkle $2/3$ pistachio sugar evenly over the puff pastry.

Starting along the long side of the pastry, tightly roll up just to the center, then roll the opposite long side to meet in the center, forming a 16-inch-long heart-shaped log. Place the log on a large rimmed baking sheet and freeze until firm, at least 15 minutes (or longer if the kitchen is hot). It shouldn't be so firm that you can't slice it.

Preheat the oven to 375°F and line two large rimmed baking sheets with parchment paper.

Place the log on a sheet of parchment paper. Brush the exterior of the pastry log with remaining egg wash and sprinkle the remaining $1/3$ pistachio sugar over all sides of the log. Use the parchment paper to help press the pistachio sugar onto the pastry. With a sharp knife, trim $1/2$ inch off either end and then cut the log into 32 slices. For even slices, cut the log in half and continue to cut each piece in half until you have 32 slices. Arrange the slices, cut sides up, on the rimmed baking sheets, spacing 1 $1/2$ inches apart.

Bake until cookies are golden brown and crisp, 28 to 30 minutes. Transfer the sheets to a wire rack and allow the palmiers to cool on the sheet for 5 minutes. Transfer palmiers to the rack to cool completely.

Cookies can be stored in an airtight container (a resealable bag works great) at room temperature for up to 5 days.

Kinako Sewing Tin Butter Cookies

MAKES 50 SMALL COOKIES

I can always count on finding a shiny Royal Dansk Danish butter cookies tin tucked beneath my pau pau's coffee table. I always hold out hope that the tin will contain a fresh batch of buttery, pretzel-shaped cookies (my preferred shape). More often than not, though, spools of thread and sewing needles will be rattling around in there instead. The disappointment! For years, I thought Pau Pau was deliberately toying with my emotions, but thanks to internet memes, I now know that pretty much everyone's grandma does the same thing.

While they might not be traditionally Chinese, these are nostalgic cookies from my childhood. Of course, I had to give my version a twist. Have you ever tried *kinako*? It's roasted soybean flour, a popular ingredient in Japanese desserts. You'll find it most commonly dusted on mochi. Its nutty flavor is reminiscent of peanut butter! Here, kinako blends easily into the creamy butter-cookie base, to add extra depth of flavor. I hope to start keeping a tin of cookies beneath my own coffee table, but it might take a while to graduate to true grandma level—I'll leave out the needles and thread . . . for now.

250g (2 cups) all-purpose flour

24g (¹/4 cup) kinako (roasted soybean flour)

1 teaspoon coarse salt

226g (1 cup; 2 sticks) unsalted butter, softened

100g (¹/2 cup) sugar

¹/2 teaspoon pure vanilla extract

1 large egg

Preheat the oven to 350°F and line two large rimmed baking sheets with parchment paper.

In a medium bowl, whisk to combine the flour, kinako, and salt.

In the bowl of an electric stand mixer fitted with the paddle attachment, mix the butter and sugar on medium speed until very light and fluffy, 3 minutes. Add the vanilla and egg, mixing until incorporated. Add the flour mixture and mix until a smooth and slightly airy dough forms, 1 minute.

Fit a piping bag fitted with a medium (at least ¹/4-inch) star tip. (If the piping tip is too small, it will make piping the cookie difficult.) Fill with the cookie dough. Pipe roughly 1 ¹/2-inch cookies into desired shapes (circles, hearts, pretzels, or whatever you prefer) onto the baking sheet, spacing them 1 inch apart. Refrigerate the cookies until firm, 15 minutes (or longer if the kitchen is hot).

Bake until cookies are golden brown, 10 to 12 minutes. Transfer the sheets to a wire rack and allow the cookies to cool on the sheets for 5 minutes. Transfer cookies to the rack to cool completely.

Piping notes: The cookie dough should be smooth and airy in order to pipe without too much difficulty. Piping does require a bit of hand strength. The first few cookies may be harder to pipe but the dough gets easier to manage as it warms up in your hands. If you find the cookie dough too difficult to pipe, use a larger piping tip, or place the cookie dough near the preheated oven for a few minutes to warm up slightly.

Matcha and Hojicha Cream Puffs

MAKES 16

For the Diplomat Cream Filling

3 large eggs

70g (¹/3 cup) sugar

20g (2 tablespoons) cornstarch

¹/4 teaspoon coarse salt

460g (2 cups) milk

18g (3 tablespoons) hojicha tea leaves

42g (3 tablespoons) chilled unsalted butter, cut into pieces

115g (¹/2 cup) heavy cream

For the Craquelin Topping

50g (¹/4 cup) sugar

50g (¹/3 cup plus 1 tablespoon) all-purpose flour

4g (2 teaspoons) food-grade matcha powder

55g (4 tablespoons) unsalted butter, softened

For the Choux Pastry

75g (¹/3 cup) milk

75g (¹/3 cup) water

65g (4 ¹/2 tablespoons) chilled unsalted butter, cut into pieces

¹/4 teaspoon coarse salt

75g (¹/2 cup plus 1 tablespoon) all-purpose flour

150g (3 large) eggs

You might be surprised to hear that there's a decent amount of crossover between studying architecture and developing recipes. I feel like my technical architecture training has prepared me most for multicomponent *Great British Baking Show*–level patisserie. I only have enough energy to be this meticulous and disciplined about once a year, so if I'm going to expend my patisserie energy on anything, it's got to be heavenly Matcha and Hojicha Cream Puffs.

These puffs are a tea lover's dream. The matcha is in the craquelin topping, which provides lovely color and sweet, slightly grassy flavor. Hojicha, a variety of green tea that is toasted over charcoal for a deeply roasted flavor that borders on smoky, flavors the cream filling.

Yes, this recipe requires that you make pastry cream (then diplomat cream, which is just pastry cream with some whipped cream folded in, for a lighter texture), craquelin (a sugary topping), and pâte à choux. No, you won't dissolve into a puddle of tears at the end. Just take it slow, read through the steps and ingredients carefully, and remind yourself that if someone on *The Great British Baking Show* can make this in a hot tent in the middle of summer with a time limit and icy-blue eyes staring down the back of their necks, then you can easily do this on a lazy Sunday in PJs in the comfort of your own kitchen. You've got this!

Make the filling: In a medium bowl, whisk to combine the eggs, sugar, cornstarch, and salt until smooth. In a medium saucepan, combine the milk and tea leaves and bring to a simmer over medium heat. Turn off heat, cover with a fitted lid, and steep for 10 minutes. Strain the milk through a fine-mesh sieve. Discard the tea leaves.

Pour half of the strained milk into the egg mixture, whisking to combine. Pour in the remainder of the milk, whisking until smooth. Transfer the mixture back to the saucepan. Heat over medium heat, whisking constantly, until the mixture has thickened and the whisk leaves a trail in the cream, 3 to 4 minutes. Turn off the heat and add the butter, a tablespoon at a time, whisking until the butter has melted and the mixture is smooth, 1 minute. Transfer to a bowl and cover with plastic wrap, pressing the plastic wrap on the surface of the custard to prevent a skin from forming. Refrigerate until chilled, at least 2 hours (or up to 3 days).

In a separate medium bowl, whisk the cream until medium peaks form. Using a flexible spatula, fold the whipped cream into the chilled hojicha pastry cream until evenly combined. Refrigerate the hojicha diplomat cream until ready to fill the choux. (This is enough cream to fully fill each puff. If you have any extra cream, you can save by refrigerating or freezing for another use.)

Make the matcha craquelin topping: In a medium bowl, combine the sugar, flour, matcha powder, and softened butter with a flexible spatula until smooth. Place the craquelin pastry between two sheets of parchment paper and roll out until slightly less than 1/8 inch thick. Freeze until very firm, at least 45 minutes or up to overnight.

Preheat the oven to 450°F and line a large rimmed baking sheet with parchment paper.

Make the choux pastry: In a medium saucepan, combine the milk, water, butter, and salt over medium heat. Bring the mixture to a simmer and then immediately turn off the heat and add the flour. Using a flexible spatula, stir to form a thick, smooth paste. Return the saucepan to medium heat and continue to cook to dry out the pastry, stirring constantly, 3 to 4 minutes. There will be a thin layer of cooked pastry at the bottom of the pan.

Transfer the pastry to the bowl of an electric mixer fitted with the paddle attachment. Mix on low speed to release the steam from the pastry, 2 to 3 minutes. The bowl will feel very warm still. Increase the speed to medium and add eggs, one at a time, fully incorporating each before adding the next. (The mixture will look curdled at first). Continue to mix on medium until the pastry is smooth and thick, scraping down the sides as needed, about 2 minutes.

Fit a pastry bag fitted with a large (about 1/2-inch) round piping tip. Fill the bag with the pastry dough and pipe 1 1/2-inch-diameter rounds, about 1 inch tall, on the rimmed baking sheet, spacing at least 2 inches apart. Position the bag perpendicular to the surface and as you're piping, gradually pull away from the surface to give the pastry height.

Using a 1 1/2-inch round cookie cutter, cut out 16 rounds of matcha craquelin. Using a small offset spatula, lift the craquelin rounds and place one on each round of dough. If the craquelin starts to soften, place it back in the freezer until firm again.

Place the baking sheet in the oven and immediately reduce the temperature to 375°F. Bake for 20 minutes and then open the oven to release the steam. Close the door again and bake until the pastry is deep golden brown (the craquelin will still have a green tint), 15 to 20 minutes. Transfer the baking sheet to a wire rack and allow the puffs to cool on the sheet for 5 minutes, and then transfer to the rack to cool completely.

To assemble the cream puffs, fill a piping bag fitted with a large (about ½-inch) star tip with the cream. Split each of the puffs like a hamburger bun, and pipe a generous amount of cream over the bottom of each. Place the top of each puff on top of the cream. Alternatively poke a hole at the bottom of each puff and fill a piping bag fitted with a small round piping tip or a Bismarck tip; fill each puff with cream. Serve immediately.

The puffs and cream can be stored separately until ready to serve. Store puffs in an airtight container at room temperature for up to 4 days. Cream can be refrigerated in an airtight container for up to 3 days. Assembled cream puffs can be refrigerated in an airtight container for up to 2 days.

It is very important to weigh the ingredients for the pâte à choux, including the eggs. The success of a well puffed and hollow choux relies on the perfect balance of all its ingredients.

Sesame Crisps

MAKES 12

These perfectly sweet, snappy crisps are the epitome of a Chinese cookie: plenty crunchy, full of seeds, and just sweet enough. The sesame crisp is similar to a tuile cookie, or the base batter of a fortune cookie. (This is the closest we're going to get to a fortune cookie.) You'll find stacks and stacks of sesame cookies in Chinese bakeries. My cookies are essentially half sesame seeds, so if you aren't a fan of sesame, skip this recipe.

The seeds are suspended in a thin batter of sugar, flour, butter, egg whites, and a hint of vanilla. It's not a typical cookie-dough consistency; the desired "dough" texture is more like thick pancake batter. The melted butter helps the cookies spread into thin wafers, and the granulated sugar gives them their extra-crispy texture and essential snap!

65g (2 large) egg whites

65g ($^1/3$ cup) sugar

$^1/4$ teaspoon coarse salt

$^1/2$ teaspoon pure vanilla extract

50g ($^1/3$ cup plus 1 tablespoon) all-purpose flour

56g (4 tablespoons) unsalted butter, melted

55g ($^1/2$ cup) roasted white sesame seeds

55g ($^1/2$ cup) roasted black sesame seeds

Preheat the oven to 350°F and line two large rimmed baking sheets with silicone mats.

In a medium bowl, whisk the egg whites vigorously until light and foamy, 1 to 2 minutes. Add the sugar, salt, and vanilla extract and whisk until the sugar has fully dissolved. Add the flour and melted butter, whisking until combined. Add the white and black sesame seeds and mix until the seeds are evenly dispersed in the batter. (The batter should be thin, like pancake batter.)

Using a 1 $^1/2$-tablespoon cookie scoop or spoon, drop the batter onto the prepared baking sheets, spacing 2 inches apart (fit six rounds per sheet; the cookies spread as they bake). Smack the baking sheets a few times on the counter to help flatten the cookies.

Bake one sheet at a time, until the edges of the cookies are golden brown, 14 to 16 minutes. Transfer the sheet to wire racks, and allow the cookies to cool on the sheet for 5 minutes. Using an offset spatula, transfer the cookies to the rack to cool completely (they will continue to crisp as they cool). Serve warm or at room temperature.

Specialty equipment: These cookies are best baked on a silicone mat. The mat distributes the heat better, allowing the cookies to spread really thin.

Cookies can be stored in an airtight container (a resealable bag works great) at room temperature for up to 4 days, but the longer they sit, the more they lose their crisp texture.

Chocolate-Hazelnut Macau-Style Cookies

MAKES 10

Delicate almond cookies, vastly different from Goong Goong's Almond Cookies (page 194), are popular in Macau. Their texture is unique—tender as tender can be, and prone to crumbling in your hands if you handle them even a bit too forcefully. There's always a few of these cookies on the dessert platter at Chinese New Year, and normally Pau Pau is within eyesight, to shout across the room that you need a napkin before you even think about taking a bite. Despite their fragility, the nutty flavor is irresistible. The traditional Macau almond cookie is made with two flours (almond and mung bean) and shaped in a mooncake mold. To be honest, I can never find mung bean flour, so I use *kinako* (roasted soybean powder), swapping out one bean flour for another. The substitution still achieves that crumbly texture, and also provides a lot of wonderful peanut buttery flavor. Kinako is easy to find at Asian markets and online.

To take things a few more steps away from tradition, I swapped in hazelnut flour for the usual almond flour, and added a hint of cocoa powder as well. As a result, the cookies taste exactly like the gold foil–wrapped Ferrero Rocher hazelnut chocolates, which are also a quintessential gift for special occasions and holidays in Chinese culture (we can't seem to get enough of confections wrapped in gold). Within one crumbly bite, the cookie tastes of tradition, nostalgia, and modern flavors.

Even with a few modifications, these are still a fragile cookie, especially when you bring a mooncake mold into the picture. The cookie dough is crumbly but should stick together when you press it, sort of like wet sand. The dough will stick to all the intricate carvings of the mooncake mold, unless you liberally dust the mold and dough with confectioners' sugar. Use a little more sugar than you think you'll need—it will melt into the cookies as they bake. Cookies fresh from the oven will still be soft and somewhat sticky; resist the urge to move them or sneak a taste until they have fully cooled and set up. The reward for your patience will be tender, chocolatey, nutty, and intricately stamped cookies.

155g (1 ¼ cups) hazelnut flour

70g (¾ cup) kinako (roasted soybean flour)

15g (2 tablespoons) cocoa powder

18g (2 tablespoons) cornstarch

75g (½ cup) confectioners' sugar, plus more for dusting

½ teaspoon coarse salt

70g (6 tablespoons) vegetable shortening, chilled and cut into ½-inch pieces

Preheat the oven to 300°F and line a large rimmed baking sheet with parchment paper.

In a large mixing bowl, whisk to combine the hazelnut flour, kinako, cocoa powder, cornstarch, sugar, and salt. Add the shortening, mixing it into the dry ingredients with a pastry cutter or with your fingertips. The dough should be crumbly, resembling wet sand, but should stick together when pressed.

Divide the dough into ten pieces (about the size of golf balls), pressing tightly so it sticks together. Arrange the balls on the lined baking sheet, spacing 3 inches apart. Gently flatten the balls until they are about ½ inch thick.

Using a pastry brush, generously dust the tops of the balls and the mooncake mold with confectioners' sugar. Place the mold over a dough ball and firmly press down with the plunger. Release pressure to gently release the dough from the mold. Repeat with remaining balls of dough, generously dusting the mold between each.

Bake cookies until slightly set around the edges but mostly still soft and a little sticky, about 25 minutes. Transfer the baking sheet to a wire cooling rack and allow the cookies to completely cool and set before serving or moving, 35 to 40 minutes.

Cookies can be kept in an airtight container at room temperature for up to 5 days.

Phoenix Bakery
LOS ANGELES, CALIFORNIA

Los Angeles Chinatown is one of the oldest standing Chinatowns in the United States. Its current home, just north of downtown Los Angeles, was founded in 1938. Chinatown's original location, Old Chinatown, was established back in the 1880s, where Union Station stands today. As the new Chinatown was laying down its foundations, so was Phoenix Bakery. It is still there today, serving its famous strawberry and cream cake, crunchy almond cookies, flaky winter melon pastries (fondly known as "old wife cakes"), and addictive sugar butterflies: twisted pieces of wonton wrappers that are deep-fried and then dipped in syrup (and not to be confused with butterfly palmiers).

Fung Chow Chan and his wife opened Phoenix Bakery in 1938 because they dearly missed the sweets they loved from back home in Guangzhou, China. They had no culinary training but worked hard to achieve the flavors and textures they remembered from home. Chan's brother, Lun F. Chan, who did have pastry training at the Culinary Institute in Los Angeles and in Hong Kong, later joined the business as their head baker. After eighty-two years in operation, it remains one of the longest-running shops in Chinatown. Today the Chans' daughter, Kathryn Chan Ceppi, along with her brothers and cousins, run the show.

From the beginning, Phoenix Bakery's motto has been "Sweets for the Sweet." "Even in hard times, people celebrate with something sweet," said Ceppi. This ethos has sustained their business from a small storefront in 1938 to the expansive bakery it is today. It also has cultivated an incredibly loyal community over the years, with generations of customers visiting daily. Like any small business, Phoenix Bakery has faced hardships, but customer loyalty has kept their doors open. During the pandemic, it was one of the few businesses in Chinatown that remained open for business, underscoring the family motto that even during the darkest of times, people want to celebrate, and sweets bring joy to your day.

What resonates with me is the devotion of the community. It's obvious that the bakery's longstanding history in Chinatown and their fresh cakes, buns, and cookies keep people coming back. But Ceppi's family also had an interesting role in the foundation and growth of Chinatown. Fung Chow Chan was the first Asian to get a charter to open a bank. His bank, Cathay Bank, opened in 1962 and quickly became a trusted bank for the Los Angeles Chinese community (he also founded East West Saings and Loan in 1973). It was a bank that spoke their language and understood their culture. Old-school Chinese people are historically distrustful with their money, especially when they're immigrants and working tirelessly to survive in this country. Instead of hiding money in paper bags or coffee tins, the Chinese community in Los Angeles finally had an establishment they trusted to protect their hard-earned cash. The bank was a game changer that helped the Chinese community grow and prosper. Today, Cathay Bank has an international reach, spread across the United States and Asia.

Phoenix Bakery's unique history represents a vital contribution to the rich culture and history of Los Angeles Chinatown. Fung Chow Chan and Lun F. Chan and their generation left a legacy for his children and future generations to carry on. And thanks to the little bakery that keeps on chugging, Angelenos and lucky visitors like me know exactly where to go for the freshest cream cakes and the most perfect sugar butterflies.

In other words, family, trust, loyalty, and a really good cookie can carry a business a long way.

ALMOND COOKIES
NET WEIGHT: 10 oz

INGREDIENTS:
FLOUR, SUGAR, LARD, EGGS, ALMOND, EGG
SHADES (MIXTURES OF FD & C NO. 5, NO. 6,
& FLOUR SALT.)

PHOENIX BAKERY INC.

969 NORTH BROADWAY
LOS ANGELES, CA 90012
(213) 628-4642
www.phoenixbakeryinc.com

"Sweets for the Sweet"

Sweets for the Sweet

chinese breakfast

Chapter 6

There are no rules when it comes to Chinese breakfast. Dishes you might consider more appropriate for lunch, dinner, or even dessert find a spot in the morning ritual. Cafes and popular street stalls offer a wide range of specials for breakfast: stir-fried noodles, savory soy milk, freshly steamed dumplings, jook, French toast, or waffles. *Youtiao* (Chinese doughnuts) are a common accompaniment because it's hard to say no to fried dough for breakfast. And cold cereal doesn't make the cut.

Besides venturing out for our favorite dim sum, normally breakfast was spent at home. Some mornings my parents whipped up warm bowls of instant ramen with Spam, or rice bowls with leftovers and a runny egg. If we were lucky, we'd have a few dumplings too. Breakfast was typically hot and savory, but every once in a while, we made Hong Kong–Style French Toast, with a healthy drizzle of condensed milk (never syrup). The best natural alarm clock is the sound of my mom working on breakfast in the kitchen and the smell wafting through the house of jasmine rice cooking down for jook. Can you think of anything better to help rouse you out of bed?

Crystal Shrimp Dumplings (Har Gow)

MAKES 32

For the Filling

1 pound shrimp, peeled and deveined

1/3 cup canned bamboo shoots, finely chopped

2 cloves garlic, grated or minced

2 tablespoons cornstarch

1 tablespoon oyster sauce

1 teaspoon canola or other neutral-flavored oil

1/2 teaspoon sesame oil

2 teaspoons sugar

1 teaspoon coarse salt

1/2 teaspoon ground white pepper

For the Dough

120g (1 cup) sweet potato starch

90g (3/4 cup) tapioca starch

60g (1/2 cup) wheat starch

1/4 teaspoon coarse salt

200g (scant 1 cup) boiling water

2 tablespoons canola oil

Cornstarch, for dusting

A morning spent feasting on dim sum is never complete without at least a few orders of *har gow*. Crystal shrimp dumplings have been a favorite as far back as I can remember. The wrapper is made of a blend of starches, giving it a satisfying bouncy texture and a semi-translucent, gemlike appearance. When I was a young, picky eater, I loved the wrapper so much I'd remove the shrimp filling, sneak it onto Goong Goong's plate, and eat just the wrappers, with a little soy sauce. I've since wised up and find myself craving the tender shrimp filling as well.

I like to compare har gow to French macarons, because they're similarly finicky. If you've never worked with crystal dumpling dough before, my best advice is to get yourself a digital scale and use a light touch. And know that if the water isn't hot enough or the humidity in the kitchen is off, things can start to go haywire. Since the dough has no gluten, it lacks the same stretch and strength of regular wheat-based wrappers, so folding the dough into dumplings can be a delicate process. Don't feel discouraged if your first few dumplings are misshapen or have a few tears or holes (after you steam them, any tears will be barely noticeable). The art of making dumplings (whether crystal or wheat-based) is completely reliant on repetition. The more you practice, the better you get. Once your hands start to feel comfortable with all the subtle movements, pleat after pleat, the act of folding dumplings takes on a meditative feel. Making dumplings, especially these har gow, is my favorite relaxing weekend activity for just that reason.

Make the filling: Finely chop the shrimp until it resembles a thick paste, with a few larger chunks (alternatively, you can quickly pulse the shrimp in a food processor, though I prefer the texture you get from chopping by hand). Transfer to a medium mixing bowl. Add the bamboo shoots, garlic, cornstarch, oyster sauce, canola oil, sesame oil, sugar, salt, and white pepper, mixing with flexible spatula until well combined. Cover the bowl with plastic wrap and refrigerate until chilled, at least 15 minutes, or until ready to form dumplings (up to overnight).

Make the dough: In a large mixing bowl, whisk to combine the sweet potato starch, tapioca starch, wheat starch, and salt. Pour the boiling water over the starches and, without mixing, cover immediately with plastic wrap. Allow the boiling water to steam the starches for 10 minutes. Remove the plastic and add the canola oil, mixing with a flexible spatula until a crumbly dough forms. Knead with your hands until the dough is very smooth, 3 to 4 minutes.

Divide the dough in half, keeping one half well-wrapped in plastic. Working with the other half, form the dough into a 1-inch-thick log. With a bench scraper, divide the dough into 16 equal pieces. (The easiest way to do this is by continually dividing the dough portions in half until you have 16 pieces). Working with one piece at a time (cover the remaining dough pieces with a clean towel), roll into a smooth ball. On a work surface lightly dusted with cornstarch, flatten the ball of dough with your palm and then, using a dowel rolling pin, roll out to a 3 1/2-inch round. Lift the round of dough off the work surface (use the bench scraper to help, if needed), and top with 2 teaspoons shrimp filling. Carefully pull up and pleat the dough to enclose the filling. Only pleat one half of the wrapper, making overlapping pleats with one hand. Bring the unpleated side to the pleated side and pinch closed. Place the dumpling on a large rimmed baking sheet dusted with cornstarch. Repeat to form 32 dumplings with the remaining dough and filling.

Prepare your steamer setup (page xxviii) and bring water to a boil. Working in batches, arrange the dumplings in the bamboo steamer, spaced at least 1/2 inch apart. Steam for 7 minutes. Place the steamer basket on a wire rack and remove the lid. Allow the dumplings to cool for at least 5 minutes before serving. (The dumplings will be sticky and opaque at first but will become more translucent and less sticky as they cool.)

Raw dumplings freeze well: Fill a small rimmed baking sheet or plate with pleated dumplings and freeze until solid, then transfer to a resealable plastic bag and store in the freezer for up to 3 months. To prepare frozen dumplings, steam as you would fresh dumplings, but increase the steam time to 10 minutes. Never defrost frozen dumplings.

A Lesson in Starches

This crystal dumpling dough is naturally gluten-free, thanks to a blend of starches—sweet potato, tapioca, and wheat—each with properties that work in harmony with one another to produce easy-to-handle dumpling wrappers with a great texture. Everyone has their own textural preferences for crystal dumplings. Some like them softer or less translucent; others prefer them firmer or more opaque. The starch proportion in recipes can therefore be tailored to the desired texture, whether you use one starch or a blend of all three. You can adjust the starch ratios according to your own preferences, but first you have to understand the particular properties each starch contributes to the dough:

Sweet potato starch gives the dumpling its semi-translucent appearance and a peek at the tasty filling inside. Some crystal dumplings are made with 100 percent sweet potato starch, for a super-glassy appearance, but the dough tends to be extremely delicate to handle.

Tapioca starch lends a softer, chewier texture than sweet potato or wheat starch, and gives the dough a slight stretch that's helpful when pleating the dumplings.

Wheat starch provides strength and some rigidity to the dough. I'm not a fan of really sticky and soft crystal dumplings, so I like to add a little wheat starch to help stiffen the dough (and make it a lot easier to handle). It also makes dough more opaque, so if you prefer a transparent look, you'll want to balance the wheat starch with sweet potato starch.

Rose Siu Mai

MAKES 32

I was really into origami as a kid. I was fascinated by how a square sheet of paper could morph into endless designs, with merely a few strategic folds and tucks. That's probably why I love folding dumplings so much and finding imaginative ways to make dumplings look out of the ordinary. Though they look impressive, rose dumplings are easy to form and require no real pleating. I normally don't advise people to bring out a pasta roller and cookie cutter to make wrappers—it's not necessary for regular dumplings, when a rolling pin and some elbow grease will do the trick. But if you're expending the time and energy to make dumplings look like flowers, the extra tools will give you more control over the dough and a cleaner, more consistent aesthetic. Since this recipe requires assembling three dumpling wrappers into one rose dumpling, you'll want to make sure the wrappers are on the smaller, thinner side. Too much dough, and you start to lose the delicate definition of the petals (and a too-doughy dumpling isn't as appetizing). A pasta roller helps achieve the thinness you need, without tearing the dough, and a standard 3-inch cookie cutter will ensure that each fold of the rose is uniform and graceful.

Siu mai are open-faced dumplings, traditionally filled with pork and shrimp and topped with a little fish roe. They're my second favorite dim sum dumplings, right behind har gow (page 219). Creating open-faced rose-shaped dumplings seemed like a natural combination of two concepts—siu mai and the folded rose dumpling—with each petal slightly open and the filling revealed. But because these dumplings are open-faced, you can only steam or pan-fry them. I prefer to steam them—it's the gentlest way to cook dumplings and preserves all the work you put into shaping each dainty, edible rose.

For the Dough

300g (2 ¹/2 cups) all-purpose flour

¹/2 teaspoon ground turmeric

¹/4 teaspoon coarse salt

170g (³/4 cup) hot water

For the Filling

¹/2 pound ground pork

¹/2 pound shrimp, peeled and deveined, finely chopped

3 green onions, whites and greens, finely chopped

2 tablespoons oyster sauce

1 teaspoon sugar

¹/2 teaspoon coarse salt

¹/2 teaspoon ground white pepper

Cornstarch, for dusting

Specialty equipment: *This recipe requires a pasta roller and cookie cutter.*

Make the dough: In a medium mixing bowl, whisk to combine the flour, turmeric, and salt, then pour in the hot water. With a flexible spatula, mix to form a shaggy dough. Knead with your hands until the dough is smooth-ish (a few lumps and dimples are okay). The dough should be tacky and not stick to your hands. If it feels too dry, add a tablespoon of hot water (or a little more, if needed); if it feels too sticky, add a tablespoon of flour (or a little more, if needed). Form the dough into a ball and tightly wrap in plastic. Allow the dough to rest at room temperature for at least 30 minutes or up to 2 hours.

Make the filling: In a medium bowl, combine the pork, shrimp, green onions, oyster sauce, sugar, salt, and white pepper, mixing with a flexible spatula until evenly combined. Refrigerate for at least 15 minutes or until ready to fill the dumplings (up to overnight).

On a work surface lightly dusted with cornstarch, unwrap the dough. Using a knife or bench scraper, divide the dough into four equal portions. Working with one piece of dough (keep the rest of the dough covered with plastic wrap or a kitchen towel to prevent it from drying out), form into a ball and flatten into a 1/2-inch-thick oval using a dowel rolling pin. Lightly dust the dough with cornstarch. Starting on the thickest setting, run the dough through the pasta roller, increasing the setting with each pass and dusting with more cornstarch if needed, until the dough is fairly thin. (I go up to setting 6 on the KitchenAid pasta roller attachment.) Place the rolled dough on a work surface dusted with cornstarch and repeat with remaining pieces of dough. Allow the sheets of dough to dry out for about 15 minutes, which will make the wrappers easier to handle.

Using a 3-inch cookie cutter, cut out rounds. Gather the dough scraps to knead and run through the pasta roller for more dumpling wrappers. You should have enough for 60 wrappers. Stack the rounds on top of each other, making sure to dust in between with cornstarch to prevent sticking.

Prepare a small bowl of water to dip your finger into and dust a large rimmed baking sheet with cornstarch. To form a rose, arrange three dumpling wrappers side by side, overlapping the edges by 1/4 inch, like a Venn diagram. Use your finger to dab a little water where the edges of the dumpling wrappers meet. Spread a heaping tablespoon of filling along the centerline of the wrappers. Fold over the wrappers in half lengthwise. Here you have the option to press the wrappers closed or leave them unsealed (as shown); either option is fine and the decision is purely aesthetic. With your finger, dab some water along the straight edge of the wrappers to help them stick when rolled up. Starting at one end of the wrappers, roll the dumpling up into a tight coil and apply a little dab of water at every end of the coil to ensure it sticks. Adjust the petals of the rose if needed and then place directly onto the rimmed baking sheet lightly dusted with cornstarch. Repeat with remaining wrappers and filling to form 20 dumplings.

Prepare your steamer setup (page xxviii) and bring water to a boil. Working in batches, arrange the dumplings in the bamboo steamer, spacing at least 1/2 inch apart. Cover with the lid and steam for 8 minutes. Place the steamer basket on a wire rack and remove the lid. Allow the dumplings to cool for at least 5 minutes before serving.

Raw dumplings freeze well: Fill a medium rimmed baking sheet or large plate with pleated dumplings and freeze until solid. Transfer the frozen dumplings to a resealable plastic bag, seal, and freeze for up to 3 months. To prepare frozen dumplings, cook as you would fresh dumplings, but steam for 12 minutes. Never defrost frozen dumplings.

Bacon and Kale Potstickers

MAKES 32

On a few occasions, I've been met with puzzled faces when I tell people I eat dumplings for breakfast. When dim sum is a cornerstone of your upbringing, dumplings are a logical breakfast food. Siu mai? Wonton soup? Soup dumplings? Potstickers? All ideal breakfast options. Since determining which meal a dish is most appropriate for has always been pretty fluid in my family, I wanted to create a dumpling stuffed with traditional breakfast flavors, a gateway potsticker to feed the dumplings-for-breakfast skeptics. I managed to fit a classic Western-style breakfast of smoky bacon, greens, and tender potatoes inside a dumpling wrapper. Try these hearty, incredibly satisfying dumplings with a generous amount of hot sauce on the side (or ketchup, if that's your jam).

For the Dough

300g (2 1/2 cups) all-purpose flour, plus more for dusting

1/4 teaspoon coarse salt

170g (3/4 cup) hot water

For the Filling

6 strips thick-cut bacon

1/2 medium yellow onion, diced

2 medium yellow potatoes, peeled and grated

1 bunch (about 4 cups) kale, stems discarded and leaves finely chopped

1 tablespoon oyster sauce

1 teaspoon sugar

1/2 teaspoon coarse salt

1/2 teaspoon ground white pepper

1 tablespoon cornstarch

Canola or other neutral-flavored oil, for cooking

Make the dough: In a medium mixing bowl, whisk to combine the flour and salt, then pour in the hot water. With a flexible spatula, mix to form a shaggy dough. Knead with your hands until you have a smooth-ish dough (a few lumps and dimples are okay). The dough should be tacky but not stick to your hands. If the dough feels too dry, add a tablespoon of hot water (or a little more if needed); if the dough feels too sticky, add a tablespoon of flour (or a little more if needed). Form the dough into a ball and wrap tightly in plastic. Allow the dough to rest at room temperature for at least 30 minutes or up to 2 hours.

Make the filling: In a large cast-iron skillet over medium heat, cook the bacon strips in an even layer until crisp, 6 to 8 minutes, flipping halfway through. Transfer the bacon to a paper towel–lined plate to drain. Allow the bacon to cool until warm and then chop into medium-size pieces.

In the same skillet with the bacon fat, turn the heat up to medium-high, add the onion, and cook until starting to brown around the edges, 3 to 4 minutes. Add the grated potatoes and cook until the potatoes are tender, 7 to 8 minutes. Add the kale, oyster sauce, sugar, salt, and pepper, tossing to combine. Cook until the kale is wilted, 4 to 5 minutes.

Transfer the filling to a medium bowl. Add the chopped bacon and cornstarch, mixing to combine. Cover the bowl and refrigerate until chilled. (You can prepare the filling in advance and refrigerate until ready to fill the dumplings, up to 2 days.)

Unwrap the dough and divide in half, keeping one half well wrapped in plastic. Working with one half, form the dough into a 1-inch-thick log. With a bench scraper, divide the dough into 16 equal pieces. (The easiest way to do this is by continually dividing the portions in half until you have 16 pieces.) Working with one piece of dough at a time (keep the remaining pieces covered with a clean towel), pinch the dough into a round resembling a thick coin. On a work surface lightly dusted with flour, flatten the dough with your palm, then use a dowel rolling pin to roll it into a 4-inch round. Lift the round off the work surface (use the bench scraper to help, if needed), and top with a heaping tablespoon of filling. Carefully pull up and pleat the dough together to enclose the filling, then place the dumpling directly onto a large rimmed baking sheet dusted with flour. Repeat with the remaining dough and filling to form 32 dumplings.

In a large nonstick pan, heat 2 tablespoons oil over medium heat. Working in batches, arrange dumplings in the pan, they can be close but not touching. You should hear a gentle sizzle when the dumplings hit the pan; if the oil is crackling too much or loudly, your oil is too hot, and you should reduce the heat slightly. Fry dumplings until the bottoms are lightly golden brown, 1 to 2 minutes. Hover a fitted lid over the pan and carefully add ¼ cup water to the pan. Cover the pan with the lid and allow the dumplings to steam for 6 minutes (since the filling is cooked already, you're mainly cooking the dough now). If the water evaporates too quickly, add another tablespoon of water. Remove the lid and cook until any remaining moisture cooks off and the bottoms of your dumplings are crisp, 1 to 2 minutes. Transfer the dumplings to a platter to cool for a few minutes. Repeat the cooking process with remaining dumplings, adding a little more oil to the pan in between batches. Serve the dumplings immediately.

Raw dumplings freeze well: Fill a small rimmed baking sheet or plate with pleated dumplings and freeze until solid. Transfer to a resealable bag and store in the freezer for up to 3 months. To prepare frozen dumplings, cook as you would fresh dumplings, but increase the water to ⅓ cup and the steam time to 9 to 10 minutes. Never defrost frozen dumplings.

The Simplest Jook

SERVES 4

The single most comforting bowl of food I can think of is my mom's *jook*. Everyone in my family was practically raised on this creamy rice porridge. Instead of testing to see if I took a liking to pureed carrots or applesauce as a baby, my parents gave me lightly seasoned jook . . . and I obviously loved it. It's a magical food that instantly consoles you if you're heartbroken, settles your stomach if you're feeling unwell, and cures a bad case of homesickness. Also, the fact that 1 cup of rice plus water can be easily transformed into a meal for four is extraordinary.

Making jook is a slow process. When I lived in San Francisco, if I woke up with a craving and couldn't wait an hour to stir a pot of rice, I would walk over to Good Luck Dim Sum on Clement Street for a pint container to go. It is hard to mess up jook, and as much as I love making it at home, I often find it fun to try all the varieties offered in different cafes and bakeries. Water and rice essentially become a blank canvas for pork, fish, ginger, dried scallops, or anything else you can dream of.

This version of jook is the simplest one in my mom's repertoire. Lots of times, she'll load it up with dried scallops, pork shoulder, or leftover Thanksgiving turkey. But when she wants to keep things basic, she'll crumble in some ground pork. It's an accessible, effortless way to add a lot of flavor and a little more heft to your breakfast. This would also work with any other ground protein. After you've patiently stirred your bowl of rice for about an hour (a great time to call your mom, by the way), don't forget the toppings. Jook needs texture from crispy onions (like the kind you top green bean casserole with!), and also makes an excellent dipping situation for a side of youtiao (page 27).

12 cups water

1 cup jasmine rice (do not rinse)

1 tablespoon chicken bouillon

1 teaspoon salt

8 ounces ground pork

Suggested Toppings

Chinese Doughnuts (Youtiao, page 27)

Sautéed gai lan

Crisp fried onions

Pork floss

Chili oil

Soy sauce

In a large pot over medium-high heat, bring the water to a boil. Add the rice and bring back up to a simmer. Reduce the heat to maintain a simmer and stir in the bouillon and salt. Continue to cook, stirring the pot every 5 minutes with a wooden spoon and making sure to scrape the bottom so the rice doesn't stick, until the jook is creamy but still loose, 35 to 45 minutes.

Crumble in the ground pork and continue to cook and stir the rice until thick and creamy, 15 to 25 more minutes.

Remove from heat, spoon into bowls, and serve with your favorite toppings.

Store jook in an airtight container in the fridge for up to 4 days. Reheat in the microwave until warmed through, 1 to 2 minutes, or in a saucepan until warmed through, 5 to 8 minutes. If the jook is too thick, stir a little water in to loosen it up.

Fan Tuan

MAKES 2 LARGE ROLLS (SERVES 4)

Fan tuan is the carb-on-carb breakfast of your dreams. This burrito-like roll of sticky rice is stuffed with youtiao (Chinese doughnuts), a just-runny-enough fried egg, spicy kimchi, and the magical fluff known as pork floss. The roll is heavy overall, literally and flavor-wise, so the kimchi lightens it up, with its bright, tart flavor. Eat one (or more likely half a roll) for breakfast, and you won't feel hungry for a very long time. Eating sticky rice and a doughnut in the morning has that effect.

2 Chinese Doughnuts (Youtiao, page 27)

1 ½ cups sticky rice (uncooked)

2 cups water

2 tablespoons olive oil

2 large eggs

2 tablespoons furikake

4 tablespoons kimchi

3 tablespoons pork floss

In the bowl of a rice cooker, rinse the rice under cold water and drain a few times until the water runs mostly clear. Drain the rice and add 2 cups fresh water. Press "cook." (Alternatively, cook the rice in a saucepan on the stovetop by simmering for 20 to 25 minutes.) Fluff the cooked rice and then allow it to cool until warm, 5 to 10 minutes.

Preheat the oven to 350°F. Place the youtiao on a large rimmed baking sheet and bake until crisp and warmed through, 10 to 12 minutes.

In a medium skillet, heat the oil over medium-high. When the oil is hot and shimmery, crack the eggs in. Fry the eggs until the whites are set and the edges are crispy, 3 to 4 minutes. Flip and cook the other sides until set and crispy, another minute. Transfer the eggs to a plate to cool.

Place a bamboo rolling mat on a work surface. Place a sheet of plastic wrap on top of the mat. Transfer half of the sticky rice to the plastic wrap. Using a flexible spatula, spread the rice into an 8-inch square. Sprinkle a tablespoon of furikake over the surface of the rice. Place a fried egg in the center of the rice and then place a youtiao on top. Add 2 tablespoons kimchi and 1 ½ tablespoons pork floss on either side of the length of the youtiao. Using the plastic wrap and the bamboo mat to assist you, roll everything up into a tight, burrito-like log. Twist the ends of the plastic wrap to keep the fan tuan well-wrapped until ready to serve. Repeat with remaining rice, youtiao, and fillings.

While the fan tuan is still wrapped in plastic wrap, cut it in half with a sharp knife and serve. These are best eaten by hand, and the plastic wrap helps keep fingers clean.

Specialty equipment: *This recipe requires a bamboo rolling mat, like the ones used for rolling sushi.*

Fan tuan are best eaten fresh and warm, but are quite good cold! They should be kept wrapped in plastic wrap until ready to serve, and can be refrigerated for up to 3 days. You can reheat in the microwave for 45 seconds to 1 minute.

Maple Bubble Waffles

MAKES 2 LARGE WAFFLES

Bubble waffles (also known as egg waffles) border on snack territory for me. After I touch down in Hong Kong, hug all my family members, and eat a few dumplings, I go in search of a bubble waffle. The interconnected web of batter is so crispy and the "bubbles" deliciously puffy that I almost always order my waffles plain: no extra flavors, ice cream, or toppings for me, please. It's a wonderful handheld treat. I tear off a few bubbles as I stroll, making it last as long as I can.

I gave my mom an egg waffle iron for her birthday a few years ago. Since then, she's developed her own egg waffle recipe and taken to making it for breakfast when my brother and I come home. (So who was the waffle iron a gift for, really?) The wonderful chew of my mom's waffles comes from the addition of tapioca starch, while eggs and a hint of vanilla give them a lovely custardy flavor. Maple syrup in the batter imparts amazing flavor and helps the waffles get extra crisp. When I eat these for breakfast and not just as a snack, I love them topped with fresh fruit and a drizzle of sweetened condensed milk. Dress them up however your heart desires.

140g (1 1/4 cups) cake flour (not self-rising)

50g (1/4 cup) sugar

25g (1/4 cup) tapioca starch

20g (2 tablespoons) cornstarch

1 1/2 teaspoons baking powder

1/4 teaspoon coarse salt

2 large eggs

170g (3/4 cup) water

70g (1/4 cup) maple syrup

20g (2 tablespoons) canola or neutral-flavored oil

1 teaspoon pure vanilla extract

Nonstick spray, for the waffle iron

In a medium mixing bowl, whisk to combine the flour, sugar, tapioca starch, cornstarch, baking powder, and salt. In another bowl or large liquid measuring cup, whisk to combine the eggs, water, maple syrup, oil, and vanilla extract. Pour the wet ingredients into the dry ingredients and whisk until the batter is smooth. Cover the bowl and allow the batter to rest at room temperature for at least 1 hour (or refrigerate up to overnight).

Preheat the bubble waffle iron. (If using an electric bubble waffle iron, set to medium. If using a stovetop bubble waffle iron, preheat both sides of the iron over medium-low heat.) Using a ladle, quickly pour the batter into the iron, trying to fill all the indentations three-quarters of the way full. For an electric iron, cook until both sides are golden brown, 4 to 6 minutes. For a stovetop iron, immediately flip the iron and cook for 2 to 3 minutes. Flip the iron again and cook the other side until golden brown, 2 to 3 minutes. Carefully remove the waffle from the iron with tongs and repeat with remaining batter. Serve the waffles immediately.

Specialty equipment: These waffles are made specifically in a bubble waffle iron, easily found online and at stores where kitchen gadgets and appliances are sold. You can also make them in a traditional waffle iron, however the texture will not be the same. With a bubble waffle iron, you get really thin and crispy webbing between the bubbles, which contrasts really well with the puffy chewy bubbles.

Jianbing You Can Actually Make at Home

MAKES 4

I still have dreams about the jianbing stall a few blocks from my apartment in Beijing. I didn't go there nearly as much as I should have (there was so much new food I needed to try), but when I stopped by for breakfast, I couldn't imagine starting my day any other way. Jianbing are Chinese-style crepes, similar to French crepes, made on a big, hot flat top. The street vendor cracks an egg over the top and marbles the golden yolk and whites around the surface like a Jackson Pollock painting, sprinkling on chopped green onions and sesame seeds. When the eggs are set, he effortlessly flips the huge crepe without losing a single green onion, smears on a salty, funky, spicy fermented bean sauce (doubanjiang), and layers on crisp lettuce, crunchy bao cui (a fried cracker), and whatever other filling options he has handy. He folds it up into a neat package and hands you breakfast. It takes about five seconds to devour.

You can't quite achieve the exact same product at home, because who has a 30-inch crepe pan stored in a kitchen cabinet? With a few tweaks and nuanced substitutions, however, you can make jianbing that's just as satisfying and full of textural delight. I don't own a crepe pan and I probably never will, but a 12-inch nonstick skillet works fine. The batter is loose enough that you can spread it into a thin layer by swirling the pan or spreading the batter with the back of a spoon. But first, make sure the pan is set on low heat. If it's any hotter, the batter will cook too quickly and won't spread. From that point on, the process of making jianbing at home is essentially the same as at street stalls. If you want to practice your crepe-flipping theatrics in the privacy of your kitchen, go right ahead. When you add your fillings, I suggest substituting pork rinds for the fried cracker. I've seen other recipes use fried dumpling wrappers, but I couldn't resist a reason to have pork rinds for breakfast.

For the Crepes

345g (1 ½ cups) water

150g (1 ¼ cups) all-purpose flour

30g (¼ cup) rice flour

2 tablespoon canola or other neutral-flavored oil, for brushing

4 large eggs

3 green onions, chopped

2 teaspoons black sesame seeds

For the Filling

Spicy fermented bean sauce (doubanjiang)

Romaine lettuce, chopped

Pork rinds

Make the crepes: In a medium mixing bowl, whisk to combine the water, all-purpose flour, and rice flour until smooth. Cover the bowl with plastic wrap and let the batter rest at room temperature for at least 1 hour (or refrigerate up to overnight).

Brush a little bit of canola oil onto a 12-inch nonstick skillet. Heat the pan over low until warm. Pour about ⅓ cup batter into the pan and gently swirl to cover the whole pan, or use the back of a spoon to quickly spread the batter into a thin even layer to cover the interior of the pan. Increase the heat to medium-high and continue to cook just until the batter looks set, 1 to 2 minutes. Crack one egg over the crepe and use a spatula to break the yolk and spread it over the crepe. Sprinkle 2 tablespoons green onions and ½ teaspoon black sesame seeds over the surface. Continue to cook until the egg is set and the edges of the crepe are crisp and starting to curl up, 3 minutes. Flip the crepe and cook the other side until the egg is golden brown and crisp, 3 minutes. (If you want a crispier crepe, flip it one more time and cook another 1 to 2 minutes.)

Transfer the crepe to a cutting board, egg side down, and spread 1 ½ teaspoons bean sauce over the top. Layer on the lettuce and pork rinds. Fold the crepe into thirds and cut in half.

Repeat with remaining batter and other ingredients to make four crepes, allowing time for the pan to cool and brushing with more oil between each. Serve immediately.

Turnip Cake (Lo Bak Gao)

MAKES ONE 8-INCH CAKE

The name "turnip cake" is quite deceiving. This savory cake, which is cut into squares and pan-fried, is made mostly of daikon—not turnip—along with bits of mushroom and salty meat bound together in a batter of rice flour. So, no . . . it's not a new spin on carrot cake. When a turnip cake is really, really good, it has a fighting chance of being the star at the dim sum table. The ideal turnip cake is light and not too mushy on the interior, and nicely caramelized and crispy on the exterior. Finely minced mushrooms, Chinese sausage, and dried shrimp should be evenly suspended in the batter. Most important, it should be hot! This can be a problem at cafes, where plates of turnip cake often sit around too long and slowly miss their window of peak freshness. To avoid this sad dilemma, I love making a turnip cake at home, keeping it in the fridge for a few days, and frying fresh squares each morning. Refrigerating the cake also allows it to set properly and gives you cleaner slices.

A word of caution if you haven't cooked with daikon before: it is a very odorous root vegetable. Some don't mind the smell, but be sure to let everyone in the house know when you're getting ready to cook a fresh batch of *lo bak gao.*

4 dried shiitake mushrooms

2 tablespoons dried shrimp

4 tablespoons canola or other neutral-flavored oil, divided

2 Chinese sausages, finely minced

2 green onions, whites and greens, finely chopped

450g (1 large) daikon radish, grated

2 tablespoons oyster sauce

1 teaspoon sugar

1/2 teaspoon ground white pepper

125g (3/4 cup) rice flour

35g (1/4 cup) cornstarch

Nonstick cooking spray (optional)

Hoisin sauce, for serving

Chili oil, for serving

Place the mushrooms and shrimp in two separate small bowls. Cover both with boiling water until submerged and soak until softened, 30 to 45 minutes. Drain the liquid from both, and finely chop.

In a large skillet, heat 2 tablespoons of the oil over medium-high heat. Add the mushrooms, shrimp, sausage, and green onions. Cook, stirring occasionally, until everything is crisp and the fat from the sausage has rendered, 4 to 5 minutes. Transfer to a medium mixing bowl.

In the same skillet heated over medium-high heat, add the daikon and enough water to just cover. Bring the water to a simmer and simmer until the daikon looks like rice porridge and most of the water has evaporated, at least 30 minutes. Transfer the daikon to the bowl with the mushrooms.

Add the oyster sauce, sugar, and white pepper to the bowl, stirring to combine. Add the rice flour and cornstarch and stir until well combined. (The batter will be very thick.)

Coat an 8-inch round cake pan with nonstick spray or brush with oil. Transfer the batter to the prepared pan and smooth the top with a flexible spatula.

Prepare your steamer setup (page xxviii), using a steamer big enough to fit the cake pan, and bring water to a boil. Place the cake pan in the bamboo steamer basket, cover, and steam for

35 minutes. Place the steamer basket on a wire rack and remove the lid. Allow the cake to cool for 30 to 45 minutes. The cake will initially be a little soft but will firm up as it cools. Cover the cake with plastic wrap and refrigerate until firm and set, at least 2 hours or up to overnight.

Cut the cake into squares; you'll have a few scraps left over. In a large nonstick skillet, heat the remaining 2 tablespoons oil over medium heat. Working in batches, add the cut squares to the pan and fry until crisp and golden brown on each side, 3 to 4 minutes total. Serve immediately with hoisin or chili oil.

Hong Kong–Style French Toast

SERVES 2

Sometimes when I make a fresh loaf of milk bread, I'll purposefully reserve a portion of the loaf to "age" and dry out for a few days, just so I can make Hong Kong French toast. Thick slices of milk bread are stuffed with creamy peanut butter and soaked in an egg batter, for a luscious and exquisitely custardy interior. (The light crumb of milk bread makes it an exceptional sponge.) They are then fried in a little bit of butter until brilliantly golden brown and crisp. Instead of maple syrup, top with a drizzle of sweetened condensed milk and another slab of butter for good measure.

For an even more luxurious French toast, instead of regular milk bread make French toast out of Chocolate Milk Bread (page 6) or Matcha and Black Sesame Marbled Milk Bread (page 13)!

2 (1-inch) slices Mother of All Milk Bread, preferably a few days old

3 tablespoons creamy peanut butter

3/4 cup milk

2 large eggs

Dash of cinnamon

Pinch of coarse salt

1 tablespoon unsalted butter, plus more for serving

2 tablespoons sweetened condensed milk, for serving

Trim off the bread crusts and carefully cut the thick slices in half, leaving one side intact. Spread 1 1/2 tablespoons of peanut butter inside each piece of milk bread.

In a shallow bowl, whisk to combine the milk, eggs, cinnamon, and salt. Soak the peanut butter–stuffed bread in the milk mixture for 2 minutes on each side.

While the bread is soaking, melt the butter in a large skillet over medium heat. Add the soaked bread to the pan, cover with a tight lid, and cook until golden brown on the underside, 2 to 3 minutes. Flip the bread and cook the other side, uncovered, until golden brown, 2 to 3 minutes.

Serve the French toast with a drizzle of condensed milk and a slab of butter.

Savory Soy Milk with All the Fixings

SERVES 1

Here's another way to enjoy a fried doughnut for breakfast. Along the same lines as jook, savory soy milk is a popular breakfast dish, with limitless topping combinations. Simmer the soy milk with a pinch of salt until warmed through and then start adding all the fixings! Soy milk is relatively neutral in flavor, so adding chili oil and Chinkiang vinegar (Chinese black vinegar) kicks up the heat and acidity. Pickled mustard greens are a traditional topping, but you can also swap in kimchi for a little brightness and crunch. The classic accompaniment to savory soy milk is youtiao (Chinese doughnut)—it stays nice and crisp while soaking up all that soy-milk goodness. Make sure you have a bag of youtiao in the freezer at all times, to quickly warm up in the oven.

You can easily find fresh unsweetened soy milk at your local Asian market. Avoid the typical soy milk sold in grocery stores; the flavor and texture isn't quite the same.

2 cups unsweetened soy milk

1/4 teaspoon coarse salt

Suggested Toppings

1 Chinese Doughnut (Youtiao, page 27), sliced

2 tablespoons kimchi

1 tablespoon pork floss

1 teaspoon chili oil

1 teaspoon Chinese black (Chinkiang) vinegar

Sprinkle of sesame seeds

Sprinkle of chopped green onion

Dash of ground white pepper

Warm the milk: In a small saucepan over medium heat, whisk to combine the soy milk and salt and bring to a simmer. Stir occasionally with a whisk to prevent a film from forming on the soy milk.

Pour the soy milk into a serving bowl and top with your favorite toppings.

Sausage, Egg, and Cheese Sheng Jian Bao (SEC SJB)

MAKES 16

Traditional *sheng jian bao* is a hybrid of soup dumplings and steamed bao. At street stalls in China, you'll find block-long lines of people hungry for a few of these juicy, squishy buns. Instead of steaming the buns and then pan-frying them separately, the entire cooking process is done in one big pan—similar to the pan-fry-and-then-steam method for potstickers. You might not think that would make a huge difference, but it gives the steamed buns an extra richness. The fat from the filling melts into the cooking oil and steaming water and, as the water evaporates, the flavor from the meat permeates the dough, putting sheng jian bao into a whole other league than regular steamed buns.

I've stuffed my SJB (sheng jian bao) with SEC (sausage, egg, and cheese), aka my go-to breakfast-sandwich order. The fat from the sausage and the melty cheese supplement the soupy quality of traditional sheng jian bao, packing this exceptional breakfast sandwich with flavor and a satisfying shimmer of grease.

4 large eggs

1 teaspoon olive oil

Fluffy Steamed Bun Dough (page 17), made through step 2

All-purpose flour, for dusting

10 ounces ground breakfast sausage

4 ounces cheddar cheese, cut into 16 small cubes

2 tablespoons canola or other neutral-flavored oil

1/2 cup water

Ketchup, hot sauce, or other, for serving

In a medium bowl, whisk the eggs until the whites and yolks are well combined. Heat the olive oil in a medium nonstick skillet over medium heat. Add the eggs and cook, stirring constantly with a flexible spatula, until just barely set but still a little runny, 1 to 2 minutes. Transfer the soft scrambled eggs to a bowl and cool to room temperature.

Line a large rimmed baking sheet with parchment paper.

After the first proof, punch down to deflate the dough and transfer to a lightly floured surface. Pinch and pull the ends of the dough into a smooth ball. Divide the dough into 16 equal portions (for accuracy, weigh with a digital scale if you have one). Form each portion of dough into a smooth ball by pulling the ends of the dough underneath and then rolling between the palms of your hand.

Roll out a ball of dough to a 4-inch round with a dowel rolling pin, with thinner edges and a thicker middle. Place 1 tablespoon sausage, 2 teaspoons scrambled egg, and a cube of cheese in the center of the dough. Pull up the edges of the dough and pinch together to seal the bun. Place either pleat-side up or pleat-side down on the prepared baking sheet. Repeat to make 16 buns. Cover the buns with a damp, clean kitchen towel and let them rest until they are 1 1/2 times larger, 30 to 40 minutes.

In a large nonstick pan over medium heat, heat the canola oil until warm. Working in batches, arrange the buns in the pan, allowing about 1/2 inch between each. Fry the buns until the bottoms are lightly golden brown, 2 to 3 minutes. Hover a fitted lid over the pan

and carefully add ½ cup of water to the pan. Cover the pan with the lid and allow the buns to steam until the water has completely evaporated, 8 to 10 minutes. Turn off the heat and, with the lid still on, let the buns cool for 5 minutes. (This will help keep them from collapsing.) Repeat with remaining buns, adding a little more oil in between batches.

Serve the buns immediately with ketchup, hot sauce, or your favorite dipping sauce.

After the final proof (end of step 4), place the buns on a small rimmed baking sheet or plate and freeze until solid. Transfer to a large resealable plastic storage bag. Cook frozen buns just as you would fresh, but increase the water to ⅔ cup and steam until all the water has evaporated, 12 to 14 minutes. Let the buns cool for 5 minutes as above.

Ray's Cafe & Tea House

On the outskirts of Philadelphia Chinatown is a quirky coffee shop offering breakfast sandwiches, Taiwanese beef noodle soup, handmade colorful dumplings, cake by the slice, and expertly made siphon coffee. Ray's Cafe & Tea House might just be the only location where you can order all of those things in one place. The first thing you notice when you arrive is the mauve counter topped with a delicate glass-and-metal structure reaching up to the ceiling, which, over the course of many hours, dispenses the most delicious cup of cold brew. Only an avid coffee connoisseur would recognize it as an Oji Co. water dripper. Behind the structure is most likely Grace Chen, the owner of Ray's Cafe. She runs the coffee shop with the help of her two sons, Lawrence and Randy.

Grace grew up in Taiwan, in a family that knew how to feed a crowd. Her uncle owned a steel factory, and her family cooked for all six hundred employees. Every. Single. Day. As a child, she watched her grandma efficiently prepare food for a small army and accompanied her on grocery runs. She was also inspired by an aunt who insisted on making everything from scratch. If you could buy it at the store, she'd want to figure how to make it even better at home. Grace brought this focus on homemade food and the desire to feed lots of people with her when she moved to the States in the 1980s.

Thirty years ago, coffee shops weren't as ubiquitous in America as they are today. In Philadelphia at the time, there were only two coffee shops, one of them a coffee roaster in Reading Terminal. Grace missed the coffee shops she so dearly loved in Taiwan, the aroma of coffee being brewed at her favorite cafes. They were a space of respite, a place to sit and enjoy great coffee and food. So Grace took it upon herself to fill that void in Philadelphia.

Grace opened Ray's Cafe in 1989 and had the Oji Co. water drippers and siphon coffee apparatus from the beginning. The process of making siphon coffee feels like watching a science experiment. I had the pleasure of enjoying a cup of coffee at Ray's, and the delicate, deeply flavorful brew didn't disappoint. Nowadays, siphon coffee makers are common in Blue Bottle and other trendy third-wave coffee shops. But Grace was making coffee this way over thirty years ago. She invested in the next-level equipment after a deep dive into coffee research at her local library. Today, parts for this apparatus are almost impossible to source or only found in museums.

Coffee is king at Ray's Cafe, but Grace pours just as much thoughtfulness into her collection of imported teas from Taiwan, naturally colored dumpling wrappers, and the most comforting bowl of Taiwanese beef noodle soup. Everything tastes expertly made but with a homemade touch. It's all made from scratch and by hand, from the dumpling dough and chili oil to the side of pickled mustard greens accompanying each bowl of noodle soup. It's what keeps generations of regulars coming back daily and weekly. The unwavering community support has kept the doors open at Ray's Cafe over Philadelphia's ever-changing coffee landscape.

Grace was obviously way ahead of the times when it came to craft coffee, cold brew, and curated teas. Her intuition and attention to detail is inspiring. What's refreshing is that her offerings are presented so humbly, without the pretentiousness that often comes with *craft* anything. At its heart, Ray's Cafe is a homey coffee shop and cafe where Chinatown locals, daily civic employees, and coffee connoisseurs come in for a damn good cup of coffee, and so much more.

sips

Chapter 7

The first hour of my day is a rare time of quiet and stillness, while I wait for the rest of the world to wake up. More often than not, my mornings involve sipping on something caffeinated, while I prepare breakfast and watch the Bay Area fog slowly dissipate. On a cozy, crisp morning, there's nothing better than swirling a generous spoonful of sweetened condensed milk into my tea and licking the spoon for a delicious little sugar rush. In the summer, an effervescent sparkling matcha with a squeeze of lime (grown in our yard) is the jolt I need to shake off that last bit of grogginess. If I'm lucky enough to start the day with family gathered around a table at dim sum, I know I'll have my fill of chrysanthemum tea for the day.

All of the following sips, from rich and creamy to bubbly and fruity, complement just about any part of any meal, whether a simple bun, a platter of dumplings, or a generous slice of cake. They're satisfying on their own too.

Chrysanthemum Tea

SERVES 4

The aroma of chrysanthemum tea instantly takes me back to Sunday dim sum with my family. I can practically hear the clinking of dishware and teacups, the squeaky wheels of the dim sum carts, the Cantonese chatter echoing through the vast banquet hall. Instead of coffee and bottomless mimosas, our version of Sunday brunch includes steaming pots of freshly steeped chrysanthemum tea. This floral tea is on the drier side, which helps balance out the rich and savory flavors of siu mai, braised chicken feet, and other delectable small plates.

Chrysanthemum tea not only tastes wonderful, but it's full of medicinal benefits. From a young age, we were taught that some foods can overheat your internal balance, a concept called *yeet hay*, which means "hot air." Fried and greasy foods increase your internal temperature, leading to headaches and a scratchy throat. You can counteract yeet hay by cooling your internal balance with foods like chrysanthemum tea, bitter melon, and seemingly every soup my pau pau makes. Yeet hay has nothing to do with the actual temperature of foods, because fruit such as pineapple and lychee, consumed in large quantities, can contribute to yeet hay. As a kid I thought of yeet hay as an Chinese old wives' tale meant to force children into eating vegetables and finishing their tea, but now I see the wisdom behind it. At the very least, it's a reminder of moderation and balance. So if I want to eat more dumplings, I'm just going to keep sipping my chrysanthemum tea.

Brewing tea is as simple as combining hot water with loose tea leaves (or tea bags, if that's all you can find). You should, however, pay close attention to the tea-to-water ratio and the length of time you steep the tea, to avoid an overly bitter flavor. Thankfully, chrysanthemum is a very forgiving herbal tea and hard to oversteep. I love brewing flower-based teas in a glass teapot, so I can peacefully sit and watch the buds slowly plump and bloom as they steep.

2 tablespoons dried chrysanthemum flowers

3 cups boiling water

In a teapot, combine the flowers and water and allow the tea to steep for 5 minutes. Strain out the flowers and serve.

Hong Kong Milk Tea (Li Cha)

SERVES 4

The moment you step into a Hong Kong diner or bakery, the air will be thick with the scent of aromatic Ceylon tea and sweetened condensed milk. Ceylon is a robust black tea from Sri Lanka that, when brewed strong, has almost as much caffeine as a cup of coffee. Its flavor is a little chocolatey, with a hint of citrus brightness. *Li cha* is made with Ceylon tea and two milks: sweetened condensed gives it a distinctive, creamy sweetness, and evaporated delivers a slightly caramelized flavor and velvety smooth finish. If you see freshly brewed li cha offered at your local cafe, order it. Or, make a big batch at home to keep in your fridge all week. Serve it on ice or warm it back up—either way, you can't go wrong.

1/4 cup (8 to 10 tea bags) Ceylon tea leaves

4 cups water

1/2 cup evaporated milk

2 tablespoons sweetened condensed milk

In a saucepan over medium heat, combine the tea leaves and water and bring to a simmer. Turn off the heat, cover, and allow the tea to steep until strongly brewed, 6 to 8 minutes.

Strain out the tea leaves and pour the tea into mugs or a heat-proof pitcher. Add the evaporated milk and condensed milk and stir to combine. Serve warm or chilled over ice.

Yuenyeung

SERVES 1

Along with pure black coffee, this is my partner Reuben's preferred caffeinated beverage in the morning. *Yuenyeung* is a blend of Hong Kong milk tea and coffee, yet it somehow tastes like neither. It tastes distinctively like, well, yuenyeung. Everyone has their opinion on the ideal tea-to-coffee ratio. I think yuenyeung is best with more tea than coffee. The bright citrus notes of Ceylon tea really come through and enhance the deeper, roasted flavors of the coffee (coffee flavors vary vastly, obviously). What you get is a complex and refreshing cup to start your day.

1 tablespoon (about 2 tea bags) Ceylon tea leaves

1 cup water

1/2 cup brewed coffee

1 teaspoon sweetened condensed milk

1 tablespoon evaporated milk

In a saucepan over medium heat, combine the tea leaves and water and bring to a simmer. Turn off the heat, cover, and allow the tea to steep until strongly brewed, 6 to 8 minutes.

Strain out the tea leaves and pour the tea into a mug. Add the coffee, sweetened condensed milk, and evaporated milk. Serve warm or chilled over ice.

Sparkling Lime Matcha

SERVES 1

Matcha has such an ethereal flavor: inherently sweet, a little grassy, and decidedly earthy. Its complexity may take a while to grow on you. Give it a few chances, find some quality matcha, and you'll soon crave it in all its forms—in ice cream, lattes, buns, cake. Yes, combining matcha with rich ingredients like white chocolate and heavy cream is a *matcha* made in heaven (I had to), but I love sipping on matcha in its more stripped-down form. Effervescent sparkling water lightens up the matcha, and a squeeze of lime lends some juicy brightness.

I recommend a ceremonial-grade matcha powder here, as opposed to the food-grade recommended for other recipes, for better flavor and color. Lower-quality matcha powder won't be as bright green and might give your drink a less-than-appealing swamp-water aesthetic.

2 teaspoons ceremonial-grade matcha powder

1/4 cup cold water

Ice cubes, for serving

3/4 cup sparkling water

Juice of 1/2 lime

In a small bowl, combine the matcha powder and water, whisking until smooth. Fill a glass of ice with the sparkling water and lime juice. Pour the matcha over the ice and serve.

Strawberry Jasmine Milk Tea

SERVES 1

Here's my version of a "pink drink." It is tart, fruity, creamy, and springy, and feels just a wee bit fancy—but with minimal effort. I steep my favorite jasmine tea, throw it into a blender with strawberries and coconut milk, and serve over ice. Feel free to boil some boba if you have it handy, to turn this into Strawberry Jasmine Bubble Tea.

1 tablespoon (about 2 tea bags) jasmine tea leaves

1 cup water

¼ cup canned full-fat coconut milk

¼ cup coarsely chopped hulled strawberries

Ice cubes, for serving

In a saucepan over medium heat, combine the tea leaves and water and bring to a simmer. Turn off the heat, cover, and allow the tea to steep until strongly brewed, 5 to 6 minutes.

Strain out the leaves.

In the bowl of a blender (or with a handheld immersion blender in a bowl), combine the tea, milk, and strawberries and blend until smooth, 1 minute. Pour over ice and serve.

Lychee-Lemon Iced Tea

SERVES 4

It was a good day when my mom packed a Vita Lemon Tea in my lunch box. The sweet drink inside the little yellow juice box with the bold graphic design was low on tea flavor but tart enough to make my lips pucker. I loved it so much. This bright and refreshing lychee-lemon tea is an ode to my favorite childhood juice box. The tea flavor is much more in-your-face, however—I like to steep the tea until it is borderline bitter. When you add lemon juice and concentrated lychee syrup (from a can of lychees), the bitterness mellows, and the tea flavor shines through. I prefer to use canned lychees, because not only do you get sweet, ripe fruit to snack on and toss into your tea, but the pure, lovely lychee syrup is magical.

4 cups water, divided

3 tablespoons loose black tea leaves

1/4 cup fresh lemon juice

3/4 cup lychee syrup (from canned lychee)

1/2 cup lychee fruit (from canned lychee)

Ice cubes, for serving

Lemon slices, for serving

In a medium saucepan over medium heat, bring 2 cups water to a boil. Turn off the heat and add the tea leaves. Cover and steep until the tea is very strong in flavor, 8 to 10 minutes.

Place a fine mesh sieve over a large pitcher, and strain the tea through it. Discard the tea leaves.

Add the remaining 2 cups water, lemon juice, lychee syrup, and lychees to the tea.

Refrigerate until cold, at least 2 hours, and serve over ice with lemon slices.

Coffee with Grass Jelly

SERVES 1

How do you know when you've officially turned into your parents? Is it when commercials start to make you cry, like they do to your mom? Or when you start to uncontrollably sneeze insanely loud, like your dad? My moment was when I realized I genuinely enjoy grass jelly. If you don't know what grass jelly is, imagine Jell-O that's sweet and earthy tasting.

For practically my whole life, I would watch with disgust as my parents ordered grass jelly drinks at cafes. It tasted medicinal, and seemed like something only adults would enjoy. How can something that looks like Jell-O taste like dirt? I avoided anything grass jelly–related for years—decades, really—until I decided to try it again for the sake of research. Either my taste buds have matured, or years of loving matcha has calibrated my palate to appreciate earthy flavors. I can finally say it: Grass jelly is not terrible. It's even—dare I say?—delightful, with sweet, a little caramelly, even herbaceous notes. The jelly is flavored from a variety of Chinese mint, which gives it almost a root beer flavor. Root beer Jell-O sounds pretty good, right? (I will add that I sampled a few canned grass jelly "drinks" in my research and, for the record, those still taste pretty awful to me.)

I like to buy grass jelly powder (found at Asian markets or ordered online) and make it myself, so I have more control over the texture and level of sweetness. This grass jelly is on the firmer side, so if you prefer a softer texture, reduce the powder by a tablespoon or two. Same for the sweetness: simply adjust the amount of brown sugar to suit your taste.

Ice cubes, for serving

1/3 cup (1/2-inch) cubes Grass Jelly (recipe below, or store-bought)

3/4 cup strongly brewed coffee or cold brew

1/4 cup milk (whatever kind you prefer)

Fill a glass with ice and the cubes of grass jelly. Pour the coffee and milk into the glass and serve.

Grass Jelly

MAKES 2 CUPS

1 1/2 cups water

55g (1/4 cup) brown sugar

60g (1/2 cup) grass jelly powder

In a small saucepan over medium heat, whisk to combine the water, brown sugar, and grass jelly powder. Bring to a simmer and then turn off heat.

Pour the mixture into a 6-inch-round cake pan or a small heat-proof container and allow to cool to room temperature. Cover with a fitted lid or plastic wrap and refrigerate until firm and set but still jiggly, at least 4 hours or up to overnight.

Slide a small offset spatula around the edges of grass jelly to loosen, invert the cake pan over a cutting board, and gently tap on the bottom of the pan to release the jelly. Cut into 1/2-inch cubes and refrigerate in an airtight container for up to 1 week.

Some Assembly Required

Building Your Own Pink Box

Walking out of a Chinese bakery with a pink box is like a badge of honor. It means you bought enough buns and treats to warrant one, and everyone should be jealous of your bounty.

Every so often, I like to make a double or sometimes triple batch of milk bread, bake a few different buns, and assemble my own pink boxes to hand out to loved ones. They make wonderful gifts for holidays, birthdays, housewarmings—or sometimes for no real reason at all! Buying the bakery boxes (at a store or online) is the easy part. Baking a variety of buns in one go requires a little strategy, but it's not difficult. The milk bread recipe (page 6) doubles easily, and a standard-size electric stand mixer accommodates the larger volume.

The majority of the bun recipes in chapters 2 and 3 make 12 buns each. You could make a triple batch of milk bread dough to bake up three different bun varieties. And there are a handful of bun recipes that don't require a full batch of filling or a topping, so you could make an even wider variety of buns. For example, you can make six of one kind, three of another—you get the idea.

After-School PB&J Buns (page 60)

Hot Dog Flower Buns (page 94)

Very Chill Jam Buns (page 79)

Taro Leaf Buns (page 76)

Red Bean Swirl Buns (page 52)

Everything Bagel Bao (page 114)

Sambal and Parmesan Buns (page 111)

If you have leftover red bean or taro paste, peanut butter and jam, a jar of sambal in the fridge, or some hot dogs leftover from a BBQ, you can make an assortment of buns with minimal effort.

Ultimate Steamer Basket

The best part of making dumplings and steamed buns (other than eating them right away) is freezing them for a quick, easy future meal. At any given time, I have a few different bags of homemade dumplings and buns in my freezer, and I'm always thankful for them after coming back from a trip or when I have zero energy to cook for myself. What's even better is that frozen dumplings and buns generally steam in the same amount of time. So, in a single steamer you could have a few har gow (page 219), Rose Siu Mai (page 223), and a couple of different steamed buns all hanging out together. No need to defrost anything. Just arrange everything in the steamer baskets, steam for 10 to 12 minutes, and get ready for a feast!

Holiday Cookie Box

I love assembling cute cookie boxes during the holidays. For a few days, my kitchen transforms into a cookie factory as I listen to "All I Want for Christmas Is You" on repeat. The game plan is simple: Find some cookie tins or boxes at a craft store, select four or five cookies (or however many varieties you think will fit in each box) ranging in size, shape, and flavor, and start baking.

Mentally envision sections in the cookie boxes for each type of cookie so that it looks neat and orderly. If you want, use cupcake liners to help create some physical division.

For a final festive touch, wrap the boxes in decorative string and tie a gift tag and small sprig of rosemary for some wintry flair.

Acknowledgments

This book would not have been possible without my partner, Reuben. My love, best friend, and on-call taste tester. Thank you from the bottom of my heart for constantly cheering me on, emotionally (and sometimes physically) picking me back up after numerous recipe fails, and always being honest with your feedback, so I can try again better. I love you and the amazing pizza you fed me when I couldn't cook anymore.

Everything that I am is all thanks to my family. Thank you, Mom, Dad, and Tyler, for always fully supporting my dreams, allowing me to follow my own unique path, and indulging me whenever I felt like commandeering the whole kitchen. Thank you, Mom, for always taking my calls to work through family recipes together. Thank you, Dad, for passing down your major sweet tooth and love of all things chocolate. Thank you, Tyler, for being the first person I ever had to "cook" for, with after-school snacks and reheated leftovers.

I'm eternally grateful to my grandparents, Goong Goong and Pau Pau, for taking the biggest risk by moving to America. Thank you, Pau Pau, for letting Mom record you as you made batches of white pizza and steamed cupcakes, so I could reverse engineer your recipes. Goong Goong, I love and miss you dearly. I'm so grateful to be your Yee Yee and have the privilege of passing on your love of food and teaching.

To Jim and Susan, my amazing in-laws, I'm so thankful to have you both as my biggest fans. Jim, thank you for being my unofficial copy editor and correcting each and every mistake I make in each blog post and Instagram caption. Susan, thank you for always washing the dishes for me and feeding me the best matzo ball soup and noodle kugel.

A million thanks to my wonderful literary agent, Kitty Cowles. I still feel like I don't deserve you. Thank you for believing in me as a writer and guiding me through the whole cookbook pitching and writing process. Without you, my dream of writing this book wouldn't have been possible. And thank you, Alexis Kraft, my old project manager, for casually mentioning me to Kitty when I was just a wannabe food blogger.

To my team at Harper Horizon, Andrea Fleck-Nisbet, Amanda Bauch, and John Andrade, thank you for being so enthusiastic about and believing in this project. You all trusted me with my vision and gave me such freedom to bring it to life.

The recipes in this book wouldn't have been nearly as organized and thoughtful without the help of Ellen Morrissey. Thank you, Ellen, for your endless wisdom and incredible attention to detail. I learned from you how to be a confident recipe writer.

To the bakers and bakery owners I interviewed, thank you for trusting me with your stories. I'll never forget your generosity. This book is so much more than a baking book because of you.

Thank you to my best friends, Jeff Brown and Katie Polenick, for enduring my endless panic texts throughout the cookbook writing process and always responding with genuine support and humor. Our group chat is one of the great joys of my life.

Jess Chen, how I could I ever thank you for testing so many recipes from the book and discussing every complication and detail with vigor and insight? You're such an inspirational baker and having you as a friend is such a gift.

Thank you to all my friends and fellow bloggers for being so generous with your time and energy by testing recipes for me.

And finally, thank you to all the readers and followers of *Eat Cho Food*. Your enthusiasm and support made this book a reality.

Index

About the Author

Kristina Cho is a Bay Area–based food blogger, recipe developer, and cooking instructor. She's originally from Cleveland, Ohio, where her family owned and operated a Chinese restaurant. Cooking and sharing culture through food were always a huge part of her life. Before becoming a food blogger, Kristina studied and worked in architecture and interior design. Architecture instilled in her a designer's attention to detail, a disciplined approach to iteration, and creative artistry. But between sketching and coordinating construction drawings, she spent all her time exploring new flavors, shopping for the freshest ingredients at her local farmers markets, and developing recipes for her blog, *Eat Cho Food*.

Today she has dedicated her professional career to making, teaching, writing about, and photographing her unique interpretations of Chinese food—everything from noodle soups to dumplings and, of course, baked goods.